LABOUR MARKET EFFICIENCY
IN THE EUROPEAN UNION

The deregulation of labour law in the European Union was thought to be a spur to lasting growth of employment and an increase in labour market efficiency. In particular, it was hoped that facilitating fixed-term contracts would help many Europeans out of continued unemployment and back into the workforce. Based on data from the European Labour Force Survey, *Labour Market Efficiency in the European Union* reveals that the results of such policies have been far from those expected.

This study provides a country-by-country overview of the legal regulations concerning employment protection and fixed-term employment in the twelve Member States of the European Union (prior to its expansion in 1995). Employment patterns of fixed-term employees are compared with those of employees in standard employment relationships, with the analytical focus on age-, gender- and industry-specific differences. The authors then look beyond country-specific patterns and assess the probability of fixed-term employment within the European Union. They offer hypotheses concerning the impact upon the labour market of deregulation and of reregulation.

Drawing upon solid research and rigorous analysis, this is a valuable discussion of how legal, sociological and economic labour market theories contribute to an understanding of atypical employment.

Klaus Schömann is a Senior Research Fellow at the Wissenschaftszentrum Berlin für Sozialforschung, Germany. **Ralf Rogowski** is Senior Lecturer in Law at the University of Warwick, England. **Thomas Kruppe** is a Research Fellow at the Wissenschaftszentrum Berlin für Sozialforschung, Germany.

ROUTLEDGE STUDIES IN THE EUROPEAN ECONOMY

GROWTH AND CRISIS IN THE
SPANISH ECONOMY, 1940–1993
Sima Lieberman

WORK AND EMPLOYMENT IN EUROPE
A New Convergence?
Peter Cressey and Bryn Jones

TRANS-EUROPEAN
TELECOMMUNICATION NETWORKS
The Challenges for Industrial Policy
Colin Turner

EUROPEAN UNION – EUROPEAN
INDUSTRIAL RELATIONS?
Global challenges, national developments and transnational dynamics
Edited by Wolfgang E. Lecher and Hans-Wolfgang Platzer

GOVERNANCE, INDUSTRY AND LABOUR
MARKETS IN BRITAIN AND FRANCE
The modernising state in the mid-twentieth century
Edited by Noel Whiteside and Robert Salais

LABOUR MARKET EFFICIENCY IN
THE EUROPEAN UNION
Employment Protection and Fixed-term Contracts
Klaus Schömann, Ralf Rogowski and Thomas Kruppe

LABOUR MARKET EFFICIENCY IN THE EUROPEAN UNION

Employment Protection and Fixed-Term Contracts

Klaus Schömann, Ralf Rogowski and Thomas Kruppe

London and New York

First published 1998
by Routledge
11 New Fetter Lane, London EC4P 4EE

Simultaneously published in the USA and Canada
by Routledge
29 West 35th Street, New York, NY 10001

© 1998 Klaus Schömann, Ralf Rogowski, Thomas Kruppe

Typeset in Garamond by M Rules
Printed and bound in Great Britain by Biddles Ltd, Guildford and King's Lynn

British Library Cataloguing in Publication Data
A catalogue record for this book is available from the British Library

Library of Congress Cataloging in Publication Data
Schömann, Klaus, 1961–
Labour market efficiency in the European Union: employment protection and
fixed-term contracts / Klaus Schömann, Ralf Rogowski, Thomas Kruppe.
p. cm. – (Routledge studies in the European economy; 6)
Includes bibliographical references and index.
1. Job security–European Union countries.   2. Job security–Law and
legislation–European Union countries.   3. Labor contract–European
Union countries.   I. Rogowski, Ralf.   II. Kruppe, Thomas, 1958–   .
III. Title.   IV. Series.
HD5708.45.E85S36   1998
331.12'094–dc21   98–11170
CIP

ISBN 0–415–15734–X

CONTENTS

List of figures and tables   vii
Acknowledgements   ix

1   Introduction   1

2   **Legal and economic theories of labour market regulation**   2

    Legal theories 2
    Economic theories 13
    A multi-layered theoretical design and research hypotheses 19

3   **Employment protection systems and the regulation of
    fixed-term contracts in the European Union**   24

    Introduction 24
    *Employment protection and fixed-term contracts in the Member States
        of the European Union 25*
        Belgium 25
        Denmark 29
        France 32
        Germany 38
        Greece 42
        Ireland 44
        Italy 48
        Luxembourg 52
        The Netherlands 54
        Portugal 56
        Spain 60
        United Kingdom 65
    Atypical employment and European law 70

4 **Fixed-term employment patterns in the European Union** 72

Evidence on the extent and patterns of fixed-term employment contracts 74
Aggregate trends in fixed-term employment 74
Is fixed-term employment an issue of gender? 83
The age structure of fixed-term employment 101
Working fixed-term and part-time: accumulating risks or just what
  you wanted? 111
Does higher education work as insurance against fixed-term employment? 116
Implications of a changing occupational structure on fixed-term employment 117
Industrial sector differences 128
Labour market dynamics 130

5 **Multivariate analysis of country patterns** 133

Gender differences 134
Age structure 134
Nationalities 139
Selectivity by level of education 140
Impact of employment status last year 141
Industrial sector effects 144
Occupational segregation 147

6 **Fixed-term contracts and their relationship to**
   macro-economic conditions 149

The example of Spain 149
Comparative aspects of macro-performance 155

7 **Conclusions** 158

Appendix 168
Notes 192
References 197
Index of authors cited 209
Subject index 211

FIGURES AND TABLES

Figures

2.1	Fixed-term employment and human capital	16
2.2	Unemployment as a worker discipline device	18
4.1	Fixed-term employment as a percentage of total dependent employees in the EU	75
4.2	Women in fixed-term employment in the EU, 1991	85
4.3	Women in fixed-term employment in the EU, 1996	86
4.4	Fixed-term employment by age as a percentage of all fixed-term employment, 1991	107
4.5	Total employees by age as percentage of total dependent employment, 1991	108
4.6	Fixed-term employees by age as percentage of all fixed-term employment, 1983	109
4.7	Total dependent employment by age as percentage of all dependent employment, 1983	110
4.8	Percentage of part-time employment in fixed-term and total employment in the EU, 1991	115
4.9a	Fixed-term employees as percentage of total dependent employment by occupation in selected EU Member States, 1991	126
4.9b	Fixed-term employees as percentage of total dependent employment by occupation in selected EU Member States, 1991	127
6.1	Flows into new contracts, Spain 1985–95	154

Tables

2.1	Legal and economic theories and fixed-term contracts (FTCs)	20
4.1	Index 1987 of fixed-term employment	77
4.2	Index 1987 of total dependent employment	78
4.3	Annual rates of change in total dependent employment	79

4.4   Fixed-term employment as percentage of total dependent
employment   81

4.5   Annual rates of change in fixed-term employment   82

4.6   Total dependent employment by gender; fixed-term
employment by gender   87

4.7   Fixed-term employees as percentage of total dependent
labour force by gender   94

4.8   Annual change in gender in (a) permanent employment
(b) fixed-term employment   97

4.9   Total dependent employment by age   103

4.10   Fixed-term employment by age   105

4.11   Fixed-term employees as percentage of total dependent
employment by full-time/part-time   112

4.12   Fixed-term employees as percentage of total dependent
employment by level of education attained   118

4.13   Total dependent employment by level of education attained   119

4.14   Fixed-term employees by level of education attained   121

4.15   Total employees by occupational status   123

4.16   Fixed-term employees by occupational status   124

4.17   Fixed-term employees as percentage of total dependent
employment by occupational status   125

4.18   Fixed-term employment as percentage of total dependent
labour force by industrial sectors in the EU in 1991   129

4.19   Current employees with a permanent or fixed-term contract
by selected labour force status one year earlier   131

5.1   Summary table of estimated coefficients for fixed-term
employment in the EU in 1991   135

6.1   Dependent employment by duration of contracts and
gender as percentage of all dependent employees   153

6.2   Dependent employment by duration of contracts and
sectors as percentage of all dependent employees   153

6.3   Dependent employment by duration of contracts and
sectors as percentage of all dependent employees of the
specific sector   153

7.1   Regulations of fixed-term contracts in the EU   160

ACKNOWLEDGEMENTS

We are grateful for financial support by the Commission of the European Communities DG V. We would also like to thank Geoff Thomas, Laurent Freysson and Didier Lesnicki of Eurostat for their assistance with calculations of the European Labour Force Survey. The whole staff of the labour market policy and employment unit of the Social Science Centre in Berlin (WZB) provided either helpful comments on earlier drafts or has been directly involved in the preparation of the manuscript at some stage. We would like to thank Günther Schmid, the director of the unit, for his continued encouragement of this research.

1

INTRODUCTION

Labour market efficiency has become a major topic of political debates and legal reforms in the European Union during the 1980s and 1990s. Supported by neo-liberal economic policies at the national and supranational level, the majority of Member States of the European Union embarked on policies of deregulation of labour markets based on the neo-classical concepts of the market economy and reduced or minimal welfare states. In some countries these efforts form part of a wider programme of deregulation of economies and privatisation of nationalised industries and public enterprises.

The debate and policies of deregulation of the labour market are characterised by a bias in favour of flexibility. An increase in flexibility is assumed to correlate with higher productivity. In this perspective the booming United States labour market appears to be the product of flexible policies and the European labour markets in contrast are suffering from 'Euro-sclerosis' as a result of rigid labour markets. However, such a view is caught in a binary thinking of rigid versus flexible and is hardly able to grasp the complexity of employment systems. Employment systems contain both flexible and rigid elements which only occasionally serve as functional equivalents but often complement each other. Furthermore, in order to avoid the pejorative undertone conveyed by the term rigidity we use instead the term stability to denote the opposite of flexibility. In analysing the development of employment systems we prefer a gradual concept which accepts the need for both regulation and deregulation and which tries to assess the various mixes of flexible and stable elements (see also Nielsen 1991).

The general aim of our book is to evaluate the balance between flexibility and stability in European labour markets by using the criterion of labour market efficiency. Our concept of efficiency is thereby based on a Pareto notion of efficiency, according to which an economic advantage of one or more persons is efficient, and thus justified, if it does not entail the worsening of conditions for other economic actors. In addition, we apply the Kaldor and Hicks compensation criterion, according to which policies are efficient if the gains achieved by these policies compensate for their losses.

Policies of deregulation of the labour market target primarily so-called 'burdens on business'. A particular concern of the public debate and policy initiatives are costs associated with employment protection. The fact that most flexibilisation policies aim at reducing existing levels of protection granted by labour law and collective agreements has triggered lively political and scientific debates between governments and interest groups about the effects of these policies. In these debates trade unions tend to defend existing employment protection, whereas employers are more likely to endorse flexibilisation policies.

Policies of labour market flexibilisation usually favour new or atypical forms of employment over permanent, life-time jobs which used to be characteristic of the standard or typical employment relationship. During the last two decades most Member States of the European Union altered their regulations on atypical employment. Although the scope of these changes varies considerably among countries, the principal goal is fairly similar: to increase flexibility in the labour market in order to facilitate higher rates of job creation.

Among atypical forms of employment, fixed-term employment contracts have received special attention. This form of employment is seen as cost-saving because the employer is in general void of legal obligations which occur in case of dismissal of a permanent employee. In addition, fixed-term employment is perceived as a possible remedy for Europe's unemployment problem. The underlying rationale is that lower labour costs to employers enable labour-intensive production, ease the pressure of rationalisation and support employment-intensive growth which ultimately leads to a higher number of employees in the economy as a whole.

We can distinguish a macro-economic and a micro-economic line of argumentation in the debate on fixed-term employment. In comparing the duration of job tenure among employees in the Member States of the European Union and the United States, it is evident that, on average, the duration of employment in a single job is longer in Europe than in the North American labour markets.[1] In a macro-economic perspective, an increase in fixed-term contracts in Europe narrows the structural differences between Europe and the United States.[2] Furthermore, in this perspective employment systems are determining factors in the location of new plants, and a reduction of levels of employment protection increases the chances within the global competition for new investments (OECD 1994). However, this argumentation is valid only if it can be assumed that capital investments are taking place on a global scale and that the European Union cannot dissociate itself from these developments.

In contrast to the macro-economic line of argumentation, according to which the labour market is shaped by international competition for capital investment, the micro-economic discourse deals with flexibility considerations of employers and employees. It is, for example, concerned with ways in which personnel policies match tasks and employment status. If tasks are performed for specific periods during the year, it is in the interest of the employer to engage a person only for a period which corresponds to the duration of the task. Seasonal work is the most common type of employment in this context, for which most labour law systems traditionally provide specific contractual arrangements. Some European Union Member States have introduced new regulations which extend these arrangements to other forms of discontinuous employment.

Furthermore, micro-economic analyses study the relationship between innovations in production methods and employment relationships. The evolution of new forms of contractual relationships between firms in product markets, reduced stocks of products and lean or just-in-time production have led firms to reconsider their employment strategies. Long-term attachment of workers to firms is more often replaced by shorter and more flexible arrangements favouring employment for a fixed duration. In addition, increased flexibility is obtained through the introduction of new working time arrangements (Blanpain and Köhler 1988, Commission of the European Communities 1994).

Lean personnel management policies require innovative manpower strategies. An issue of increasing importance is the replacement of employees who are absent due to sickness, maternity leave, vacations or longer sabbaticals. The substitute employees for temporary replacements are increasingly drawn from the 'external' labour market (OECD 1995). This tendency reinforces the role of employment agencies which provide fast access to 'flexible' employees and thus offer temporary solutions in situations of labour shortage. In the case of agency work the employee has a contract with the temporary work agency and works on the premises of a third party, the contractor of the agency. Employment or temporary work agencies are regulated differently in each Member State of the European Union and the triangular employment relationship between the employee, the agency and the firm poses a particular problem for European-wide regulations (Blanpain 1993). Agency work is a form of 'atypical' employment which may serve as a functional equivalent to a fixed-term contract and thus requires special attention in any analysis of fixed-term employment in Europe.

Fixed-term employment increases labour turnover and competition among employees. In the wider context of cultural changes in Western societies fixed-term employment is not only an instrument of human resource management policies of companies but creates a voluntary option for employees as well. The dissolution of traditional work patterns particularly among women has transformed the meaning of fixed-term employment for many employees (OECD 1993: 28). Due to changes in the organisation of the employees' life-course – for example, multiple transitions between working and learning or between working and unpaid work in the household (Schmid 1993), and interregional or international migration and job shopping of employees – fixed duration employment is a matter of choice for an increasing number of individuals (European Foundation 1992).

The idiosyncratic development of each country's system of employment

3

protection and the regulation of fixed-term employment as part of this system require that specific attention is paid to the comparative method. In particular in the case of a multi-country survey, which deals with both legal regulations and socio-economic developments, a close observation of the comparative dimensions is indispensable. The discussion of comparative methods must thereby develop an understanding of the paradoxical relationship of the autonomy of any legal system and its embeddedness in the countries' employment and economic system as well as its dependence on supranational and international developments.

Unfortunately, the comparative practice reveals so far that there exists no 'single best' method, but rather a mixture of methods in conducting comparisons in law, economics and social sciences (Rogowski 1996a). A fashionable approach in studying national economies and the welfare state is the comparison of so-called 'model' cases (Esping-Andersen 1990), for example the Japanese model of production and employment (Hashimoto and Raisian 1992; Matsuda 1992) or the Swedish model of a corporatist labour market (Calmfors 1994). The reference to a system as a positive model suggests in these studies the potential transfer of a system of regulations to another country, as if a 'model' automatically implies a superior form of regulation. Conversely, the reference to a negative model implies a generally applicable criticism of certain developments. However, the mere use of the word 'model' should warn against simplistic references to national systems of regulation and patterns of employment. Indeed, with respect to employment protection, atypical employment and regulations of fixed-term employment, there is no particular model of regulation or a model use of fixed-term contracts. Instead, we observe a number of interesting patterns within the European Union which require other conceptual devices than the search for country models.

The potential and limits of comparative methods have been discussed in comparative law and in comparative sociology for quite some time. These debates have highlighted a number of fallacies in comparing national employment systems and legal cultures (Rogowski 1996b). Some of the specific problems in conducting comparative studies of law, and in particular labour law, can be summarised as follows (see also Blanc-Jouvan 1993):

1   Conceptual splits, like individual and collective labour law, are misleading when they disguise an actual overlap in the practice of law. The dominant comparative perspective of law tends to treat legal regulations as 'abstract' and 'static', instead of conceptualising them as 'fluid' or 'dynamic'. Written law develops when it is applied and interpreted in legal and judicial practice. Thus comparative accounts have to incorporate historical and sociological perspectives in contrasting labour law systems. Adequate comparisons of labour law require an approach which combines an internal legal analysis of the legal system and an external socioeconomic analysis of the employment system (Zielinski 1982).

2   The legal sources differ among countries. They can consist of one com-
    prehensive source, e.g. a labour code, or of many statutes and other legal
    instruments. Most countries acknowledge within labour law a range of
    legal sources which reach from statutes to collective agreements, company
    agreements, customs and practice, and, in addition, the employment con-
    tract. This range of legal sources poses a particular problem for
    comparative analyses of labour law. If, for example, only statutory regu-
    lations are compared and other relevant legal sources are not included, the
    study is likely to result in misleading comparisons of specific legal
    aspects.

3   Advanced comparisons of national legal systems use an approach which
    operates with functional equivalents at the conceptual and institutional
    level (Zweigert and Kötz 1987: 28–46). The functional approach assumes
    that social problems constitute the same point of reference for different,
    country-specific legal solutions. It thereby suggests to define the social
    problems with reference to influences of the surrounding societal context,
    e.g. in the case of labour law the system of industrial relations, the level of
    economic development, industrialisation or 'tertiarisation' of the economy
    etc. However, the functional approach is confronted with the problem of
    labelling substantively different aspects of law, which sometimes even
    might carry the same name, as equivalent. In the language of comparative
    law the problem has been coined as the occurrence of 'faux amis' or a 'mis-
    conception' of functional equivalence (Blanc-Jouvan 1993). This
    fundamental fallacy can be contained if comparisons of functional equiv-
    alents are based on sufficiently detailed legal and social indicators in
    depicting the institutional infrastructure of regulations (Rogowski 1996a:
    220–2).

Although the terminology is different, the problems and fallacies with which
sociologists and other social scientists are confronted in conducting comparisons are similar to the methodological problems of comparative law systems.
For example, Ragin (1991, 1987) defines as the primary goal of comparative
research the use of sophisticated theoretical concepts in analysing relationships
which nevertheless can be translated into observable variables or indicators. He
distinguishes between cases and variables, and criticises social science com-
parativists who treat specifically selected cases falsely as meaningful wholes. If
countries are reduced to a set of variables, country systems as a whole become
almost invisible behind the predominant issue of selection of observable and
available variables.

Janoski (1991) proposes the combination of qualitative and quantitative
methods. He distinguishes between an internal analysis of events and processes
within cases, and an external analysis of patterns across cases. Both parts of the
comparative analysis can be qualitative or quantitative.[3] Janoski's approach
could be further improved through precise references to time which enable

concrete historical analyses as well as precise references to geographical space of legal changes (Schömann 1994).

Previous comparative studies of employment protection systems have used a variety of methods in assessing national systems (Emerson 1988, Walwei 1991, Mosley and Kruppe 1993, Büchtemann 1993). However, most of the surveys consist of studies of a limited number of rather arbitrarily chosen countries in which separate descriptions of the countries are simply added together without much comparative analysis. The reason for their limited engagement in comparisons seems mainly due to the complexity of the task. Our own study attempts to strike a balance between single country studies (characteristic of the description and analysis of the legal systems of the Member States) and discussions of patterns and variables (the predominant approach in the empirical parts of the report). We thereby combine a qualitative comparison of the institutional settings and legal systems and a quantitative comparison of country patterns of employment in general and fixed-term employment in particular. Our analysis at the level of both cases and variables demonstrates the need for comparisons to be embedded in historical accounts of country-specific labour regulations and patterns of employment.

In addition, our study evaluates the policy area of labour market regulation from a target-oriented perspective (Schmid *et al.* 1996). It assesses regulatory goals with respect to underlying assumptions and their chances of implementation. For example, if the increase in flexibility of the labour market is adopted as the principal goal of (de)regulating fixed-term contracts, it is assumed that increased flexibility in labour regulations will enhance the efficiency of labour allocations, which in turn leads to higher levels of employment. However, existing legal frameworks which consist of national labour law, collective agreements between the social partners and Community regulations are mitigating factors in the implementation of flexibilisation policies.

The principal objectives of our book can be summarised as follows: to analyse the interaction between established legal frameworks and deregulation measures; to list economic factors which support or resist the spread of atypical employment; and to assess distributional aspects of policy changes, including equity effects related to age, gender and ethnicity as part of anti-discrimination policies. The particular policy field in which these aspects are studied is the (de)regulation of fixed-term contracts in the Member States of the European Union.

The book analyses the development of fixed-term employment in the twelve Member States of the European Union before its enlargement in the beginning of 1995. It is structured as follows: Chapter 2 is devoted to a discussion of theoretical approaches in law and labour economics which constitutes the foundation for our socio-economic analysis of atypical employment. Chapter 3 describes the legal context of employment protection with special reference to dismissal law and fixed-term contracts in twelve Member States of the European Union. In Chapter 4 we analyse the empirical evidence and evolutionary processes of fixed-term employment in the European Union on the basis of data from the Labour Force Survey provided by Eurostat.[4] Results of a multivariate analysis of country patterns are presented in Chapter 5. Chapter 6 reviews macro-economic assessments which are concerned with employment adjustment and labour market regulations. Finally, Chapter 7 summarises the comparisons and draws conclusions for future research.

2

LEGAL AND ECONOMIC THEORIES OF LABOUR MARKET REGULATION

Economic studies of employment protection systems tend to view law as an external reference system without considering that legal systems are based on dynamic factual and contractual relations and thus evolve over time. For us, legal regulations are a result of political compromises and unforeseeable legislative action, and labour law in particular is shaped by processes of implementation and control exercised by the industrial relations and employment protection systems. In order to analyse and compare various national labour regulations it is misleading in our view to rely on a single discipline approach. Our aim in this chapter is to show that legal and economic labour market theories, which assess the impact of regulation on labour market efficiency, are to some extent complementary and can be used to develop a multi-disciplinary theoretical design for the analysis of employment relationships.

The chapter starts with a comparison of two legal theories, the theory of the standard employment relationship and the theory of reflexive labour law. Thereafter we review some economic theories from which hypotheses concerning changes in the employment relationship, in particular fixed-term employment, can be retrieved. Finally, the legal and economic theories are combined into a multi-layered theoretical design for our empirical analyses in Chapters 4 and 5 of the book. The section presents testable rival hypotheses based on the theoretical designs which guide the ensuing empirical analyses of fixed-term contracts and their implementation in Europe.

LEGAL THEORIES

A new legislative interest in atypical employment emerged in a number of Member States of the European Communities in the 1980s. Non-standard forms of employment were discovered as instruments to combat unemployment in Europe. New policies were adopted under the general heading of 'flexibilisation' and 'deregulation' of the labour market. Employment protection was declared to be a 'burden on business' and labour law in general came under attack for neglecting business interests. Governments embarked on policies which aimed at 'liberalising' labour law and 'flexibilising' labour markets (Standing 1993). This free-market version of deregulation meant both less restrictions on personnel policies of companies and a decrease in employment protection for workers, especially for so-called atypical employees.

The national deregulation policies were pursued in the 1980s and 1990s without coordination at the European level. Attempts to introduce at the supranational level measures to harmonise regulations on atypical employment were blocked by the Council of Ministers. The European Communities, and now the European Union, were until recently impaired by the strong resistance of some Member States, in particular the United Kingdom, to grant European bodies competences in designing European labour law measures. However, even after the adoption of a positive attitude towards European Social Policy by the new British Labour government since May 1997, there are few reasons to expect the development of a comprehensive system of labour law at the European level. It is indeed highly unlikely that European Social Policy will be a replication of national policy-making in the areas of labour law and employment protection. National policies are often the result of corporatist arrangements which do not exist to the same extent at the European level. Instead we find the attempt to instrumentalise national policies for a neo-liberal European economic integration policy. In this process Member States are more or less voluntarily adopting European measures which flexibilise their employment laws. Deregulation at national level is thereby positively or negatively linked to neo-voluntarist European social and economic policies as well as the process of globalisation (Streeck 1996, Rogowski and Schmid 1997).

The neo-liberal reforms of the labour market at national and supranational level have forced labour lawyers to adapt to a new view of their field. The main function of labour law is no longer seen as restricting atypical contracts for the sake of employment protection. Instead atypical employment contracts are to be interpreted as instruments of labour market policies in line with the goals of legal norms which were introduced to facilitate the use of atypical employment.

Legal theories vary in their assessments of the new 'deregulatory' trend in the regulation of atypical employment. Broadly speaking there are two approaches which differ considerably with respect to their assumptions about functions and factors influencing the development of legal regulations. These approaches emphasise either 'external' factors related to the economic, the political or the industrial relations system or 'internal' factors related to the legal system itself. In the following we present briefly two theories which represent the 'external' and the 'internal approach'. These are the theory of the standard employment relationship and the reflexive labour law approach. We shall first introduce their main features and then attempt to demonstrate how

9

these apparently diametrically opposed theories can nevertheless complement each other.

The theory of the *Standard Employment Relationship* distinguishes between the contract of employment and the employment relationship (Mückenberger 1985b, see also Streeck 1990). Whereas the contract of employment refers to express agreements between the employer and the employee, the employment relationship is defined as a status which in legal terms is constituted by a floor of rights (Deakin and Mückenberger 1989). These rights are granted by statutory employment protection which defines rights independent of the terms agreed upon in the actual contract of employment.

In this view, statutory employment protection aims primarily at the employment relationship and not at the contract of employment. Employment protection measures are thereby understood as means to shape the employment relationship in legal terms and to equalise a socially unequal relationship between the employer and the employee. Furthermore the legally protected employment relationship is seen as a minimum condition for an adequate participation of employees in social life. The fact that the employment relationship constitutes the economic basis for the employee means that legal protection participates in guaranteeing the subsistence of the employee.

The theory conceives the standard employment relationship both as a factual relationship and as a legal relationship. The theory assumes a determining influence of factual changes on legal developments. Thus the legal model of a standard employment relationship is threatened by factual changes in the forms of employment. Furthermore, the theory assumes a factually unequal relationship between the employer and the employee. This inequality is the main reason for legal measures of employment protection. Since the employment relationship is dominated by powerful employer interests, legal regulation is required to restrict and counter the company interests. Labour law's function is seen as a balancing act between the interests of the employer and employee through protection of minimum standards which the employer has to observe (Mückenberger 1990).

The theory of the standard employment relationship was originally explicitly normative or prescriptive. Based on a so-called politico-economic assessment of social processes, it viewed new forms of employment as predominantly expressing employer demands. The function of labour law was therefore to protect employees against one-sided demands (Mückenberger 1989 and Deakin and Mückenberger 1989). From this perspective, atypical employment, including fixed-term contracts, are seen as undermining the standards which the law provides for a typical employment relationship. The growth of atypical forms of employment appears as a process of gradual 'erosion' of the standard employment relationship (Mückenberger 1985b).

One weakness of the theory lies in its distinction between typical or standard employment conditions and atypical forms of employment. The notion of a standard employment relationship assumes that there are one or more typical forms of employment. However, it is unclear how many of the typical elements (permanent, full-time, etc. employment) need to be changed, and to what degree, to turn typical into atypical work. The theory also appears unable to accept fixed-term contracts as being incorporated into the system of employment standards.

Meanwhile the theory of the standard employment relationship has adopted a pragmatic attitude towards new forms of employment. The previously rigid defence of a standard employment relationship is widely regarded as supporting the preservation of an increasingly unrealistic model of a male wage-earner who is responsible for a family of non-wage-earners (Bosch 1986). Furthermore, fixed-term contract and other new forms of employment are no longer seen as inspired exclusively by employer demands, but rather as an expression of general trends and cultural changes in lifestyles. An increased female participation in the labour market means that not only employers but also employees demand new forms of employment, in particular part-time jobs. The task for labour law cannot be to prevent the flourishing of these new types by insisting on a negative appraisal of them as an erosion of a sacred standard employment relationship. Labour law must instead develop notions of social protection compatible with these new forms of employment (Keller and Seifert 1993, 1997; Mückenberger 1993).[1]

The theory of *Reflexive Labour Law* is based on the assumption that legal development is only indirectly influenced by economic development. It postulates that in modern labour law systems, legal innovations are most likely to be reactions to social or legal consequences of previous legal regulations. This approach is interested in the 'feedback loop from legal norm to social consequences to legal norm' (Teubner 1986: 309). In particular reflexive labour law thematises the awareness of limits of legal regulation within labour law (Rogowski and Wilthagen 1994).

The theory of reflexive labour law analyses the concept of an employment relationship as an internal legal construction of an external world of social relations. Factual changes in the forms of employment can only influence the legal construction if they are recognised as a problem within the legal discourse. Law is conceived as cognitively open to social changes but normatively closed with respect to its basic operations of self-reproduction. New social constellations have no determining effect on the legal system because the legal system enjoys autonomy in deciding on adjustments to its legal construction of reality.

Furthermore, the reflexive law theory assumes that regulation is dependent on self-regulation. Political attempts to reduce unemployment through a reform of labour law ('deregulation') are limited by conditions within the labour law system (Rogowski and Schmid 1997). Labour law can accept the new political guidelines only to the extent to which it is able to reform itself. If the new legislation does not fit within the system of employment protection measures, labour courts and labour law doctrine are likely to interpret the new law in the light of the existing system of norms (Blanke 1994). In the end, it is self-reference of labour law communications to labour law communications which constitutes the labour law discourse.

The reflexive law theory tends to view the regulation of atypical employment foremost as an internal affair of an increasingly complex labour law system. In particular the regulation of fixed-term contracts is interpreted as a reaction to problems created by the employment protection measures themselves. A reflexive process of 'protection of employment protection' is suggested to be characteristic of labour law's reaction to economic and political challenges (Rogowski and Schömann 1996). However, this labour law tendency can be recognised by other function systems as detrimental to their objectives, and it can then lead to hostility towards labour law objectives and foster further demands for deregulation.

We can conclude our overview of legal theories with remarks on the complementarity of the theories. The theory of the standard employment relationship and the theory of reflexive labour law agree that an analysis of the legal norms themselves as well as their political and economic contexts is required for an adequate understanding of the development of legal norms. However, they differ with respect to the relative weight each of the theories attaches to legal and non-legal factors in explaining the development of regulation of atypical employment. Nevertheless, they seem compatible if the political and economic analyses of the standard employment relationship theorists are reconstructed as attempts to explain the non-legal use of law and the studies following the reflexive labour law concept as concentrating on the legal view of law. Both perspectives add dimensions of research which must be taken into account in order to gain an adequate picture of the development of the law on atypical employment.

In particular, a study of the effects of deregulation requires analyses of the use of law in both legal and non-legal contexts. It then becomes possible to see that the impact of deregulation on the use of fixed-term contracts, for example, is mitigated by a large variety of legal and non-legal factors. This result reinforces the need for country-specific studies and an analysis of the relations between the extent of (de-)regulation and the actual number of fixed-term contracts.

An analysis of the regulations on fixed-term contracts in the Member States of the European Union thus requires an evaluation of country-specific approaches to employment protection. Such an analysis includes a number of different analyses of legal provisions. First, the regulations themselves must be outlined, including the law of the employment contract and the basic floor of rights granted by employment protection legislation. Secondly, the evolution of nationally specific features of labour law regulations needs to be assessed. And thirdly, it is necessary to include various contexts of labour regulations consisting of information on legislative processes, labour market conditions and traditions of industrial relations. Information regarding the first and second types of analysis is provided in our legal overview in Chapter 3.

ECONOMIC THEORIES

The earliest theoretical approach to employment security and fixed-term employment is actually found in the writings of Adam Smith. In chapter X part 1 of the *Inquiry into the Nature and Causes of the Wealth of Nations* (1776 cited from 1976 edition Vol. I: 120) Smith writes:

> The wages of labour in different occupations vary with the constancy or inconstancy of employment. . . . What he (a mason or bricklayer) earns, therefore, while he is employed, must not only maintain him while he is idle, but make him some compensation for those anxious and desponding moments which the thought of so precarious a situation must sometimes occasion. . . . The high wages of those workmen, therefore, are not so much the recompense of their skill, as the compensation for the inconstancy of their employment.

In Smith's work the notion of a compensating wage differential is already present. A compensating wage differential is to be expected for inconstancy of employment as he puts it. The concept of wage differentials assumes a relative ranking of groups of workers along specific dimensions. Most commonly in labour market theories these are occupational or regional wage differentials. For example, occupations with more hazardous health conditions are supposed to compensate for these health risks through higher wages. Similarly, Smith's hypothesis concerning the constancy of work is to test for the presence of a compensating wage differential in a country's legal provision for fixed-term contracts, which offsets the disadvantage incurred by the insecurity of the employment relationship in certain occupations.

In the empirical analysis it should be possible to identify such occupational or industrial sector compensating wage differentials. It is, however, an open empirical question whether such compensation is organised along the lines of wage differentials between occupations or industries, or whether in addition to this wage differential a specific compensation is attributed to fixed-term employment independent of occupation or industry. However, if earnings of fixed-term employees are lower than those of employees with a more permanent job during the period of fixed-term employment, they might receive a lump sum recompensation at the beginning or end of a fixed-term contract which makes up for job insecurity.

The Nobel laureate, Ronald Coase, questions the price mechanism as a valid explanation of job mobility within firms. Factor allocations within the firm, in his view, do not obey a price mechanism, but they are more likely to follow the directions of the entrepreneur. 'If a workman moves from department Y to department X, he does not go because of a change in relative prices, but because he is ordered to do so' (Coase 1937: 387). Coase cuts short an extensive analysis of the costs involved in the coordination mechanism or during the process of coordination. He deems it more expedient to think of an employment contract as a contract which establishes a hierarchical relationship between employer and employees. The production factor labour is expected to obey, within certain limits, is the directions of the entrepreneur.[2] With more or less fixed factor payments to labour, the contracted services of labour remain largely unspecified and subject to the discretion of the entrepreneur.

This view of the nature of labour contracts might appear implausible, but Coase explains it by referring to the economic rationale which is behind the need for long-term contracts. In his explanation of why firms supersede the price mechanism as an instrument of coordination, Coase stresses the cost advantage of long-term work contracts. The advantage results from the fact that any other form of work contract would have to specify more precisely the content of the work to be carried out. The cost-effectiveness of long-term contracts stems from the difficulty to foresee which tasks might be required from the employee at a later point in time. Due to uncertainty about future requirements, it is in the firm's interest to be able to decide more or less freely which specific services should be provided by the employee at a later point in time (Bertola 1990).

A labour contract of this kind is cost-saving for the firm because in the event of changing work requirements, it can redeploy employees with more flexibility without having to first renegotiate work contracts. In cases where learning-by-doing is an important implicit component of the work contract, fixed-term contracts increase the probability that employees will want to renegotiate the terms of their contract. Renegotiation would allow employees to participate more fully, or earlier, in the returns from the increased productivity during this process of learning-by-doing.

In the following section we discuss three economic approaches to analysing labour relationships and employment protection. We start with classical and neo-classical economics, in particular the human capital theory. We then discuss briefly the theory of labour market segmentation and its contribution to an understanding of employment durations. Finally, the efficiency wage theory is dealt with in some detail with particular reference to its attempt to link the micro- and the macro-economic levels.

Human Capital Theory

Within the framework of human capital theory (Becker 1964 and Mincer 1974), fixed-term employment is not dealt with directly. However, in a more indirect manner individual investment decisions in education and training are linked to the expected returns of education. As soon as employment security deteriorates this is likely to have consequences for investment decisions. Both employment uncertainty associated with a fixed-term contract and the risk of unemployment after termination of a fixed-term contract[3] have negative consequences on the returns to investment in education, training and further training. The incentive to invest in general and in firm-specific human capital is reduced due to the uncertainty of continuous employment over the entire life-cycle.

The reduced 'constancy of employment' Smith (1976: 120) shortens the accumulated duration over which investments can be recouped (Becker 1964). Later birth cohorts are, therefore, expected to reduce the amount of investment in human capital for the society as a whole. These macro-economic consequences of individual-level action are caused by lower employment security for a growing number of fixed-term employees. For example, if the transition from full-time education to the labour market has become more difficult in a specific subject area and involves many short-term jobs before finding a more stable employment situation, the choice of this track of full-time education is likely to be reduced. Hence, for a four-year course it might take about five years until changing labour market insertion patterns will have an effect on educational choices of later born cohorts.

Figure 2.1 depicts the changing life-time patterns of labour earnings (E) for an individual with s and a second individual with s-d years of schooling or training. If fixed-term contracts become a widely-used feature of the labour market independent of the level of education, this should be neutral to the returns to education. But in cases where the risk of unemployment after termination of a fixed-term contract is relatively high for those with higher investments in education or training, then the returns to higher education will be reduced.[4] On the other hand, if those with little or no investment in education and training have the unstable employment patterns, the labour earnings relative to persons with higher levels of education are reduced and earnings differentials increase. Such higher earnings differentials between low and highly educated employees will increase the demand for higher education. Hence the observed 'run' to achieve higher education in most Member States of the European Union could also be a reaction to the increasing gap between well-paid and stable jobs for graduates on the one hand, and badly paid and insecure jobs for the less well educated. Sorting of job applicants according to their educational attainment into fixed-term or more stable employment relationships might be observable.

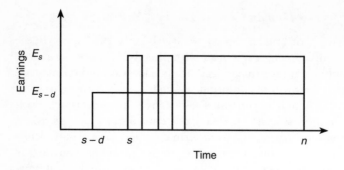

Figure 2.1 Fixed-term employment and human capital

Since initial investments in human capital will depend on the probability of stable employment, it is an empirical question whether recruitment of specific groups of labour force participants into fixed-term employment occurs. If educational sorting of fixed-term employees is present, repercussions of this process on initial human capital investments of later birth cohorts is very likely.

In a cross-national analysis we expect countries with generally more unstable employment patterns to have lower levels of initial investment in education than countries with low risks of unemployment and few fixed-term employees. Findings of a cross-country comparison of 'hire and fire' practices of employment, more common in the United States and the United Kingdom, might reveal that those at risk of unstable work patterns have insufficient incentives to invest in general human capital or even firm-specific skills.

Theory of Labour Market Segmentation

Employment stability plays an important role in the theory of labour market segmentation (Doeringer and Piore 1971, Stinchcombe 1979, Schömann 1994). Segmentation theories distinguish between primary and secondary segment jobs. Primary segment positions offer long-term, continuous employment in connection with structured career ladders. Secondary segment jobs offer lower wages, no further training possibilities, no or few career prospects and generally unstable and precarious employment prospects.

Stinchcombe's (1979) version of the segmentation theory applies a cross-classification of the position of firms in product markets (competitive versus monopolised) and labour market demand (skilled versus unskilled labour). Secondary and precarious jobs in this theory are likely to be fixed-term jobs offered in specific industrial segments. These are mainly small competitive

16

industries like textiles, wood, paper, printing and in the service sector of the economy like in private services, catering and hotels. The differentiation into skilled and unskilled jobs is of particular importance in explaining labour earnings as well as probabilities for employees to be employed on a fixed-term contract.

The theory of labour market segmentation argues that there are persistent wage differentials between fixed-term employees and standard contract employees. These differences cannot be explained by compensating wage differentials in the sense that employees working under bad working conditions or precarious employment will receive a wage premium to compensate for this. Evidence is even unconclusive about the fact that bad weather conditions, more polluted air and heavy work are compensated for (Schmidt and Zimmermann 1991).

If fixed-term employment is perceived by employees as having characteristics of 'secondary jobs' – that is, offering lower wages, few career prospects and no further training possibilities – employees with occupations or in industrial sectors with high demand for labour will tend to avoid employers offering such labour contracts. Employees are likely to interpret fixed-term contracts as a negative signal of a firm's employment record. Employers recruiting employees with fixed-term contracts in secondary industrial segments will find it difficult to attract highly-skilled labour.

As a hypothesis we derive that competitive, large-scale engineering, professional and bureaucratic labour market segments are less likely to offer fixed-term contracts than those segments which rely mainly on unskilled labour. In a cross-national analysis countries will differ in the distribution of fixed-term employees across industrial segments according to the lines of labour market segmentation usually found in a specific country.

Efficiency Wage Theory

The efficiency wage theory is based on the basic assumption that the productivity of workers depends on the real wage paid to them. An individual's utility is assumed to be a function of the wage received (w) and the level of effort on the job (e). Wage cuts therefore have negative effects on a worker's productivity and increase costs of production possibly by more than the wage cut saves money for the firm (Shapiro and Stiglitz 1984).

Further basic assumptions are: (1) there is a specific probability b for exogenous separations from the firm due to firm closures for example, (2) if a worker shirks there is a specific probability q that the worker will be found out and have to leave the firm. In this model it is rational for a firm to pay a wage above the full employment equilibrium wage, since workers are expected to reduce shirking because of the high costs of a job loss. This latter effect constitutes the discipline function of aggregate unemployment for individual work efforts. Another result of this modelling is that labour turnover will be reduced, causing lower training and administrative costs (Akerlof 1982).

In respect to our major concern of labour market efficiency, employment stability and the use of fixed-term contracts we can derive hypotheses on likely effects of deregulation of dismissal protection. In a slightly augmented version of the basic theoretical model (Levine 1989: 902), it is shown that government policies which discourage labour turnover through introduction of just cause employment policies (increasing the evidence required for a dismissal) can increase labour market efficiency. In the original model by Shapiro and Stiglitz (1984: 51) using comparative statics it can be shown that increasing the quit rate b, or decreasing the monitoring intensity q, shifts the non-shirking condition (NSC) upwards (to NSC'), while leaving the labour demand curve unchanged.

Facilitating the use of fixed-term contracts by legislation, however, works in the opposite direction. Even with the same monitoring intensity q of newly hired persons on fixed-term contracts it involves little or no costs to dismiss at the end of the contract. Within efficiency wage models, fixed-term contracts operate as an additional worker discipline device, since fixed-term contracts increase the risk of losing one's job at expiry of the contract. Therefore, changing legislation to allow for more widespread use of fixed-term employment is shifting the no-shirking condition in the aggregate labour market downwards (i.e. the shift downwards from NSC' to NSC", compare Figure 2.2). This has the effect of reducing the level of wages in the aggregate. The no-shirking condition is based on the rationale that setting w^* sufficiently high will prevent workers from shirking. The deregulation of just cause dismissal protection legislation reduces the wage w^* which will prevent workers from shirking.

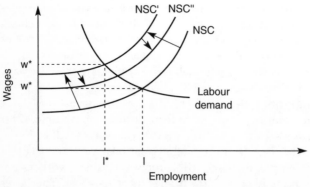

Figure 2.2 Unemployment as a worker discipline device

Note: NSC means aggregate no-shirking condition

The efficiency wage theory allows for the integration of the reflexive labour law theory discussed above into the economic modelling of the labour market. The ample jurisdiction on cases of just or unjust dismissal which has evolved in many European countries has, over many years, led to an upward shift of the no-shirking condition (NSC to NSC') requiring a higher wage w^* to discourage workers from shirking. The introduction of increased job insecurity due to deregulation of fixed-term contracts redresses this balance (in a reflexive way) and shifts the no-shirking condition back to its original level or some lower level NSC". In the realm of this model, the legal facilitation of fixed-term employment in a previously highly-regulated labour market will have the effect of reducing the aggregate wage w^*.

On the micro-level, however, it is not as obvious who among all workers will be adversely affected by this shift, since this is a statement about the distribution of wages among the employed. The existence of a 'worker discipline device' suggests that this outside pressure mainly comes from the unemployed who, by offering to work for lower wages, present a possible alternative for employers. Fixed-term contracts might in this model contribute to the effectiveness of aggregate unemployment in increasing the pressure on worker wage restraint. It is a prediction by Shapiro and Stiglitz (1984: 443) that their model might be most suited in labour markets for lower-quality workers since the unemployed are more able to compete with these workers. However, at times of high levels of unemployment, even among recent university graduates in many European countries, the wage pressure effect of the unemployed can be widely spread.

A MULTI-LAYERED THEORETICAL DESIGN AND RESEARCH HYPOTHESES

The socio-legal and socio-economic theories mentioned in the previous two sections are not mutually exclusive. They emphasise different aspects and offer different perspectives for an empirical comparison of legal regulations and economic trends. In the following we want to show how the two legal theories and the three economic theories can be combined to provide a multi-layered concept for an analysis of fixed-term contracts. Table 2.1 summarises the theories.

The table is an attempt to synthesise the theories by highlighting the specific perspectives of the different approaches which can guide our analysis of legal and economic aspects of fixed-term contracts in the European Union. The table distinguishes between explanatory dimensions and reasons which the theories emphasise in explaining the occurrence and the rates of fixed-term contracts.

The theory of the standard employment relationship highlights reasons for the occurrence of fixed-term contracts which relate to changes in the factual

Table 2.1 Legal and economic theories and fixed-term contracts (FTCs)

	explanatory dimension	reasons for FTC	rates of FTC
Standard Employment Relationship	employment relationship and empl. contract	changes in the employment relationship	post-Fordism, cultural and value changes
Reflexive Labour Law	autonomy of labour law	complexity of empl. protection	degree of legal control
Human Capital	costs and investment	cost saving strategies	change in regime of production, low wage, low skill
Segmentation	industrial context	secondary labour markets	decline of industrial relations
Efficiency Wages	motivation and productivity	concern with worker discipline	high unemployment service economy

relationship of the employer and the employee. Employment is conceived as a status which is only marginally regulated by the actual employment contract. With respect to rates of fixed-term contracts the theory refers to economic (post-Fordist) as well as cultural and value changes which erode the basis of the standard employment relationship. Thus the forms of atypical employment are determined by societal factors rather than individual needs.

The theory of reflexive labour law gives prominence to internal legal developments. It assumes autonomy of the labour law system in shaping legal forms of employment. It describes in particular problems related to the legal complexity of employment protection and attempts of legal control which explain the occurrence as well as the rates of fixed-term contracts.

The human capital approach views atypical employment in the light of investment strategies in the education of workers. Fixed-term contracts are uninteresting if there are high company investments in the education of an employee. However, if the work force consists mainly of employees with low skills and low wages, atypical forms of employment are more suitable.

The theory of labour market segmentation argues on the line of changes in the industrial context in explaining the occurrence of fixed-term contracts. The split of the labour market into a primary segment of stable employment and a secondary labour market consisting of atypical forms of employment is related to changes in the industrial relations system and in governance structures of industrial sectors. In particular, a decline of collective bargaining and of regulation through tripartite arrangements involving trade unions, employer associations and the state supports the emergence and expansion of secondary industrial segments.

Finally, the efficiency wage theory stresses the threat of unemployment as a disciplinary device in establishing wage levels. Fixed-term contracts occur as an additional disciplinary device to favour moderate wage agreements. However, its functioning is linked to high levels of unemployment and the growth of employment in the service sector of an economy.

This multi-layered design provides the theoretical basis for our empirical analysis and the supply of testable hypotheses. It indicates the dimensions in which concrete hypotheses for a study of fixed-term contracts are located. In the following we suggest some concrete hypotheses based on the five theories discussed above.

Based on the theory of the standard employment relationship we expect that the use of fixed-term contracts is limited to a small number of occupations or specific industrial sectors. These sectors or professions will have specific characteristics for which the 'new' type of fixed-term employment is particularly suited. Hence in an empirical analysis of the selection into fixed-term contracts we expect that personal characteristics of fixed-term employees will differ from characteristics of employees holding standard open-ended work contracts.

In countries where fixed-term contracts require the express mentioning of a reason to justify the use of a fixed-term contract (like in Spain, Italy, Luxembourg, France, Germany and Greece), the difference between groups of employees with these two types of contracts should be easily identifiable. Employment with one or the other form of a contract will be based on 'objective' reasons related to the type of work rather than characteristics of employees like age or gender.

According to the theory of reflexive labour law, an extensive use of fixed-term employees in an economy is to be understood as a development within a national system of employment protection. A country's employment system which protects the standard employment relationship is expected to create a specific group of fixed-term employees, whereas a country's system of labour law which acknowledges the need of fixed-term contracts is expected to reveal a 'less discriminatory spread' of fixed-term contracts among employees.

We also expect quite different patterns of change in the spread of fixed-term employment. Following the reflexive labour law theory we should be able to observe so-called vintage effects of these new types of contracts. Once new regulations of fixed-term contracts are officially introduced, they are likely to be applied across the whole range of newly hired employees. However, for both theoretical and empirical reasons it would be interesting to investigate in detail the time structure of the evolution after a change in regulation. Countries may react similarly to a policy change but differ in the speed of application of new labour law.

The theory of reflexive labour law comments on the process and the sequences of legislative and other regulatory activities, for example judicial intervention and collective agreements. We expect to observe within countries regulatory activities which reveal the reflexive nature of this process. In a country where statutory employment protection is left largely unchanged for many years, other legal activities become likely to flexibilise the employment relationship in the subject area of fixed-term contracts. No or little change in one area of regulation, for example employment protection, will be compensated by extensive activities in another area of labour law, like judicial interpretation of fixed-term contracts.

The empirical part of the study (Chapter 3) on country patterns of employment protection legislation tries to keep track of reflexive processes within employment protection systems by portraying the chronological order[5] of the various types of legal activities, mainly legislative activities, but also court decisions and collective agreements. This enables our analysis to measure the degree of reflexivity in each country against the background of the legal context of a country's employment system.

Unlike socio-legal theories of the employment relationship socio-economic labour market theories emphasise the dominant role played by wages.[6] The notion of compensating wage differentials presents a topic in economic theories of the labour market raised in the writings of Adam Smith (1976). Economic labour market theories assume that, even if other characteristics of the employment relationship are acknowledged to be important to determine productivity on a job or of a specific employee, factors which have an impact on productivity will ultimately be reflected in wage levels or wage growth (Schömann 1994). A leading hypothesis for the empirical analysis is: (1) employees holding a fixed-term contract are performing more hazardous jobs or tasks and (2) if this is the case, fixed-term employees are likely to receive a kind of (additional) compensation for this. A comparative analysis of wage rates due to fixed-term employment versus standard-type contracts in each country is indicated if a rigorous test is to be carried out.[7]

In the accounting system of a firm employees' wages are usually subsumed under labour costs[8] to the firm. These costs to the employer do not only consist of the gross or net wage paid to the employee, but also the potential dismissal costs in case specific legal or contractual arrangements have been agreed upon. Profit maximising firms will try to keep these costs as low as possible. However, Coase (1937) actually argues that long-term work contracts might be a cost-effective alternative to fixed-term and short-term employment, since future requirements of tasks to be performed by an employee are hard to predict. In the case of hiring on the basis of very general job descriptions, long-term standard employment contracts are preferred by employers for reasons of lower costs to employers. It is an empirical question to identify and compare the level of determinacy of labour contracts between countries. Besides effects of custom and practice, the level of economic development and the industry structure of a country will shape the employment relationship.

In the three socio-economic theories – human capital, segmentation and efficiency wage theory – wages play a major role in the motivation of individuals.

In the framework of the human capital theory higher wages operate as a motivation to invest more in education due to the higher wages paid to higher educated employees. The introduction of more fixed-term contracts, if applied only at the hiring of lower educated employees, will have the effect of widening wage differentials. In both segmentation and efficiency wage theory the motivational effect of wages is directly linked to the effort provided on the job. Introducing fixed-term contracts into the employment relationships is likely to increase the gap between groups of employees with favourable and unfavourable employment conditions. It is unlikely to introduce a new economy-wide divide into the labour force.

All socio-economic theories claim a wage reducing effect for employees holding a fixed-term contract. However, they disagree on the distributional implications of a change in legislation facilitating fixed-term employment contracts. Human capital theory predicts a narrowing of the wage gap if fixed-term contracts are applied equally across all levels of education and professional groups, but a widening of the wage gap if applied selectively. Segmentation theory forecasts a wider gap in earnings as well as a deepening of the split in the labour force between those employed in the primary segment and those with precarious employment relationships. Finally, efficiency wage theory offers the most detailed rationale for the mechanism which leads to the wage reducing effect of more fixed-term employment on the individual as well as the aggregate level of an economy. In fact, efficiency wage theory underlines the importance of the level of unemployment, as a credible threat for dismissal, as a major factor for wage attainment and the distribution of wages.

3

EMPLOYMENT PROTECTION SYSTEMS AND THE REGULATION OF FIXED-TERM CONTRACTS IN THE EUROPEAN UNION

INTRODUCTION

Legal regulations of fixed-term contracts differ widely among the Member States of the European Union. In addition, there are attempts to regulate atypical employment relationships at the European level. In the following we shall present basic information on the legal situation in the twelve Member States as it existed in general in September 1994, and on attempts to harmonise these regulations at the European level.

Our overviews of national regulations are, to some extent, guided by a theoretical concern which we derive from the reflexive labour law approach (see Chapter 2). The basic assumption of this approach is that legal regulations of fixed-term contracts are shaped in developed labour law systems by their surrounding legal context and by national approaches to regulating employment protection rather than by economic trends or political fashions (Rogowski and Wilthagen 1994). More precisely, regulations of fixed-term contracts 'reflect' in particular regulations on unfair dismissal.

In accordance with this hypothesis, the following presentation contains information not only on the law of fixed-term contracts, but also on legal regulations of dismissal. The main purpose of the following analysis is not, however, theoretical, and should not be read as a test of the reflexive labour law hypothesis. Our aim is more modest. The goal is to expose the legal approaches in the Member States of the European Union and at the European level in order to provide the basis for a future, indepth comparison of national and supranational regulations of fixed-term contracts.

EMPLOYMENT PROTECTION AND FIXED-TERM CONTRACTS IN THE MEMBER STATES OF THE EUROPEAN UNION

Belgium

Characteristics of the Belgian system of employment protection regulations

In order to understand the nature of Belgian labour law it is necessary to emphasise the importance of collective agreements as a source of regulation. The centralised system of collective bargaining is the outstanding feature of the Belgian industrial relations system and influences its approach to the regulation of employment matters. There are four levels of collective bargaining: national or inter-industry bargaining, resulting in central framework agreements; negotiations in the bipartite National Labour Council (*Conseil National du Travail*, CNT), leading to central national agreements; bargaining at the sectoral or regional level; and negotiations at the company level resulting in company agreements.

The CNT is of particular interest. It is empowered to conclude collective agreements (*Conventions collectives de travail*, CCT) on major issues of employment protection, including working time, collective redundancies, works council rights, minimum wage levels (Commission 1992, Supplement 4/92, 52) as well as 'flexible' employment conditions. The Belgian government is obliged to seek advice from the CNT on all reform proposals in the area of employment. Furthermore, the implementation of labour law statutes is in a number of cases delegated to the National Labour Council (Blanpain 1985. Also EIRR 183, April 1989: 24–6, and 186, July 1989: 20–2).

In the field of employment protection, there are a number of statutes which contain provisions on employment contracts and dismissal protection.[1] The first Act on Standard Labour Contracts came into force in 1900, and a special Act on Employment Contracts was introduced in 1922. The main statutory regulations in the area of statutory employment are now incorporated in the Act on Employment Contracts of 1978. This Act also contains regulations on dismissal protection. Collective agreements provide additional protection for the employee in the case of termination of the contract of employment.

It is noteworthy that the regulations on dismissal focus on notice periods rather than on substantive standards or requirements of reason and reasonableness (Kronke 1990: 212). Notice periods, regulated in the Act on Employment Contracts, are different for blue-collar workers and for salaried or white-collar employees. Workers have a right to a minimum notice period of seven working days for employment which has lasted less than six months. The normal notice period thereafter for the employer is twenty-eight days and for the employee fourteen days (Articles 59 and 60). These periods double after twenty years of service.

25

In the case of salaried or white-collar employees, the law distinguishes between levels of income. Employees earning less than BF 699,000 per year enjoy a minimum notice period of three months until they reach five years of service. The notice period increases for every additional five years of service by another three months. The maximum notice period for termination by these employees is three months. For employees having an annual income in excess of BF 699.000, additional notice periods can be negotiated (Commission 1992, Supplement 4/92: 72); in this case the maximum notice period for an employee termination is four and a half months (six months for very high wage earners). The dismissal protection for white-collar employees is regulated in Articles 82 to 84.[2]

Only blue-collar workers – but not white-collar workers – are further protected by the legal requirement of a reason for dismissal. The unilateral dismissal of a blue-collar employee is only legal if it is justified by a reason relating either to misconduct or incapability of the employee or to reorganisation of the company (Art. 63). Long-term sickness of the employee for more than six months is deemed a valid reason for dismissal. In this case the employer has to pay compensation equivalent to the amount of wages to be paid during the period of notice.

Absolute protection from dismissal is given by collective agreements to works council members, trade union delegates, and members of safety and health committees. Special protection is given by statute to pregnant employees if the principal reason for dismissal is pregnancy.[3] In addition, statutory dismissal protection exists for company doctors, employees with a political mandate, and employees who are involved in disposing of toxic materials. Furthermore, the Act of 1985 on Revitalisation of the Economy has introduced protective measures for so-called career breaks, which include protection against dismissal and the right to return to work. The two main cases of specially-protected career breaks are child-minding of either or both parents after the birth of their child (Art. 101) and a break for purposes of further training (Art. 118).[4]

Since 1966 employees have had a right to redundancy payment in the case of closure of a company with more than twenty employees. Employees with a minimum of one year's service can claim a legally fixed sum as basic redundancy payment plus a compensatory payment subject to a statutory maximum. For employees over the age of 45 there is an additional payment subject again to a statutory maximum.

A national collective agreement has extended the basic concept of the right to redundancy payments to cases of mass dismissals for economic or technical reasons. In these cases, at least 10 per cent of the employees must be affected by dismissal. The redundancy payment is calculated on the basis of the difference between unemployment benefits and the previous net salary. The employee is entitled to this payment for up to four months.

Temporary or agency employment has received special recognition in Belgium in the Act on Temporary Work of 24 July 1987. It restricts agency work to the replacement of permanent employees, extraordinary increase in the workload, and exceptional work (Art. 1). Exceptional work is defined by the national agreement CCT No. 36, concluded in the CNT on 27 November 1981 (Blanpain and Oversteyns 1993: 45–75). The regulation of the relationship between agency and agency worker follows the pattern of regulations for fixed-term replacement contracts (discussed below).

Outplacement, i.e. services offered by third parties to accompany individual or collective redundancies, is further regulated by Collective Agreement or CCT No. 51 of the National Labour Council, adopted in February 1992 (EIRR 179, December 1988: 22).

The regulation of fixed-term contracts in Belgium

The Belgian regulations on fixed-term contracts, which were introduced in the 1980s, have to be interpreted in the context of government initiatives to combat unemployment through the promotion of non-standard forms of employment. Given the importance of industrial relations and collective bargaining for the system of employment protection, the reaction of the Belgian employer associations and unions to these government proposals on atypical employment have been crucial (Alaluf 1989: 249–66). In general, the industrial relations system has supported the reforms on flexibilisation of employment conditions in exchange for stable wages and reduction in working hours. The unions have actively participated in the National Labour Council, which has implemented labour legislation through collective agreements. The unions have acted as 'social agencies', i.e. as quasi-public institutions responsible for social management and regulation at the expense of traditional militant demands (Rosanvallon 1988. See also the critique of Alaluf 1989: 260–2).

The Belgian regulations protecting atypical employment derive both from general law on employment contracts and from specific laws and collective agreements on atypical employment. There are specific regulations regarding fixed-term contracts in the Act on Employment Contracts of 1978, in the above-mentioned Act on Temporary Work of 24 July 1987, which includes regulations on fixed-term employment, and in a national collective agreement of 1987 (EIRR 179, December 1988: 22). Fixed-term contracts must be in writing. Furthermore, an employment contract is automatically permanent if no special arrangements are made regarding a fixed term.

However, if the parties want to enter into a fixed-term contract, they are not, in general, required to be covered by legally prescribed reasons. In the case of fixed-term contracts, it is not necessary to distinguish between temporary employment contracts, contracts for a fixed term, contracts for a specific task and contracts for reasons of replacement. The main dismissal protection regulations do not apply to these contracts. Furthermore, sick pay benefits are modified with respect to these contracts.

The Act on Employment Contracts of 3 July 1978 limits the continuous use of fixed-term contracts. Art. 10 contains the general principle that successive fixed-term contracts automatically transform into a permanent contract. However, if the interruption of contracts relates to a change of circumstances of the employee (e.g. military service), the legal stipulation does not apply. A successive use of fixed-term contracts is also justified upon the request of the employee, and in cases where the employer can prove that the nature of the work, or an economic crisis situation of the company, requires a fixed term. These so-called continuation clauses are subject to co-determination.

If the contract continues after the expiry of the fixed term, the parties are legally treated as having concluded a permanent employment contract. This is regulated in Art. 11 of the Act on Employment Contracts.

In general, the parties are free to agree on an automatic expiration of the contract aimed at specific performance. However, this right is limited, according to Art. 36 of the Act on Employment Contracts, if such a contract is meant to circumvent dismissal protection. It is also limited where the condition for expiry is marriage or pregnancy.

Replacement contracts can be concluded for a maximum of two years. Typical reasons for a replacement contract are military service or maternity leave. However, replacement of employees who are suspended for economic reasons, bad weather, strikes or lock-outs is illegal. A replacement contract which continues over two years automatically becomes permanent (Blanpain and Oversteyns 1993: 49).

Replacement contracts and employment contracts for a specific task are further regulated by the 1987 Act on Temporary Work. The relation of this Act to the previous law is debatable but it seems that the new Act has largely replaced the older regulations for these specific types of contract (Kronke 1990: 45). According to the 1987 Act, the employer and the employee must agree on the length of and the reason for a fixed-term contract, which must be laid down in a written document. If the parties fail to obey the formal legal requirements, the contract automatically transforms into a permanent employment contract (Art. 4 (2) of the 1987 Act).

The 1987 Act expressly mentions the right of the employer and the employee to conclude successive fixed-term contracts for replacement purposes (Art. 3). However, the 'portfolio' or framework law (*loi de programme*) of 22 December 1985 has limited the use of successive fixed-term contracts. On-call labour contracts, stipulating that the employee may be asked to work anywhere from 0 to 40 hours per week, at times and on days specified by the employer, are considered to be a single open-ended contract by the law (see note 2). The government has, however, proposed in its 'Global Crisis Plan', issued in the autumn of 1993, to ease the use of successive fixed-term contracts in order to introduce more 'flexibility' into the labour market (EIRR 239, December 1993: 5). Fixed-term contracts can be renewed up to four times within two years. In addition, new so-called insertion contracts have been introduced for young job-seekers. They allow for reduced notice period and salaries below the sectoral minimum wage during the first twelve months of employment.

In summarising the Belgian labour law on atypical employment and fixed-term contracts, it seems fair to say that it is more concerned with regulating the conditions of employees in atypical employment than limiting the use of non-standard, including fixed-term, employment contracts through a require-ment of specific reasons for entering these contracts.

Denmark

Characteristics of the Danish system of employment protection regulations

The Danish employment protection system is traditionally regulated by col-lective agreements rather than statutes. Danish collective agreements do not only cover the main areas of collective labour law, including co-determination at the company level, but also contain major provisions which grant individ-ual employees protection against dismissal and regulate atypical employment. Nevertheless, state regulation has become increasingly important. In particu-lar the Act on White-Collar Workers (*Funktionærlov*, as amended) is widely seen as a general law for individual employment protection. It can be made applicable to any type of worker beyond the category of white-collar employ-ees through reference in the written employment contract (Kronke 1990: 217). There are also special statutes for agricultural and domestic workers and for mariners.

Provisions in Danish statutory labour law tend to be rather general. Specific regulation is often left to be enacted by decrees of the Ministry of Labour. These ministerial decrees are concerned with subject matters such as dis-missal protection, sick pay or maternity. Furthermore, specific regulations are most often established by collective agreements which are concluded at four levels: the main frame agreement between the two peak organisations (*hov-edaftalen*); the agreements between the main unions and employer associations (*almindelige overenskomster*); cooperation agreements which regulate industrial relations at the company level; and agreements between local unions and employers. Information on their content, except for the frame collective agree-ment concluded between the peak organisations, is unfortunately not readily available.

There are some statutory provisions with respect to notice periods. The Act on White-Collar Workers, in s. 2, grants one month's notice after six months' employment. The notice period extends to a maximum of six months after nine years' employment. However, if the employee wishes to leave employ-ment, he or she has to give one month's notice regardless of seniority.

Collective agreements for blue-collar workers usually provide shorter notice periods for those employed less than a year. After one year of employment, however, seniority rules apply which, in reality, represent functional equivalents to dismissal protection measures. Recent collective bargaining has tried to equalise the situation between blue-collar and white-collar workers with respect to notice periods (EIRR 230, March 1993: 5–6 on collective bargaining in the metal industry).

Danish dismissal law has traditionally been characterised as weak because it does not impose a requirement of reason. However, it is debatable if this view still holds true. According to s. 2 b of the Act on White-Collar Workers, the employer must supply a reason for dismissal which is either related to the person of the employee or to redundancy, if the employee has been in continuous employment for at least a year. Should the employer neglect this requirement, the employee is entitled to special compensation. Furthermore, the statute grants automatic compensation for dismissal of employees who have been employed for at least twelve years.

In addition, the above-mentioned frame collective agreement requires a reason for an ordinary individual dismissal. The agreement does not specify reasons. It only states, in s. 4 (3), that all employees should be protected from unreasonable dismissal. However, the agreement has established special dismissal protection commissions for interpretation of employer reasons for dismissal and for the handling of employee claims against dismissal. These commissions can declare dismissals unjustified and grant reinstatement or compensation (Kronke 1990: 51).

There is special dismissal protection for pregnant employees, granted by the Maternity Leave Act, and for trade union members, for employee representatives at the company level, and for health and safety officers. Summary dismissal for gross misconduct is explicitly permitted in s. 4 of the White-Collar Workers Act.

A special legal procedure exists for collective redundancies of ten or more employees for economic reasons within a period of thirty days (s. 23 a of the Placement of Workers and Unemployment Insurance Act, as amended in 1990). This procedure requires the employer to inform the employees and the labour administration as early as possible of the mass dismissal. The employer must then engage in negotiations with employee representatives and is required afterwards to inform the labour administration and the affected employees. Dismissals can only take effect thirty days after the information has been provided.

The Danish regulations on collective redundancy do not insist upon the observation of social criteria by the employer in the selection of employees for redundancy. Furthermore, fixed-term employees are exempted from the procedure, and thus do not enjoy benefits which derive from the delay due to the negotiation and information requirements.

Temporary or agency employment has been deregulated in Denmark since 1990. Previously, temporary employment was limited to two sectors, retail and office sectors, and was tightly regulated by the Placement of Workers and Unemployment Insurance Act and by a ministerial decree of 1970. Since then, the regulations have been completely repealed, and the restrictions on agency work have been abolished altogether. Not even a separate collective agreement exists for agency work. Temporary work firms are thus entirely free to operate in the Danish labour market. The only control of temporary work agencies at this moment seems to stem from their professional code of ethics (Jacobsen 1993: 77–90).

The regulation of fixed-term contracts in Denmark

Under Danish law, the parties are, in general, free to enter an employment contract for a definite or an indefinite period. Danish labour law does not restrict the use of fixed-term contracts by prescribing reasons for their conclusion. However, it is a general principle of Danish labour law that temporary and fixed-term employees enjoy the same rights as permanent employees. Collective agreements apply equally to permanent and to temporary or fixed-term employees. Furthermore, since collective agreements are considered to provide only minimum standards, any additional regulation must enlarge the level of protection. Thus fixed-term contracts are prevented from deviating from these standards if they decrease the level of protection or put fixed-term employees in a less favourable position than permanent employees.

The Danish legislature and the courts have not been very active in the field of fixed-term contracts. Successively renewed fixed-term contracts, which have been scrutinised by the courts, represent an exception. The renewed contract is illegal and null and void if it is found to circumvent dismissal protection or seniority rights contained in collective agreements. Furthermore, the original fixed-term contract transforms, in cases of illegality, into a permanent contract which can only be terminated by observing the notice period. The employer might even be sued by the trade union and subsequently be fined by the Labour Court for violating the collective agreement (Jacobsen 1993: 80).

There are only few references to fixed-term contracts in statutes. The Act on White-Collar Workers, in s. 2.4, relieves fixed-term employees with contracts of up to three months from the obligatory four-week notice period. For these short fixed-term contracts it stipulates that neither the employer nor the employee is obligated to observe a notice period and is thus free to terminate the contract at any time. Section 5 of the Act on Mariners provides for contractual arrangements of shorter notice periods for both parties. Section 37 of this Act contains a further regulation on the shortening or the suspension of notice periods in cases of replacement of an officer for up to nine months. The Act on Agricultural and Domestic Workers, in s. 2, excludes temporary employees who are employed for less than a month from statutory protection altogether.

The Act on White-Collar Workers stipulates in s. 3.3 that fixed-term employees are entitled to the same compensation for unreasonable dismissal without notice as permanent employees. Furthermore, according to s. 2 b employees are entitled to compensation for dismissal without just cause. However, white-collar employees on fixed-term contracts are often excluded from this dismissal compensation because it is only granted after one year of continuous employment and fixed-term employees often lack the necessary seniority (Jacobsen 1987: 250–6).

Fixed-term contracts for a specific task or during seasonal periods are common among blue-collar workers. In the construction industry, for example, such contracts are explicitly permitted by collective agreements. Furthermore, a special legal situation exists for seasonal and supply workers (*løsarbejdere*). They are represented by their own trade union and are covered by separate collective agreements. The regulation of their special employment relationship by collective agreement is further evidence of the Danish approach of relying on collective agreements rather than statutes to provide employment protection.

France

Characteristics of the French system of employment protection regulations

The French regulations of employment protection form part of the comprehensive Labour Code (*Code du Travail*). However, the Code does not take a systematic approach to outlining French labour law. This is partly due to the nature of the Code, which is fragmented into laws, decrees of the *Conseil d'Etat*, and other decrees, and partly a result of the practice of reforming labour law by incorporating into the Code regulations which are established by collective agreements. Furthermore, the reform laws in the area of employment protection have tended to be tainted by the conflicting economic philosophies of successive governments (Lyon-Caen 1993: 347–57).

A number of important employment protection measures were introduced during the 1970s. These laws were concerned with dismissal for reasons of economic redundancy, with securing wages, and with improving safety and health conditions. At the end of the 1970s, the legislative concern shifted towards 'flexibilisation' of employment contracts, and measures were introduced to ease the conclusion of temporary or fixed-term contracts. At the beginning of the 1980s, the emphasis shifted again, this time towards the strengthening of collective labour relations. The so-called *lois Auroux* were concerned with employee representation and safety and health committees at the company level, and collective bargaining at the regional and national levels. However, new laws were also introduced during this period in the area of temporary and fixed-term contracts, and these were further reformed by the end of the 1980s (discussed in detail below).

French dismissal law was substantially reformed through the introduction of the Law of 13 July 1973. It distinguishes between ordinary and extraordinary, or summary, dismissal. Since the reform of 30 December 1986, ordinary dismissal can take one of the following three forms: for reasons of misconduct, also called dismissal for disciplinary reasons (*licenciement pour motif disciplinaire*); for reasons of redundancy, also called economic reasons (*licenciement pour motif économique*); and for personal reasons, also called non-disciplinary and non-economic reasons (*licenciement pour motif non disciplinaire et non économique*), which apply mainly in cases of illness.

In cases of disciplinary or economic dismissal, or in other cases upon the request of the employee, the employers are obliged to inform the employee of the reason for separation. The requirement of reason for dismissal has applied since the reform of 2 August 1986 to all three types of ordinary dismissal. Dismissals must accordingly be based on a 'well-founded and serious reason' (*cause réelle et sérieuse*) (Art. L.122-14-3). There is no legislative definition of this just cause. The labour courts have made several attempts to distinguish causes, and have used this requirement to establish measures to control employer behaviour beyond dismissal for disciplinary or personal reasons. These attempts were rejected by the final appeal court in labour law, the Social Chamber of the *Cour de cassation*, on grounds that, in general, the lower labour courts imposed unreasonable restrictions upon the right of the employer to define employee conduct as disruptive (Péllisier 1986: 180).

After six months of employment, statutory notice periods amount to four weeks. They are extended to two months after two years of employment and cannot be shortened by collective agreement or individual contract (Art. L.122-6 and 7). In fact, collective agreements and local customary law require longer notice periods in a number of sectors. These extended notice periods may also cover the first six months of employment, which are exempted by statute.

French employees are protected against dismissal not only by notice periods and a requirement of reason but also by a procedure which the employer is required to follow before a dismissal can take place. In the past this procedure included the formal approval of the Labour Inspector in each dismissal case. Since the passage of the Laws of 30 December 1986 and 10 July 1987, the involvement of the labour inspector is limited to the control of procedure in cases of dismissal for reasons of economic redundancy.

The procedure is different for ordinary disciplinary or personal dismissal and for dismissals for reasons of economic redundancy. The procedure for individual disciplinary dismissal consists of three elements: summons for an interview; the interview; and written notification of the dismissal. The invitation letter for an interview must be sent by registered mail. It has to mention the right of the employee to be represented during the interview. Furthermore, the employee must have reasonable time to prepare for the interview (Art. R.122-2). The law does not specify a minimum period for preparation but it is assumed that at least 48 hours must be granted between the receipt of the letter and the interview (Kessler 1991: 406).

During the interview, the employer is required to explain the reason for the proposed dismissal and respond to questions from the employee. After the interview, the employer must send the written dismissal by registered mail (Art. L.122-14-1). Since the reform of 2 August 1989, the dismissal statement must include the reasons for dismissal. Between the interview and the posting of the letter there has to be at least a 24-hour time lapse.

There is currently a discussion of a 'right to work' (*droit de l'emploi*) which derives from French labour market policy initiatives. In particular, in the case of economic dismissals the employer is required to offer in each case a retraining contract which is financed jointly by the employer, the unemployment office and the labour administration. If the employee accepts the retraining contract, the employment contract ceases to exist. An employee who retrains (*travailleur privé d'emploi en conversion*) can claim all benefits to which the unemployed are entitled, but receives 70 per cent of the previous salary instead of 48 per cent as the normal unemployed do (Lyon-Caen 1987: 241–9, Domergue 1987: 250–5, and Enclos 1990: 335–8).

The procedure in the case of dismissal for reason of redundancy is different for individual economic redundancy, for dismissal of two to nine employees within thirty days, for dismissal of ten or more employees within thirty days, and for thirty employees or more within six months. The procedure for individual economic redundancy follows the three-phase procedure for disciplinary dismissals. In the case of economic dismissals, the employer is also required to indicate the possibility of retraining (*convention de conversion*). The written dismissal statement cannot be sent out until seven days after the interview. This time lapse is increased for executives (*cadres*) to fifteen days. Furthermore, the employer must, within eight days of the dismissal, notify the labour administration (*directeur départmental du travail*) of the dismissal and the reason for it.

For economic dismissals of two to nine employees within thirty days, the employer must observe not only the requirements for individual dismissals but must also consult the responsible employee representatives (in companies with less than fifty employees only the personnel delegates, otherwise the *comité d'entreprise* as well). The employer has to inform the employee representatives before the meeting of the economic, financial and technical reasons for dismissal, the number of employees affected, and the envisaged procedure for dismissal. However, the employee representatives have no co-determination right. The dismissal decision and the decision on retraining measures and retraining contracts remains ultimately with the employer. The labour administration must be informed at least eight days after the dismissal.

In cases of collective redundancies of ten or more employees within thirty days, or thirty employees within six months, the employer is obliged to observe a strict consultation procedure which requires negotiations with the relevant employee representatives. The employees and their representatives can ask an accountant of their choice, paid by the company, to assess the situation. The employer must observe delay periods after notification of the labour administration. These amount to 30 days in the case of dismissal of less than 100 employees, 45 days for dismissal of up to 250 employees, and 60 days for more than 250 employees. In addition, the collective parties have to agree to a social plan. The employer is, however, relieved of having to conduct individual interviews.

Neither of the above procedures applies in cases of summary dismissal for gross misconduct (*faute grave*) or criminal offences (*faute lourde*) mentioned in Art. L.122-8. In the absence of clear legislative categories, the courts have introduced the principle that summary dismissal is justified if the continuation of employment is unreasonable during the notice period. In these cases, the employee loses the right to automatic compensation for dismissal granted by statute or collective agreement (Art. L.122-9), and in the case of *faute lourde* the employee also loses holiday pay (Art. L-223-14).

Special dismissal protection is granted by the Law of 13 July 1983 to female employees who are dismissed in reaction to a claim of sex discrimination. Since the passage of the Law of 28 October 1982, personnel delegates, employee members of the *comité d'entreprise*, and union representatives at company level can only be dismissed with consent of the Labour Inspector. Without consent, the dismissal is null and void, and can lead to a claim for damages under the Civil Code (Kronke 1990: 225).

In cases of ordinary dismissal, excluding summary dismissal for gross misconduct, employees are entitled after two years of continuous employment to automatic compensation (Art. L. 122-9). This amounts to at least one tenth of the monthly salary before taxes or twenty-four hourly wages for each year of employment, Art. R.122-1.

If the employee has successfully challenged the dismissal in the labour court (*Conseil de prud'hommes*) for lack of a well-founded and serious reason, the court can order reinstatement (*réintegration*) (Art. L.122-14-4). However, if the employer, or the employee, rejects reinstatement, which is the rule (Kessler 1991: 411–12), the labour court awards compensation if the employee was employed for at least two years and more than eleven employees were employed in the company. The compensation in this case amounts to at least six monthly salaries. In other cases, the labour court can only award damages for loss of income etc., if the dismissal can be considered abusive (*licenciement abusif*) (Art. L. 122-14-6).

The regulation of fixed-term contracts in France

The French regulations of atypical employment are characterised by a close relationship between fixed-term contracts (*contrat à durée déterminée*) and temporary work (*travail temporaire*). The simultaneous regulation of temporary work and fixed-term contracts started with the Law of 3 January 1972, and has been reformed numerous times since. In particular, the Law of 2 January 1979 was intended to 'normalise' temporary work and fixed-term contracts. However, a major reform was introduced in 1982 when the new socialist government issued an ordinance on temporary work and fixed-term contracts on 5 February 1982 as part of the *lois Auroux*. It limited the use of fixed-term contracts. A sectoral collective agreement of 13 May 1985 reviewed the application of the legislative measure during the past three years and suggested modifications which were embodied in the Law of 25 July 1985. This new piece of legislation eased somewhat the restrictions on the use of fixed-term contracts and temporary work. With the change to a conservative government in 1986, this trend was supported by the Ordinance of 1 August 1986. However, after the election victory of the socialists in 1988, the government made legislative proposals which attacked alleged abuses of atypical employment and suggested again restricting the use of temporary work and fixed-term contracts in a manner similar to the 1982 reform. In response, the sectoral and national employers' association concluded a nationwide inter-occupational agreement on 24 March 1990 with three of the five large unions on all aspects of temporary work and fixed-term contracts. Most of the provisions of this agreement were included in the Law of 12 July 1990, which now constitutes the main legislative basis for the regulation of temporary employment and fixed-term contracts.[5]

The Law of 12 July 1990 reiterates the general principle that under French law, temporary employment and fixed-term contracts remain the exception to the rule that the normal contract of employment is the contract for an indefinite period. The Labour Code, Art. L.124-2-2, prohibits a position being filled by a fixed-term employee if this position is linked to normal and permanent activities. Art. L.124-2-1 of the Labour Code lists the cases under which a fixed-term contract is legal. These include the following limited and temporary tasks (*tâche précise et temporaire*) (Lefebvre 1991: 29–61):

- replacement of an absent employee (*remplacement d'un salarié absent*). Maximum duration is 18 months and compensation on expiry of the contract;
- replacement employee leaves a job early (*départ définitif d'un salarié précédant la suppression de son poste de travail*). Maximum duration is 24 months and compensation on expiry of the contract;
- substitution for another employee who will commence employment after the expiry of the fixed-term (*attente de l'entrée en service effective du nouveau titulaire du poste*). Maximum duration is 9 months and compensation on expiry of the contract;
- temporary increase in workload (*accroissement temporaire d'activité de l'entreprise*). Maximum duration is 18 months and compensation on expiry of the contract;

- unforeseen occurrence of an unusual, specific, and non-lasting task (*survenance d'une tache occasionelle, précisement définie et non durable*). Maximum duration is 18 months and compensation on expiry of the contract;
- extraordinary increase in export orders (*commande exceptionelle à l'exportation*). Maximum duration is 24 months and compensation on expiry of the contract;
- urgent task necessary for safety reasons (*travaux urgents nécessités par des mesures de sécurité*). Maximum duration is 9 months and compensation on expiry of the contract;
- work which is temporary by nature, and seasonal work (*travaux temporaires par nature ou saisonniers*). Maximum duration is 18 months but no compensation on expiry of the contract.

In addition, there are possibilities for the conclusion of a fixed-term contract introduced by special labour market policies. These include arrangements for vocational training (*acquisition d'une formation professionelle*) and the special situation of older apprentices due to depart for their military service (*ancien apprenti devant partir au service national*).

Fixed-term contracts must be in writing and are only renewable once within the maximum period, with the exception of the vocational training contract which is not renewable. Ordinary dismissal during the fixed term is excluded. Summary dismissal for gross misconduct and early dissolution of the contract in the case of *force majeur* are permitted (Art. 122-3-4). In the case of continuation of employment after expiry of the fixed term, the contract is automatically transformed into a permanent contract (L. 122-3-10).

A new type of fixed-term contract was introduced by the Law of 20 December 1993 on labour, employment and vocational training. These so-called employment solidarity contracts (*contrats emploi-solidarité*, or CES) are fixed-term contracts which provide part-time employment to groups who have special difficulties in the labour market, such as the long-term unemployed, unemployed people over 50, the disabled, or people on minimum income benefit (EIRR 242, March 1994: 17–18).

A report of the Ministry of Labour on 'precarious employment' at the beginning of 1992 concluded that the Act of 12 July 1990 did not contribute significantly to the transformation of precarious employment into stable, permanent jobs. It remarked critically that the reason of 'temporary increase in the company's workload' was used in order to conclude fixed-term contracts in a number of cases in which there was ample scope for a permanent contract. Furthermore, employees were recruited on seasonal work contracts in order to avoid 'end-of-contract' compensation, as is required with other fixed-term contracts. The report finally mentioned an increased use of fixed-term contracts as prolonged probation periods (EIRR 222, July 1992: 21–22)

Germany

Characteristics of the German system of employment protection regulation

The regulation of labour law in Germany appears rather fragmented. No unified labour code exists, and employment protection measures are contained in several separate statutes. However, judicial interpretation and doctrinal labour law have been successful in shaping the system of labour law (Däubler 1986 and Heilmann 1986). German labour law is governed by general principles, among which the so-called principle of 'beneficialty' (*Günstigkeitsprinzip*) is of particular interest. It introduces a hierarchical order of sources for the regulation of employment relations with labour law statutes based on constitutional norms at the top, followed by collective agreements (*Tarifverträge*), company agreements (*Betriebsvereinbarungen*), case law (*Richterrecht*), contract of employment, and unilateral decisions of the employer. This hierarchical arrangement of sources rests on the assumption that a lower source can only enlarge and not decrease employment protection for the employee. Thus a company agreement can, in general, only improve working conditions established by statute or collective agreement.[6] Furthermore, the individual contract of employment can, in principle, only improve the terms and conditions of employment for the employee and cannot be used to undermine furthergoing statutory protection or measures concluded in collective or company agreements.

German employees enjoy statutory protection against unilateral termination of the contract of employment by the employer. German labour law distinguishes between dismissal and situations in which the employment contract is null and void for legal reasons (for example, the contractual violation of anti-discrimination provisions, or circumvention of employment protection measures). In the latter case, the employee can claim damages under general contract law.

If the employer wishes to dismiss an employee, he must first consult the works council. Without consultation of this body of employee representatives, the employer dismissal is automatically illegal (Oechsler 1988: 397–410). However, opposition from the works council does not prevent dismissal. In practice, German works councils endorse most dismissal decisions either by remaining silent or by even actively supporting them (Höland 1985: 98). A principal reason for this behaviour of works councils lies in the German system of employee representation, which favours a trade-off between participation rights in personnel decisions and consultation rights in economic decision-making (Rogowski (forthcoming), ch. 3).

German dismissal law distinguishes between dismissal with and without notice (also called ordinary and extraordinary or summary dismissal). Dismissal without notice is regulated in s. 626 of the Civil Code (BGB) and restricted to situations of gross misconduct (persistent disobedience, fighting, theft), permanent disability due to illness, misuse of confidential information, etc. Labour courts assess this form of dismissal by asking four questions (Schaub 1992: 1000–17): Do suitable facts exist which can justify a dismissal without notice? Have all relevant circumstances of the case been considered? Have the interests of the employer and the employee been weighed against each other? Is continuation of employment no longer acceptable?

Statutory protection of dismissal with notice, or ordinary dismissal, is regulated in the Dismissal Protection Act (*Kündigungsschutzgesetz*, KSchG) of 1951, as amended in 1969. The length of notice follows from s. 622 of the Civil Code. In 1993 this provision was equalised for blue-collar and white-collar workers (Notice Period Act (*Kündigungsfristengesetz*) of 15 October 1993. See EIRR 241, February 1994: 22–3). There is now a minimum notice period of four weeks for both categories of employees, which extends with the length of service up to a maximum of seven months for twenty years' employment and above. The notice periods are frequently extended by collective agreements (Bispinck 1993: 322–5).

The Dismissal Protection Act applies only in companies with more than five employees, and the employee must have been employed for at least six months. In companies with less than six employees, the only statutory dismissal protection is through notice periods. Furthermore, the dismissal claim must be filed with the labour court within three months after the effective date of termination.

According to s. 1 II and III KSchG, a dismissal is socially warranted if it is based on either a reason of conduct (absenteeism, verbal abuses, etc.) or capability (mainly illness) of the employee (*verhaltens- und personenbedingte Kündigung*). The employer can also dismiss an employee for reasons of redundancy due to changes in production or a decrease of business or profits, if the decrease leads to a reduction in the amount of work in the company (*betriebsbedingte Kündigung*). An employer is barred from redundancy dismissal if an equivalent and suitable alternative place of work is available. Furthermore, redundancy dismissals are 'socially unwarranted' if the employer uses the wrong criteria in selecting the employee for redundancy. German labour law distinguishes between criteria which define the group of employees considered for selection, and criteria to compare employees within the group. Within the group, the employer has to take into consideration age, length of service, and financial support of dependent relatives before selecting the employee.

In addition, there is special dismissal protection for certain categories of workers. Disabled employees can only be dismissed after authorisation by a public welfare administration (s. 12 *Schwerbehindertengesetz*). In case of collective redundancies and mass dismissals, the employer is required to inform the local labour administration (s. 17 KSchG and s. 8 *Arbeitsförderungsgesetz*). If the employer fails to acknowledge these obligations, the dismissal is legally invalid.

In the case of mass dismissal, the employer must negotiate with the works council a social plan which regulates financial compensation. After agreeing on a basic award in the social plan, actual compensation is commonly calculated using the following formula: age multiplied by length of service divided by 100. This figure, multiplied by the basic award, constitutes the amount of compensation (Schaub 1992: 1802).

In the case of ordinary dismissal of an individual employee, the opposition of the works council gives the employee the right to continue employment if the employee has filed a claim against the dismissal with the labour court. This right to continued employment lasts until the court case is finally decided. In the case of a successful dismissal protection claim, the normal remedy is the legal stipulation of an uninterrupted employment relationship for which the employer is obliged to pay the regular wages. However, in a majority of court claims, the outcome is a settlement in court which does not result in continuation of employment but rather in some form of compensation (Blankenburg *et al.* 1979 and Falke *et al.* 1981).

A dismissal for which the transfer of the undertaking or its insolvency is the principal reason is automatically illegal according to s. 613a IV BGB. However, a dismissal for economic, technical, or organisational reasons which are put forward by the new employer is not excluded by this provision (Gaul 1990).

Employees employed by temporary work agencies are protected by a special law (*Arbeitnehmerüberlassungsgesetz* of 7 August 1972).[7] It stipulates that the employment relationship with the temporary work agency is permanent. A fixed-term contract with the agency is only justified on request of the employee. The legal relationships of the user and the agency are considered relationships *sui generis* – separate from the employment relationship. However, the user firm is required to observe the statutory health and safety provision. The law on temporary work operates in this respect with an implied term in the hiring contract which benefits the temporary worker.

The regulation of fixed-term contracts in Germany

In general, the principle of freedom of contract includes the right to enter a fixed-term contract (*befristeter Arbeitsvertrag*) which expires automatically without dismissal at the end of the agreed term (s. 620 BGB). However, the right is restricted by statutory provisions, collective agreements, and, most effectively, by case law. Indeed, since the 1960s the courts have virtually reversed the principle of contractual freedom to enter fixed-term contracts for reasons of 'protection of unfair dismissal protection'.

The labour courts introduced the 'requirement of reason' (*Begründungspflicht* or *sachlicher Grund*) for a fixed-term contract to prevent circumvention of statutory dismissal protection. According to this requirement, employers need a specific reason for offering a fixed-term contract instead of a permanent contract. The Federal Labour Court (*Bundesarbeitsgericht*) has developed a catalogue of legally valid reasons which can be grouped into seven categories (Schaub 1992: 196–202 and Schliemann 1991):

1   at the request of the employee;
2   probation period of up to six months; in exceptional cases fixed-term contracts can exceed six months, for example artistic and academic work, after longer breaks from work, or in order to restore trust after imprisonment;
3   temporary replacement of employees who are absent for health reasons or are on maternity leave;
4   seasonal work and other forms of work which are temporary in nature; these include temporary increases in work due to longer business hours on certain days and annual stocktaking;
5   employment of artists (singers, actors), athletes, journalists (foreign correspondents), and work students;
6   settlement in court to end an employment contract; and
7   so-called social reasons; these include transitory periods after vocational training; academic assistants after their contractual term.

The public sector is subject to separate regulations. Public employers can, in general, only enter fixed-term contracts if the job has been itemised in the budget as a fixed-term job (*Bundesarbeitsgericht* (Federal Labour Court) GS AP 20 to s. 1 KSchG). There is a separate statute of 14 June 1985 for academic personnel which enables universities to use fixed-term contracts almost without restrictions. Academically qualified personnel, other than professors, can be hired on a fixed-term basis, if it is a first-time academic appointment or if the position is linked with further academic training or participation in research projects. The maximum duration of contracts in the academic sector is five years with the same university, or two years in the case of a first-time appointment (Schweizer 1991).[8]

Renewal of fixed-term contracts (*Kettenarbeitsverträge*) is possible if the new contract is covered by one of the legally prescribed reasons. The reasons for the renewal of fixed-term contracts are, however, more closely scrutinised as there is the general presumption that renewals are more likely to circumvent dismissal protection (Zöllner and Lorenz 1992: 241–2). Dismissal of fixed-term employees is restricted. Furthermore, if employment is continued after the expiry of the fixed term, the employment contract transforms automatically into a permanent contract.

The Employment Promotion Act (*Beschäftigungsförderungsgesetz*, BSchFG) of 26 April 1985 introduced a change in attitude towards the regulation of fixed-term contracts. Their 'deregulation' was discovered as an instrument of labour market policy.[9] The predominant negative assessment of fixed-term contracts as a circumvention of dismissal protection was amended by viewing them as positive measures to reduce unemployment. However, the Act did not replace the existing regulations concerning fixed-term contracts which remain valid for all contracts not covered by the Employment Promotion Act.

The Employment Promotion Act removes the requirement of reason for entering a fixed-term contract under certain conditions. New employment contracts or employment immediately following vocational training contracts can be concluded with a fixed term of up to eighteen months (s. 1 I BSchFG). If the company has been in operation less than six months and employs less than twenty employees, the fixed term can last two years. Renewal of fixed-term contracts under this Act is possible up to the maximum fixed term. However, the Act cannot be used if there existed a fixed-term contract between the parties in the preceding four months (s. 1 I 3 BSchFG). Ordinary dismissal is possible only if permitted by an express clause in the contract of employment (Schaub 1992: 206).

The Act was originally limited to the period between 1 May 1985 and 1 January 1990. However, the Act has been renewed twice and is currently valid until the year 2000. Researchers associated with the trade unions have recommended legislation which requires mandatory compensation for each fixed term that expires (Keller and Seifert 1993).

Greece

Characteristics of the Greek system of employment protection regulations

Greek labour law has so far largely defied separate codification, at least in the area of employment protection.[10] However, some legislation was introduced in the 1980s on collective labour law. There are now statutes on works councils and union rights (Act 1264 of 1982) (EIRR 195, April 1990: 21–2) and on collective agreements and collective bargaining (Act 1876 of 1990) (EIRR 228, January 1993: 26–7). Furthermore, legislation has been introduced on working time, including part-time work (Act 1892 of 1990).

The main regulations for employment protection form part of the Civil Code, which has been in force since 1946. In addition, the Constitution of 1975, adopted after the demise of the military regime in 1974, contains a number of articles which are relevant for employment protection and the legal status of the employee. Furthermore, national as well as collective bargaining agreements provide regulations for a number of areas of employment protection.

The regulations on the conclusion of employment contracts are rather restrictive. The employer is obliged, according to Decree 763/1970, to hire new employees only from a waiting list which is kept at the local labour administration. If he intends to hire other employees, he must notify the labour administration (Kronke 1990: 76).

Protection against unjust dismissal is regulated in the Civil Code (Art. 669

and following) and in separate Acts (2112/1920 and 3198/1955). The employee must have been employed for at least two months to be covered by these provisions.

The notice period for white-collar employees is one month during the first year of employment, and then two months up to the fourth year of service. The maximum notice period is twenty-eight weeks. Apparently, there is no notice period for blue-collar workers (Koniaris 1982).

Greek employees are entitled to compensation in the case of dismissal, depending on their length of service (Act 2112 of 1920 and Act 3198 of 1955). It amounts to only 50 per cent of the normal compensation rate in cases of a justified ordinary dismissal of a white-collar employee. However, if the employer neglects the notice period the employee is entitled to one month's salary in the first year of service with a maximum of twenty-four monthly salaries, varying according to length of service. However, if employees qualify to collect pensions from a social insurance organisation, they lose their special dismissal protection and are only entitled to 50 per cent of the normal compensation for dismissal (Karakatsanis 1987: 277).

The Protection of Trade Union Rights Act of 1990 allows the dismissal of workers engaged in industrial action. Dismissal notice can be issued to those workers who remain on strike 24 hours after the strike has been declared unlawful by a court ruling. Dismissal is further permitted on grounds of intimidation of other employees who are willing to go to work, and the occupation of company premises during a strike, even if the strike has been declared lawful (EIRR 204, January 1991: 20–1).

Temporary or agency employment has been illegal in Greece since 1931. However, a diverse group of firms engages in placement outside the law. These include travel agents, insurance brokers, management consultants, accountancy firms, and advertising agencies. They actually fill a gap (EIRR 238, November 1993: 30–1). So far, however, there is no positive regulation of temporary employment. In general, temporary workers are legally treated as fixed-term employees (Koniaris 1993).

The regulation of fixed-term contracts in Greece

Due to the fact that there is no separate law on fixed-term employment, the main regulations are found in the labour law provisions of the Civil Code. Art. 669 of the Civil Code expressly permits fixed-term contracts. However, it also states that the permanent employment contract is the rule, and that the fixed-term contract is the exception.

There is no maximum limit for the fixed-term contract under Greek employment law. However, it is renewable only twice. After that it is converted into a permanent contract. Furthermore, if the fixed-term contract is continued without explicit renewal or further statements of the employer, it is likewise transformed into a permanent contract (Art. 671 of the Civil Code).

Art. 669 of the Civil Code imposes a requirement of reason. It limits the use of fixed-term contracts to the reasons of:

- urgent, limited tasks;
- emergency work;
- temporary increases in workload; and
- to carry out clearly defined work not normally in the employer's area.

Pay is regulated on the same basis as for workers with permanent contracts. As for social security and pension contributions, fixed-term employees are entitled to the same treatment as other permanent employees. The parties to a fixed-term contract are, however, free to negotiate individually over working conditions, such as holiday or probationary periods (EIRR 179, December 1988: 23). Dismissal of fixed-term employees is limited to summary dismissal without notice.

Under Greek labour law, seasonal work is considered to be permanent employment. According to Act 1359 of 1945, as amended by Act 1346 of 1983, and Act 2081 of 1952, seasonal workers are employed by seasonal enterprises. Seasonal enterprises are defined as being in operation for more than two months but less than twelve months. The Royal Decree 153 of 1972 regulates the yearly leave for seasonal workers.

Ireland

Characteristics of the Irish system of employment protection regulations

A recent feature of Irish regulations in the area of industrial relations and employment protection has been that they are shaped and reformed, to some extent, by national collective agreements between the government, trade unions, and employers' associations. This 'neo-corporatist' practice has enlarged centralised wage bargaining to include central areas of economic and social policy-making. It started with the three-year Programme for National Recovery (PNR) in 1987, which was concerned with adjusting pay levels and public financing. The second agreement, the Programme for Economic and Social Progress (PESP) of 1991, was even more ambitious by establishing objectives in most areas of Irish politics except foreign policy. It included, among other measures, specific proposals to reform labour law in the areas of part-time work, employment equality, unfair dismissal, employment agencies, and conditions of employment (EIRR 207, April 1991: 16–19). However, this programme seems to have been only modestly successful in guiding legislation and collective bargaining. The third national agreement, the Programme for Competitiveness and Work (PCW), which was ratified in February 1994, is not as all-encompassing as its predecessor. It is predominantly concerned with pay stability and active labour market policy measures (EIRR 243, April 1994: 14–16).

Irish labour law belongs to the family of common law countries, as does that of the United Kingdom, and is thus governed by case law. Nevertheless, there are also a variety of employment statutes which have not been consolidated into a comprehensive Labour Code (Prondzynski 1993: 109–10). These statutes include the Redundancy Payments Act 1967, the Unfair Dismissals Act 1977, the Maternity Protection of Employees Act 1981, and the Industrial Relations Act 1990 which contains statutory immunities for employees acting in contemplation or furtherance of a trade dispute.

In general, despite the common law context Irish regulations on employment protection are similar to those of their partners in the European Communities (Redmond 1985). However, there are a number of qualifying periods of employment relating to coverage by statutory protection, which vary among fields of regulation. A minimum notice period in the case of dismissal, for example, is granted after thirteen weeks, unfair dismissal regulations apply after one year, and redundancy payment regulations after two years. The qualifying period for dismissal protection, in conjunction with the statutory exclusion of certain types of employee, for example apprentices and employees on probation or training, exclude a considerable number of employees from protection against unfair dismissal.[11] Nevertheless, certain types of dismissal are exempted from the requirement of a qualifying period of employment. These include dismissals for trade union membership or activities, pregnancy, maternity leave, and time off (s. 6 of the Unfair Dismissals Act and s. 25 of the Maternity Protection of Employees Act).

The lengths of the notice periods in the case of termination of the contract of employment is regulated in the Minimum Notice and Terms of Employment Act 1973. The minimum period is one week for a person employed continuously for less than two years. The notice period increases to two weeks for persons employed between two and five years, to four weeks for between five and ten years' employment, and to six weeks for ten to fifteen years' employment. The maximum statutory notice period is eight weeks for fifteen years or more of continuous employment. In order to be covered by this legislation, the employee must work at least eighteen hours a week for the same employer. After one month of employment, the employee is entitled to a written statement of the reasons for dismissal. The statutory minima on notice periods are regularly extended by collective agreement and in individual contracts of employment (EIRR 42, June 1977: 2–3 and 32–6).

Dismissal without notice or summary dismissal is regulated under common law. The employer's right to summary dismissal is, however, restricted by the constitutional rights of the dismissed employee. Furthermore, it is not uncommon for the individual contract of employment to include specific provisions on summary dismissal (Kronke 1990: 227).

After one year of continuous employment, the employer can only dismiss the employee if there are reasons which justify the unilateral termination of the contract of employment. However, there are a number of reasons which render the dismissal automatically unfair. These include membership or activities on behalf of a trade union, religious or political opinions of the employee, civil or criminal proceedings against the employer to which the employee is a party or a witness, the race or colour of the employee, the pregnancy of the employee, and unfair selection for redundancy (ss. 6 (2) and (3) of the Unfair Dismissals Act 1977).

The main statutory reasons for dismissal available to employers relate to

1   the capability, competence, or qualifications of the employee for performing work of the kind which he or she was employed by the employer to do;
2   the conduct of the employee;
3   redundancy of the employee; and
4   a situation in which the employee cannot continue to work without contravention of a statutory duty or restriction.

In addition, there is a general clause of 'other substantial reason' (EIRR 42, June 1977: 2).

The dismissal claim must be filed within six months after the relevant dismissal (s. 8 (1) and (2) Unfair Dismissals Act) with the Rights Commissioner or the Employment Appeals Tribunal, which was established under the Redundancy Payments Act 1967. If the judicial body finds the dismissal to have been unfair, it can require re-employment, either in form of reinstatement into the previous job or in form of re-engagement in an alternative job with the same employer (s. 7 (1) of the Unfair Dismissals Act). However, in the majority of successful unfair dismissal claims the award is compensation. The statutory maximum award is 104 weeks' remuneration.

In the case of collective redundancies, employers have to consult the recognised trade unions under the Protection of Employment Act 1977. Furthermore, employees can claim redundancy payment under the Redundancy Payments Act 1967. In addition, there is an Anti-Discrimination (Equal Pay) Act 1974 and an Employment Equality Act 1977, which also grant enforceable rights against the employer. Part-time employment received special statutory attention in 1990. The Protection of Employees (Regular Part-Time Workers) Act 1990 grants employees who work at least eight hours a week equal protection with respect to maternity leave and other employment protection measures.

Temporary or agency work is regulated by the Employment Agency Act 1971. However, this statute is predominantly concerned with the licensing of employment businesses and less with employment protection. In fact, the employment relation with the agency is not considered a contract of employment in the strict sense. The Irish law follows, in this respect, the law of the

United Kingdom which treats the contract of the agency worker as a contract *sui generis* (Redmond 1993: 189–91). This means that temporary agency workers lie outside the scope of employment protection legislation. However, there is the possibility of extension of the basic employment protection measures to agency workers through the device of the Employment Regulation Order (Redmond 1993: 196–8).

The regulation of fixed-term contracts in Ireland

There are no statutory restrictions in Ireland on entering into a fixed-term contract of employment. The employer is not obliged to obtain authorisation or to justify the use of a fixed-term contract by recourse to a legally prescribed reason. Furthermore, the length or renewal of the fixed term is not restricted, and there are no regulations on automatic conversion of fixed-term contracts into permanent contracts in the case of illegality of the fixed-term contract (EIRR 179, December 1988: 23).

Fixed-term contracts are, however, explicitly mentioned several times in general employment protection laws. A distinction is made, for example, in the law on unfair dismissal between a contract for a fixed term and a contract for a specified purpose, whereby the duration of the contract is limited but is, at the time of its conclusion, not yet precisely ascertainable (s. 1 of the Unfair Dismissals Act 1977). In addition, Irish labour law distinguishes between seasonal work contracts, casual work, and probation contracts (Redmond 1993: 181–2).

The employee employed under a fixed-term or special purpose contract can waive the right to complain of unfair dismissal through express agreement in writing if the dismissal consists only of the expiry of the fixed term without renewal or the cesser of the purpose (s. 2 (b) of the Unfair Dismissal Act). This right to waiver does not take effect before or after the date of expiry or cesser (Redmond 1993: 193). Furthermore, a fixed-term contract may be terminated before it expires on grounds of gross misconduct.

If the fixed-term contract was expressly concluded to replace an employee who is absent on maternity or additional maternity leave, a dismissal based on the return of the previous employee is deemed a valid substantial reason for dismissal (s. 24 of the Maternity Protection of Employees Act 1981). However, the employer has to inform the employee in writing at the commencement of employment that the employment will terminate upon the return of the other employee on maternity leave. Nevertheless, the fixed-term employee has no right to continue employment if the employee on maternity leave decides not to return to work (Redmond 1993: 193).

Fixed-term contracts, except for those concluded for a specified purpose, are covered by the Redundancy Payments Act 1967, which stipulates in s. 9 that the expiry of a fixed term without renewal equals dismissal. There is no provision for waiver of the statutory right to redundancy pay, but the fixed-term employee must have two years of continuous employment in order to be entitled to statutory redundancy pay. However, s. 7 of the Protection of Employment Act 1977 excludes fixed-term contracts from dismissal protection in the context of collective redundancies.

After thirteen months of continuous employment, fixed-term employees have the same right to notice as permanent employees. They are covered by the Maternity Protection of Employees Act 1981 if employed for a fixed term of twenty-six weeks or more. Furthermore, they can bring claims under the Anti-Discrimination (Equal Pay) Act 1974 and the Equality Act 1977.

Italy

Characteristics of the Italian system of employment protection regulations

The core regulations of Italian employment protection form part of the Civil Code (Art. 2094 and subsequent articles). These regulations, introduced under Mussolini in 1942 and subsequently amended, relate to all employment contracts. In addition, there are a number of special employment protection statutes and decrees which have been enacted since the Second World War. The Dismissal Protection Act, for example, was introduced in 1966, and is known as Act 604. A particularly important statute was the Workers' Statute of 1970. These special statutes do not necessarily cover all employees. Furthermore, it has been argued that Italian labour law only covers a small percentage of the work force because of its high level of non-wage work and disguised employment (Bettio and Villa 1989).

The official Italian employment protection system follows general paths and has indeed developed a number of sophisticated instruments. Whereas permanent employment contracts do not have to be in writing,[12] fixed-term contracts are legally required to be in writing. However, according to a special law, also dating back to the Mussolini era (Law 112 of 1935), most Italian employees still need a 'work book' for legal employment, and employers act illegally if they hire employees who lack a proper work book. The work book contains personal data on the employee, such as qualifications, disabilities, decorations, etc., as well as information on previous employers and on periods of leave of absence.

The Italian dismissal protection system is partly regulated by statute and partly by collective agreement. The Civil Code mentions that both parties are required to observe a notice period in the case of termination (Art. 2118 Sec. I), but it does not specify the length of the period. For white-collar employees, the length of notice periods is regulated by statute (Law 1825 of 1924) and it varies, according to length of service, from between fifteen days and a maximum of four months. Notice periods for blue-collar workers are regulated in collective agreements. The Civil Code regulations govern the termination of the employee and form the main source of protection for a number of employee categories: executives (*dirigenti*), homeworkers, and those employed on probation for up to six months are excluded.

The Dismissal Protection Act 604 of 1966 regulates unilateral dismissals by the employer (*licenziamenti*). However, its coverage is limited. It originally excluded all employees in firms with less than thirty-six employees from dismissal protection. Although not in a technically legal sense, the Workers' Statute of 1970 has reduced this figure to sixteen employees – six in agriculture. However, this limitation still means that a third of all Italian employees are excluded from special employment protection. The Italian legislature has acknowledged the need to enlarge employment protection to include small employers. Monetary compensation in the case of unjust dismissal was extended to small companies by Act 108 of 11 May 1990 (Treu *et al.* 1993: 345).

Italian dismissal law distinguishes between dismissal with notice and without notice (*giusta causa*). A 'just cause' is usually related to gross misconduct of the employee. The employee has a right to be heard in these cases.

Dismissal with notice can be based on subjective or objective 'motives' or reasons. Subjective motives relate to severe violations of the contract of employment by the employee. Objective motives relate either to change in production or organisation of the company (individual redundancy), or to the eventual physical incapacity of the employee to perform the contractual duties. If the dismissal is based on redundancy, the employer must first offer alternative employment in the corporation (if available) before the dismissal can take place. The incapacity of the employee is normally related to a severe illness which renders contractual performance impossible. However, repeated short illnesses are regulated by the Civil Code and not by the Dismissal Protection Act. Over the years, the courts have offered different interpretations of how to treat cases of illness. According to contract law (not dismissal law), the employer can usually suspend the employee before the contract is dissolved.

Special dismissal protection exists for pregnant employees and worker representatives. A dismissal which is related to discrimination for religious, racial, ethnic, sexual or political reasons, or to trade union activities is automatically null and void.

Collective dismissals for reasons of economic hardship, organisational restructuring, or employment adjustment were excluded from dismissal protection until 1991, when Italy finally implemented the 1975 European Commission Directive on collective dismissals.[13] Prior to 1991, the courts had extended the concept of individual redundancies to cover multiple cases of redundancies (*licenziamenti individuali plurimi*). However, the employees were only granted recourse to the courts in these cases after the conciliation procedure, usually established by collective agreements, had failed. The new Law 223 of 23 July 1991 applies to collective redundancies of at least five employees in companies with more than fifteen employees within a period of 120 days.

Italian dismissal law is comparatively harsh with respect to remedies. In the case of unfair dismissal, the judge can order reinstatement with back pay according to Art. 18 of the Workers' Statute. The reinstatement order can be combined with an order for five monthly salaries as damages caused by the unfair dismissal. However, if the employee earned wages in the meantime, they count as mitigating factors. In practice, more than 40 per cent of judicial reinstatement orders lead to actual reinstatement (Treu 1993a: 386).

Agency or temporary work used to be illegal in Italy (Act 264 of 1949; Act 1369 of 1960). Private labour exchange or 'intermediation' by labour-only subcontractors was considered to be an infringement upon the monopoly of public placement services until the end of 1992. Only recently, with the Law-Decree of 30 December 1992 on temporary work (*lavoro itinerale*), was it permitted in the so-called tertiary sector, with respect to skilled workers and in cases in which a fixed-term contract is allowed. The temporary work agency requires authorisation from the labour inspectorate. The employment contract between the agency and the temporary employee can be concluded for an indefinite or a definite period of not less than twelve months. Temporary workers are entitled to the same wages as the regular workers of the user. The user firm must inform the trade unions representing regular employees of the reasons for, the duration of and the quantity of temporary work. The user has the right to exercise disciplinary powers over temporary workers (Treu 1993b).

In addition to the new law on agency work, Italian labour law considers some form of 'intermediation' in the implementation of the employment contract admissible (in contrast to illegal 'intermediation' at the time of conclusion of the employment contract). The 'subcontracting', the 'lending out', and the direct 'posting' of employees with another employer are common practices. These practices are considered legal because they constitute an actual entrepreneurial activity which does not escape the application of protective labour law, social security, and collective agreements. These forms of temporary employment are widespread among firms belonging to the same group.

The regulation of fixed-term contracts in Italy

According to Italian labour law, the permanent employment contract is the norm, whereas a fixed-term contract (*contratto a termine*) is considered an exception (Art. 2097 of the Civil Code and Art. 1 s. 1 of the Law 230 of 18 April 1962). The parties can resort to this exception only if one of the nine 'cases' outlined in Art. 1 II of the Law 230 of 1960, and in additional special legislation, applies:

1   The first legal reason for concluding a fixed-term contract is the seasonal character of employment, which requires a contract of limited duration. Further particulars are regulated in two presidential decrees, 1525/1963 and 560/1987, which are mainly concerned with employment conditions in the farming and food processing sectors.

2   A fixed term is legal in the case of replacement of a permanent employee who is temporarily absent for reasons of military service, maternity leave, illness, or other legally acknowledged reasons. Absence due to a strike is not considered to be a valid reason. The legitimacy of hiring an employee on a fixed-term contract to replace a vacationing employee is controversial and has been debated in the courts (Kronke 1990: 83).

3   A fixed-term contract is also possible where the work is of an extraordinary and occasional character and is temporary in nature. This possibility is limited if the employer is able to foresee the extraordinary need for employment.

4   In the case of work which is divided into stages, fixed-term employment is legal if it is complementary in nature and cannot be carried out by the regular work force. This case is commonly recognised in the shipbuilding industry (Treu 1993b: 206).

5   Specific mention is made of the possibility of temporary engagement for television, radio, or other artistic performances (introduced in 1977).

6   A special act (Law 876/1977) regulates fixed-term contracts for seasonal work in the tourist sector. If the regional labour office, after consultation with the relevant unions, agrees, fixed-term contracts can be concluded for a limited period within a year in which an increased demand has occurred. This law was extended by the Law 79 of 1983 to all economic sectors.

7   Another form of fixed-term contract was introduced in the air transportation industry. A maximum fixed term of four to six months (depending on the season) is considered legal if the share of fixed-term employees does not exceed 15 per cent of the work force (introduced in 1986).

8   Executives (*dirigenti*) can be hired on a fixed-term basis for up to five years. The executive has the right to resign after three years.

9   Non-employed workers between the ages of 15 and 26 (29 for women and for university graduates) who are registered at the employment office can be hired by private employers and public administrations under an education contract (*contratto di formazione e lavoro*). This form of fixed-term employment was first introduced in 1977 as part of an effort to promote youth employment and was later regulated by Law 863 of 1984 (*Contratti di formazione/lavoro*. Quaderni di Formazione. ISFOL, Nr. 2/84 and Nr. 5–6/85).

If challenged in court, the employer must prove that one of the above conditions for the fixed term existed at the time of conclusion of the employment contract. The courts have been rather restrictive in interpreting the original legal limitations on fixed-term contracts. However, both collective agreements and legislation have gradually reversed the judicial position, and have significantly enlarged the possible use of fixed-term contracts.

Dismissal of a fixed-term employee without notice is possible according to Art. 2119 of the Civil Code – regular dismissal with notice is excluded.

In general, it seems to be the case that the use of fixed-term contracts was less urgent in the Italian case as the flexibility of the Wage Supplement Fund (CIG) permitted work force adjustment despite rigid dismissal protection (Tronti 1993, Auer 1993). However, since the reform of the CIG in 1991, there seems to be a new need for atypical forms of employment. Employers who hire redundant CIG employees, placed on so-called mobility lists in the public employment service, can, since 1991, receive a wage subsidy even if the employee is only hired on a fixed-term contract. This subsidy can take the form of a rebate of social security contributions (Mosley and Kruppe 1993: 96–9).

Luxembourg

Characteristics of the system of employment protection regulations in Luxembourg

The employment protection system in Luxembourg is embedded in a harmonious industrial relations system with active collective bargaining. The system is supported by the Constitution, which expressly 'guarantees the right to work and secures for all citizens the exercise of this right' (Art. 11 IV of the Luxembourg Constitution) (Schintgen 1993: 138). In addition, there are a number of special statutes regulating the employment relationship. In the late 1980s, new statutes were introduced on fixed-term contracts (Law of 24 May 1989) and, in 1993, on part-time employment (EIRR 191, December 1989: 13–14 and EIRR 232, May 1993: 31–2).

The provisions on dismissal protection are rather restrictive in Luxembourg. Notice periods are different for white-collar and blue-collar employees. White-collar employees enjoy two months' notice for less than five years of service, and six months' notice for more than ten years of service. For blue-collar workers, these periods are respectively four and twelve weeks' notice.

The labour law of Luxembourg requires the dismissal to be based on a just cause. It operates with the three standard grounds for dismissal: misconduct, incapability, and redundancy. Employees are automatically entitled to compensation for dismissal. This is granted for both forms of dismissal – ordinary and summary dismissal. It amounts to one monthly salary after five years of service, and increases for blue-collar workers to three, and for white-collar employees to six monthly salaries after twenty years of service. An employer with less than twenty employees can choose between compensation or a prolongation of the notice period (Kronke 1990: 245).

The law of 2 March 1982 on collective redundancies and the recent law of 23 July 1993 on measures for the promotion of employment provide that collective redundancy shall be defined as redundancy implemented by an employer for one or more employees for reasons not related to an employee's conduct or person, when the redundancies envisaged apply to a total of seven or more employees in any thirty-day period, or of fifteen or more employees in any ninety-day period. The employer must negotiate with the employee representatives prior to instigating the redundancies with a view to concluding a social plan. Redundancy notices may not take effect until a period of seventy-five days has elapsed, without superseding, however, longer statutory notice periods or those provided by collective agreement (EIRR 237, October 1993: 29).

The employee must initiate a dismissal claim within three months after the effective date of termination. As remedy for an unjustified dismissal, the court awards damages. Reinstatement is not available as a remedy. In the case of unjustified redundancy dismissal, the employee is entitled to preferential treatment if the company wishes to hire new employees.

The regulation of fixed-term contracts in Luxembourg

The regulation of fixed-term contracts was reformed in 1989. The fixed-term contract (*contrat de travail à durée determinée*) should be confined to areas of work which are clearly defined and of a transitory nature. The law requires fixed-term contracts to be in writing unless the relevant collective agreement says differently.

The use of fixed-term contracts is now limited by a requirement of reason. Fixed-term contracts can be concluded for the following reasons (EIRR 191, December 1989: 13–14):

- to undertake work of a seasonal nature in the agricultural, tourist, or leisure industries;
- to engage in an activity or type of work which is temporary in nature, such as work in the media or the entertainment industry, professional sports, forestry, and construction (the industries are listed in the Grandducal Regulation of 11 July 1989);
- to carry out occasional tasks outside the scope of the firm's normal activities;
- to do work of a clearly defined and temporary nature due to exceptional extension of the company's activities;
- to undertake work of an urgent nature;
- to integrate or reintegrate an employee into working life;
- to promote employment for a specific group of employees;
- to replace an employee; or
- in cases of combination of work and training.

The maximum duration of the fixed-term contract is twenty-four months, with the exception of seasonal contracts. This maximum includes all renewals. However, the employer or a group of employers can get permission from the Ministry of Labour to extend the duration of the fixed term beyond twenty-four months. The renewal of the fixed-term contract is possible only twice. The renewal and the conditions for renewal must be specified in the contract. If the employer fails to do so, the contract converts into a permanent contract.

During the fixed term, only summary dismissal for gross misconduct (*motif grave*) is permitted. Employees can claim damages if the employer fails to abide by the rules of fixed-term contracts. The amount of damages depends upon the pay which the employee would have received until the expiry of the fixed term.

The Netherlands

Characteristics of the Dutch system of employment protection regulations

The main Dutch regulations concerning the employment contract can be found in Art. 1637 to 1639 dd of the Civil Code (*Burgerlijk Wetboek*, BW). In addition, there are a number of special laws and collective agreements which establish mandatory conditions for the individual employment contract (Korver 1993).

The current Dutch dismissal law is still regulated by the early postwar Extraordinary Decree of 5 October 1945 (*Buitengewoon Besluit Arbeids-verhoudingen*, BBA). It requires the employer to obtain permission from the Regional Director of Employment before any ordinary dismissal can take place. Exempted from the procedure are cases in which the employee has consented to the dismissal and also cases of summary dismissal without notice (Art. 6 II a BBA).[14] Employees on probation are also not covered by the dismissal law. However, the law restricts the maximum period of probation to two months (Art. 1639 n III BW).

During the authorisation procedure, the employee can demand not only to remain in employment and be paid the normal wages (Art. 1638 b, d BW), but also to be provided with work.[15] The employee must formally oppose the dismissal in order to be able to collect unemployment benefits. The labour office hears both parties during the procedure, and the decision-making process lasts about four weeks in cases which are only formally contested, and three to eight months in cases in which the employee opposes the dismissal with substantive legal arguments. The administration checks if the employer has just cause for the dismissal. In practice, only a small minority of employees are successful in challenging the dismissal in the administrative procedure (about 5 per cent according to van der Ven 1984: 815).

Dutch employment law prohibits dismissal of certain groups of employees even after the permission of the Regional Director of Employment has been granted. These include employees on maternity leave or who are absent due to pregnancy, recently married employees, and those completing their military service. In addition, employees who are absent from work due to illness enjoy protection from dismissal for the first two years of their illness.

The Dutch regulation of notice periods is rather unique. The general rule is that the employee is entitled to a minimum period of notice which equals the period between two dates of payment of wages, Art. 1639 i BW. According to Art. 1639 j BW the notice period increases with the length of service by one week for each year up to a maximum of thirteen weeks. Employees 45 years of age and older acquire an additional week of notice per year of service, again up to a maximum of thirteen weeks. Employees who have reached the age of 50 and older, and who have been employed for at least a year, are entitled to a minimum notice period of three weeks, Art. 1639 j III BW.

If the employer fails to observe the notice period, the employee can claim damages within six months after the actual ceasing of employment. The damages are normally calculated on the basis of the amount of wages the employer would have had to have paid until the effective legal date of termination (Art. 1639 o I and Art. 1639 r I BWH). The employee can also demand reinstatement. In most cases, however, compensation is granted in accordance with Art. 1639 t BW.

For quite some time, temporary or agency work has been acknowledged as a separate field of regulation in the Netherlands. It was first regulated in the Temporary Work Act (*Arbeidsvoorzieregulation ningswet*) of 1965 which was reformed and consolidated in the Employment Act of 1990. According to the new law, temporary work agency licences are granted by the Central Board (*Centraal Bestuur*) of the Employment Organisation. There is still some debate as to whether the agency worker is an employee under Dutch labour law (Asscher-Vonk 1993: 225–6 and 229–30). However, they are granted social security coverage and are protected from dismissal. Like other employees, temporary employees cannot be dismissed without the prior permission of the Regional Director of Employment.

The regulation of fixed-term contracts in the Netherlands

The requirement of administrative authorisation for each dismissal is argued to be the main reason for the widespread use of fixed-term contracts (Jacobs 1992). However, according to Dutch labour law, the fixed-term contract is still considered the exception and the permanent contract the rule (Kronke 1990: 118). Nevertheless, Dutch labour law does not prescribe certain categories for legally valid fixed-term contracts, and there are only a few regulations which restrict the use of fixed-term contracts. These include, for example, the prohibition of renewal of a fixed-term contract covering the two-month probation period (Art. 1639 n III BW).

If the fixed-term contract is continued beyond the expiry date, it is automatically renewed for the same period as the previous fixed term, but limited to one year in total (Art. 1639 f I BW). The contract continues to operate under the same conditions as the previous contract during the renewal period. The same applies if the contract is renewed within thirty-one days after the expiry of the fixed-term contract. However, if the contract is continued beyond one year without express renewal, it transforms into a permanent contract and the employer must terminate the contract, and thereby follow the normal dismissal procedure if he or she wishes to discontinue the employment relationship (de Leede 1987: 340–1).

Some regulations of fixed-term contracts derive from collective agreements. These place restrictions both on the conclusion and the possibility of renewal of fixed-term contracts. The *Hoogovens* agreement, for example, covering 35,000 employees, stipulates that fixed-term contracts can only be concluded for a maximum of twelve months, or for certain work, in categories of cases agreed upon with the trade union, or in exceptional individual cases. A collective agreement covering 290,000 employees in small engineering firms stipulates that fixed-term contracts can only be concluded in writing for a maximum period of twelve months, and only for a certain work. Furthermore, continuation of the contract after the expiry of the fixed term leads to a permanent contract which the employer can only terminate by observing notice periods and the administrative licensing procedure, unless it is the first written renewal which lasts, together with the first fixed term, no longer than twelve months. A national collective agreement for large engineering firms, which covers 200,000 employees, restricts continuation of fixed-term contracts to one written renewal with a maximum duration of six months. This agreement does not impose restrictions on the conclusion of fixed-term contracts. The *Shell* agreement, covering 2,700 employees, only requires the express agreement on the fixed term to be in writing (Jacobs 1992: 459).

However, despite the regulations contained in collective agreements, it is rather surprising that, given the strong incentive for firms to use fixed-term contracts in the Netherlands due to the preventive system of dismissal protection, there has been no strong pressure to tighten statutory regulations. It has become common practice among some employers to hire alternately temporary employees and fixed-term employees in order to avoid the prohibition on the renewal of fixed-term contracts.[16] Furthermore, the liberal approach to fixed-term contracts is linked to a general policy of promotion of atypical employment, in particular part-time work. Flexibilisation of the labour market through support of atypical employment is seen as a major measure to reduce unemployment.

Portugal

Characteristics of the Portuguese system of employment protection regulations

The Portuguese system of employment protection was reformed in the 1980s. This reform aimed at eliminating 'rigidities' and 'excessive protectionism' in the labour market (EIRR 224, September 1992: 18–21). The new laws modified employment protection measures which were enacted in the revolutionary period in 1975 (Decree-Law 372–A/1975). In particular, the regulations on dismissal and temporary employment were liberalised. The old law only permitted individual dismissals for blatant misconduct of the employee. Individual dismissal for reasons of redundancy or incapability of the employee were excluded. This 1975 law was seen by employers, academics, and politicians to be too ambitious and restrictive for small and medium-sized companies (Pinto 1987: 346–53).

The reform took place in two stages. The first stage was the introduction of the right of employers to suspend employees without pay (Decree-Law 398/1983). However, this option was not widely used by employers because it required a prior ministerial approval and did not entirely release them from their duty to pay wages. Instead, many employers, in practice, simply stopped paying wages without formal suspension. A large number of employees were subsequently entitled to wage claims from a legally existing employment relationship without any real chance of recovery (*salários em atraso*). In this situation the legislature introduced transitory regulations which enabled employees to collect unemployment benefits despite the fact that they were legally still employed (Kronke 1990: 250).

The second stage was the introduction of five sets of labour legislation enacted in February and March 1989, and in particular the reform of the law on individual termination of employment contracts by the Decree-Law 64–A/1989 of 27 February 1989, which came into force on 28 June 1989. The legislative history of this law was characterised by the intervention of the Constitutional Court in 1988. The concept of 'just cause' dismissal was interpreted restrictively by the Court to include only cases of dismissal for gross misconduct of the employee. The Constitutional Court thus limited the basis for a dismissal reform.[17]

As a consequence of this ruling, the reform law of 1989 has established separate procedures for the unilateral termination by the employer for just cause and for other reasons. First, the law lists a number of types of gross misconduct which constitute just cause for dismissal of the employee (disobedience of orders, aggravation of other workers, intentional acts of damage, fighting, false declarations, etc.). This legislative list is not exhaustive. If the employer wishes to dismiss for just cause, both the works council and the employee must be informed of the offences in writing (report of blame). The employee has a right to be heard and present further evidence (a simplified procedure applies in companies with less than twenty employees). After the works council has delivered a 'reasoned opinion', the employer can dismiss the employee within a period of thirty days. The employee can appeal to the labour tribunal and, if successful, can choose between reinstatement and severance payment (one month's wages for each year of service).

The second procedure regulates the termination of an individual job for economic, market, technological, or structural reasons. Technically, this procedure is not concerned with 'dismissal' (*despedimento*) because of the above mentioned constitutional restrictions, but with the 'extinction' of the position. The procedure only applies if the arrangements for collective dismissal or redundancy of a minimum of two to five employees (dependent on the size of the company) do not apply, and if the 'extinction' of the job was no fault of the employee or the employer. The procedure distinguishes between two stages: within fifteen days after informing the works council and the worker affected, a request can be made by either the works council or the worker to the Labour Inspector to intervene and issue a report. After another five days, the second stage begins in which the employer formally 'dismisses' the employee by communicating in writing the reasons for termination. The notice period is sixty days after notification. The employee has a right to appeal and can choose between reinstatement and severance payment if he or she is successful.

In 1991, a further set of reasons for dismissal was introduced: unsuitability or incapability (Decree-Law 400/1991). The law lists a number of possible grounds for separation: repeated reductions in productivity or quality of the work; repeated damage to the means of production; health risks posed by the worker; nonfulfilment of company targets because of the employee's failure to carry out his or her duties (EIRR 224, September 1992: 20). The procedure is similar to the procedure for termination due to 'extinction' of jobs on economic grounds, etc.

In addition to the reformed regulations on dismissal, employment contracts are regulated in the Law on Employment Contracts (*Lei do Contrato de Trabalho*) of 1969 (Decree-Law 49408/1969). The regulations concerning probation periods contained in this law are peculiar to the Portuguese. The law stipulates an automatic period of probation of 60 days for permanent employment contracts, and 30 (or, in some cases, 15) days' probation for fixed-term contracts, unless the parties expressly exclude or alter probation (Art. 43). During probation, both parties have the right to 'withdraw' from the contract without justification. The period of probation can be extended up to six months by individual or collective agreement (Art. 55) (Kronke 1990: 133). Since 1989, there has also been a special law on temporary employment agencies (Decree-Law 358/1989). It regulates the rights and duties of both the user of and the worker employed by an agency (Pinto *et al.* 1993).

The regulation of fixed-term contracts in Portugal

The use of fixed-term contracts was liberalised in 1976 by Decree-Law 78/1976. It enabled employers to conclude short fixed-term contracts and provided them with an easy means of discharging employees at the expiry of the fixed term without having to prove 'just cause'. It has been reported that these new forms of employment contracts were widely used in practice. Seventy per cent of all new employment contracts were concluded in the mid-1980s on a fixed-term basis (Pinto 1987: 348). However, it has also been stated that this meant that permanent employees enjoyed a high degree of security whereas fixed-term employees had very little legal protection (Pinto *et al.* 1993: 239).

Thus, in 1989, the dismissal law was liberalised and fixed-term contracts were reregulated. The new Decree-Law 64–A/1989 introduced limits for the use of fixed-term contracts. According to Art. 42 Nr. 3, an employment contract is legally a permanent contract as long as the parties have not reached a different agreement. In any case, if the contract is not in writing, it is automatically considered a permanent contract.

The main change in the law on fixed-term contracts initiated by the 1989 reform was the introduction of a catalogue of reasons for the conclusion of all fixed-term contracts. If the fixed-term contract is concluded for a reason other than a statutory reason, it automatically converts into a contract for an indefinite period (Art. 41 Nr. 2).

Art. 41 Nr. 1 of the Decree-Law 64–A/1989 lists eight reasons:

1 temporary replacement of an employee who is either unable to work or has been dismissed and opposes the dismissal;
2 temporary and exceptional growth of the company's activity;
3 seasonal work;
4 execution of an occasional task or a specific service which is precisely defined and limited in time;
5 introduction of a new position of uncertain duration or start of a new business;
6 execution, supervision, or control of civil or public construction work, or work of similar nature and duration;
7 execution of tasks or projects which do not form part of the regular activities of the company;
8 employment of first-time job seekers, long-term unemployed, or special cases of labour market policies.

The maximum fixed term is three years. The fixed-term contract can be renewed twice but only within the maximum limit. If it is continued beyond the maximum limit or renewed more than two times, it automatically converts into a contract for an indefinite period (Art. 47).

The employer is required to notify the employee at least eight days before the end of the fixed term of its expiry, otherwise the contract is automatically renewed for another fixed term of the same length (Art. 46 Nr. 1 and 2). The fixed-term contract converts into an indefinite contract if the three year maximum is exceeded through this procedure. The Portuguese law has introduced special protection which amounts to a penalty for the employer (Kronke 1990: 132): at the end of the fixed term, each fixed-term employee has a right to compensation consisting of two days' basic remuneration for each month of service (Art 46 Nr. 3).

If the fixed term lasted twelve months or longer, the employer is prohibited from concluding another fixed-term contract within the next three months. Fixed-term employees have a right to preferential treatment in applying for permanent jobs established by the employer for tasks previously performed by fixed-term employees.

Spain

Characteristics of the Spanish system of employment protection regulations

The Spanish regulations in the area of employment protection were first modernised after Franco's death in 1975 by the Law on Labour Relations (*Ley de Relaciones Laborales*) (Law 16/1976 of 8 April 1976). As an aftermath to the Constitutional reform of 1978 (and the Moncloa Pact of 1977), further reforms were introduced which now form part of the Workers Statute (*Estatuto de los Trabajadores*) (Law 8/1980 of 10 March 1980), and of the Basic Employment Law (*Ley Básica de Empleo*) (Law 51/1980 of 8 October 1980).

The Workers Statute contains the main regulations in the area of employment protection. It lists twelve forms of 'extinction' of the employment contract (*extinción del contrato de trabajo*) (Art. 49 to 60) (Ministerio de Trabajo y Seguridad Social 1993: 129–133). These include the dissolution of the employment relationship through mutual agreement or for objective reasons related to the employee, i.e. his or her death, retirement, or permanent disability. The employee has the right to constructive dismissal (Art. 49 Nr. 10, 50 Nr. 1) if the employer has unilaterally modified working conditions for the worse or failed to pay regular wages and has thus created a situation in which a continuation of the employment relationship agreed upon is no longer possible. In this case, the employee has a right to compensation of forty-five days' salary for each year of service with a maximum compensation of forty-two monthly salaries.

With respect to involuntary termination, the Spanish dismissal law distinguishes between unilateral termination by the employer and dissolution of the employment relationship after administrative authorisation.

Unilateral dismissal for gross misconduct (*despido disciplinario*) is regulated in Art. 49 Nr. 11 and in Art. 54 Nr. 1 and 2 of the Workers Statute. These regulations enumerate legally warranted reasons on which the employer can base summary dismissal of an employee. The six reasons include repeated absenteeism and offences against rules of punctuality; disobedience and undisciplined behaviour at the place of work; verbal or physical attacks against the employer or colleagues or their relatives; violation of contractual good faith and breach of trust; wilful and continuous reduction of the regular or contractual workload; and habitual drunkenness and drug addiction if these have a negative influence on work performance.

A further form of unilateral dismissal deals with so-called objective reasons for dismissal (*causas objetivas legalmente autorizadas*) (Art. 52 and 53 of the Workers Statute). In these cases, the employer must observe a period of notice which varies from one month to three months (for employees with more than two years of service). The employee has a right to compensation of twenty days' salary per year of service and a right to six hours off work per week during the notice period in order to look for a new job.

The reasons for this form of dismissal can relate both to the employee and to the company. The statute mentions:

1   incapability (*ineptitud*) of the employee due to poor health or lack of formal qualifications;
2   failure of the employee to adjust to technical changes in the workplace. These changes must have been 'reasonable', and two months must have elapsed since they were introduced;
3   redundancy (*amortización*) of an individual place of work in companies with less than fifty employees. The employer must prove that the job has lost its economic value and is required to make efforts to find alternative employment for the employee. The employee has the right to preferential treatment within a year if the job is reintroduced;
4   discontinuous absenteeism of the employee which amounts to 20 per cent in two consecutive months, or 25 per cent in four non-consecutive months within a year. However, because leaves of absence for sickness of more than twenty days, pregnancy, or strike activities are exempted, the practical relevance of this reason is rather limited (Kronke 1990: 267).

A dismissal for one of these reasons must be in writing and the written notice must contain the main reasons and the date at which dismissal will take effect (Art. 55 Nr. 1). Only in case of dismissal of an employee representative must the employer observe a certain procedure, i.e. have an interview with the employee and inform the other employee representatives (Art. 68). Without following the procedure, the dismissal is automatically invalid (Art. 111 of the Labour Procedure Code (*Ley de Procedimiento Laboral*)).

Spanish dismissal law distinguishes between a dismissal which is null and void (*despido nulo*) and an unfair dismissal (*despido improcedente*). In the case of a null and void dismissal, the employee must be reinstated. In the case of an unfair dismissal the employer can choose, within five days after the judgement of the labour court, to reinstate the employee or to pay compensation. The compensation award amounts to forty-five days' salary for each year of service with a maximum compensation of forty-two monthly salaries. However, if the employer refuses to reinstate an employee in the event of a nullified dismissal, the labour court will then dissolve the employment relationship and award the regular amount of compensation (forty-five days' salary per year of service) (Kronke 1990: 265).

The procedure is as follows: the employee is required to submit the case within twenty working days after dismissal first to conciliation, which in most cases is carried out by the Spanish Mediation, Arbitration and Conciliation Service (SMAC), prior to the initiation of proceedings before the Labour Court. Before a decision is reached, a second round of conciliation talks takes place at the Court. In 1991, 194,000 (82 per cent) of all individual dismissal complaints were dealt with through SMAC, whereas only 43,638 (18 per cent) were referred to the Labour Court (EIRR 236, September 1993: 24–6).

Spanish dismissal law requires administrative authorisation for collective redundancies and individual redundancies in companies with more than fifty employees, and for the dissolution of employment relationships because of *force majeure* (*fuerza mayor*) (Art. 49 Nr. 8 and 9, 51 Nr. 1 and 2 of the Workers Statute). The redundancies for economic or technical reasons (*causas económicas o tecnológicas*) are authorised by the Ministry of Labour. Its decisions are administrative acts and must therefore be challenged in an administrative court. Most requests for administrative authorisations in cases of redundancies are jointly agreed upon between the unions and the employer, and these agreements usually call for higher levels of compensation (at least double the statutory minimum). The minimum level of redundancy pay is twenty days' pay per year of service with a maximum of twelve months' pay.

The law on collective redundancies is currently under debate. The requirement of administrative authorisation deviates from the 1975 European Commission Directive on Collective Redundancies, which only requires notification of the authorities. Whereas the employers oppose the current regulation and the unions defend it, the government seems indecisive (EIRR 236, September 1993: 24).

The European Commission Directive on Transfer of Undertakings has been implemented (Art. 44 Nr. 1 of the Workers Statute). Employees are fully protected against dismissals which occur through the sale of their company and the subsequent change of employers.

The posting of employees and thus, in effect, agency or temporary work, is still prohibited by Art. 43 of the Workers Statute (with the exception of dock workers). Nevertheless, the law regulates, in Art 15 Nr. 1 d, the legal status of the temporary employee and the obligations of the two employers with respect to social security matters, the employees' right to permanent employment by either of the two employers, and administrative and criminal sanctions against the employers (Rodriguez-Sanudo 1993: 254–5). However, a new law permitting temporary work agencies was enacted in 1994 (EIRR 242, March 1994: 22).

The regulation of fixed-term contracts in Spain

The current Spanish regulations on fixed-term contracts must be interpreted against the background of the strict regime which was introduced during the

Franco era to secure rights of workers as individuals in exchange for a lack of union freedom. It has been stated that after the Franco regime, the Spanish employers were granted the right to temporary employment in exchange for union freedom (Larrea Gayarre 1992: 136). However, temporary employment contracts were already permitted under Franco, though subject to the limitation that the economic activity of the firm justified them, i.e. the realisation of temporary jobs and seasonal tasks (Jimeno and Toharia 1993: 301).

The first regulations of fixed-term contracts after Franco were contained in Art. 15 of the Workers Statute of 1980. The legal regulations on fixed-term contracts were liberalised by Law 32/1984 of 2 August 1984, modifying the Workers Statute, which has itself been amended by decree, for example by the Royal Decree 2104/19843 of 21 November 1984. The use of fixed-term contracts was permitted by these regulations under quite general circumstances and without the previous constraints.

All fixed-term contracts must be registered with the local employment office, and the contracts themselves must be in writing and lodged with the National Institute for Employment (INEM). Renewals are possible for up to three years. Pay levels are regulated by statutory minimum wage policies, and working times by statute or collective agreements.

If the employer fails to pay social security contributions, the contract will, in general, automatically convert to a contract for an indefinite period, unless the employer can prove during the legal procedure that the conditions for a fixed-term contract are met. The same rule applies if the contract is not in writing.

Spanish labour law distinguishes between eleven forms of fixed-term contract (on *Tipos de contrato de trabajo* see Ministerio de Trabajo y Seguridad Social 1993, 84–110 and EIRR 158, March 1987: 15–17):

1 Employment-creating contracts (*contrato temporal de fomento del empleo*). The minimum period for which a contract of this sort can be concluded was recently raised to one year to encourage employers to conclude a large number of permanent employment contracts (EIRR 220, May 1992: 13 and *inforMISEP* Nr. 44, Winter 1993: 4–5). The maximum period is three years and they are renewable up to this period. The Law 18/1993 of 3 December 1993 allows an extension of eighteen months under certain circumstances.

2 Relief contracts (*contrato de relevo*) are part-time contracts covering at least 50 per cent of the regular working time for a fixed term. They are concluded between employers and unemployed workers registered with the unemployment office to replace employees between the ages of 62 and 64 who take partial retirement and receive a partial pension until full retirement at the age of 65. The employment contract of the partial retiree is converted into a part-time contract. Both part-time contracts need to be registered with the unemployment office. The law grants the employer an

incentive to convert the relief contract into an 'open-ended' contract: he is entitled to a reduction in his social security contributions over a period equal to that of the relief contract.

3 Practical work contracts (*contrato en prácticas*) are a special type of fixed-term contract which gives young academics and those with medium- to high-level vocational qualifications the opportunity to obtain work experience. The minimum duration is six months and the maximum two years. The employee must apply within four years after the completion of studies. Remuneration may not fall, within the first year, below 60 per cent, and in the second year 70 per cent, of the wages provided by collective bargaining. The employer is entitled to a 75 per cent reduction in social security contributions. The employer receives a subsidy if the fixed-term contract is converted into a permanent contract after the expiry of the fixed term (Law 18/1993 on urgent measures to promote employment).

4 Apprenticeship contracts recently replaced training contracts. They allow young employees between the ages of 16 and 25 (no age limit for disabled employees) to combine theoretical and practical training on the job. These contracts last between six months and three years (*inforMISEP*, No. 45, Spring 1994: 9–10).

5 Contracts for specific purposes (*contrato de obra o servicio determinado*) can be concluded if the exact duration of the contract is unknown at the time of the agreement. The work or service must be specific and final and completed at the time of expiry. Two weeks' notice must be given if the contract lasted for over a year. This type of contract is common in the construction industry (Kronke 1990: 150).

6 Casual employment contracts (*contrato eventual por circunstancias de la producción*) can be concluded for a maximum fixed term of six months within a twelve-month period if it becomes necessary to adjust employment to special circumstances of the market, accumulation of work, or excess of orders.

7 Temporary work contracts (*contrato de iterinidad*). See p. 62 above.

8 New launch contracts (*contrato por lanzamiento de nueva actividad*) can be concluded in new enterprises or in existing enterprises which are launching a new production line, product, or workplace. The minimum fixed term is six months.

9 Home-working contracts (*contrato de trabajo a domicilio*) can be concluded for a definite or an indefinite period. The employee works outside the employer's supervision. This type of contract must be registered with the local Employment Office, and the employer must provide the employee with a written contract of employment specifying, for example, the type of work and the system of pay.

10 A group contract (*contrato de trabajo de grupo*) is concluded between an employer and a group of up to five workers. A leader represents the group

and receives the pay for the group. The employer must be informed of the names of the workers and the method of distribution of pay. The contract must specify its duration, the working time, the remuneration, and social security contributions. This form of contract is common among theatre groups, ensembles and circus troupes (EIRR 236, September 1993: 17).

11 Community work (*trabajos de colaboración social*) is carried out by unemployed who receive their benefits while working on community projects. Their contracts can be for a fixed term (EIRR 236, September 1993: 17).

Seasonal work, normally a main form of fixed-term employment, is actually regarded in Spanish labour law as a form of permanent employment. It is called a contract for intermittent work (*contrato de trabajadores fijos de carácter discontinuo*) (Art. 15 Nr. 6 of the Workers Statute). The regulation assumes that this contract is open-ended and is only suspended at the close of each period of activity. If the activity is not resumed, the employer must obtain authorisation from the Employment Office, and the employee can file a dismissal claim.

United Kingdom

Characteristics of the system of employment protection regulations in the United Kingdom

Comprehensive statutory employment protection is still a recent affair in the United Kingdom. Traditionally, British[18] labour law was characterised by a deliberate policy of abstentionism of the state, i.e. non-interference with statutory law in industrial relations. Until the 1960s, the regulation of both industrial relations affairs and employment protection was largely delegated to voluntary collective agreements concluded between a trade union and one or more employers or an employer association. The state made only selective use of statutory law as a means of worker protection (Hepple and Fredman 1992: 40–50, Kahn-Freund 1983). However, the voluntary system fell apart in the two decades after the Second World War, partly due to an increase in fragmented bargaining on the shop floor and a subsequent erosion of multi-employer bargaining (Sisson 1987).

British labour law was fundamentally reformed during the 1960s and 1970s. Special adjudicatory bodies in the form of Industrial Tribunals were introduced in 1964, which, in the beginning, had only limited jurisdiction to hear employer complaints against training levies. However, their jurisdiction was soon enlarged by the Redundancy Payments Act of 1965, which granted a certain category of employees compensation for dismissal by reason of redundancy. In the early 1970s, a major statute, the Industrial Relations Act 1971, was introduced. It implemented, to some extent, recommendations of the Royal Commission on Trade Unions and Employer Associations (Donovan

Commission).[19] This statute introduced for the first time unfair dismissal protection. It failed, however, to achieve acceptance within industrial relations, mainly because it neglected the Donovan Commission's warning to abstain from legislating collective industrial relations in conjunction with employment protection (Weekes *et al.* 1975).

The Industrial Relations Act was repealed in 1974 as one of the first acts of the new Labour government. However, the provisions on unfair dismissal were kept, and additional legislation on trade union rights, the reform of equal pay, and discrimination in employment were introduced in 1975 and 1976. The most important employment laws were merged into a single statute, the Employment Protection (Consolidation) Act (EPCA), which, since 1978, has been the main statutory basis of British individual labour law. The EPCA includes regulations, among others, on notification of terms and conditions of employment, maternity rights, notice periods, unfair dismissal, redundancy payments, and industrial tribunals.

To a considerable extent, legislative activities changed their objective after 1979, when the Conservative government of Margaret Thatcher adopted its so-called deregulation policy. New laws restricted a number of industrial relations and employment regulations. The gradual increase of the qualifying period of employment, for example, which was raised from six months to one year in 1980 and then to two years in 1986, led to the exclusion of a considerable number of employees from the unfair dismissal protection and redundancy payment legislation. However, it is necessary to emphasise that the main object of the Conservatives' legislative fervour was the restriction of trade union power. The basic approach to employment protection, which was adopted in the 1970s, remained unchanged. Reforms of employment law were mainly instigated in the 1980s and 1990s by European law, the latest being the Trade Union Reform and the Employment Rights Act of 1993 which includes, among other changes, reforms of maternity rights and redundancies (Deakin 1990).

In general, the British laws contain similar regulations on employment protection in comparison with their continental European partners. The lengths of the notice periods in case of termination of the contract of employment, for example, is regulated in s. 49 EPCA. The minimum period is one week for a person employed continuously for one month to two years. The notice period increases by one week for each additional year of continuous employment. The maximum statutory notice period is twelve weeks. In the case of violation of a notice period, the employee can claim damages for wrongful dismissal. This claim must be filed with the county court.

Dismissal without notice or summary dismissal is still regulated by common law, although qualified by statutory law. However, judicial attitudes on the notion of 'dismissal for cause' have changed since the nineteenth century, when they were based on the law of master and servant. It is now largely reduced to cases of gross misconduct (Smith *et al.* 1993: 267–70).

After two years of continuous employment, British employees have a right to a written statement of the reasons for dismissal (s. 53 EPCA). This includes summarily dismissed employees. Furthermore, British employees can leave their employment, with or without notice, and then claim compensation for constructive dismissal by reason of the employer's conduct (s. 55 (2)(c) EPCA). In this case the employee must prove that the employer has repudiated the contract,[20] and has acted unfairly in a way which renders it no longer feasible for the employee to continue employment.

After two years of continuous employment, the employer can only dismiss the employee if there are reasons which justify the unilateral termination of the contract of employment. However, there are four reasons which render the dismissal automatically unfair. These include trade union membership or activities, refusal to belong to a trade union, selection for redundancy in breach of an agreed procedure or customary arrangement, and pregnancy and confinement.

The main statutory reasons for dismissal available to employers are listed in s. 57 (2) EPCA. They relate to

1   the capability or qualification of the employee to perform work of the kind which he was employed by the employer to do;
2   the conduct of the employee;
3   redundancy of the employee, i.e. the job or the position ends or work of a particular kind for which the employee was employed diminishes or ceases; and
4   a situation in which the employee cannot continue to work without contravention of a statutory duty or restriction.

In addition, there is a general clause of 'some other substantial reason of a kind as to justify the dismissal of an employee' (s. 57 (1)(b) EPCA). A reason under this general clause relates, for example, to a dismissal which is motivated by an economic, technical or organisational reason entailing changes in the workforce in connection with a transfer of an undertaking (s. 8 (2) of the Transfer of Undertakings (Protection of Employment) Regulations (TUPE) 1981).[21]

In the case of dismissal for reason of redundancy, the employer is required to select the employee according to customary arrangements or agreed procedures relating to redundancy. The employee can claim either unfair dismissal or compensation in form of a redundancy payment. If unfair dismissal is claimed, the employee must argue that the employer acted unreasonably during the dismissal.

British unfair dismissal law takes a rather unique approach in assessing the legality of a dismissal. It restricts industrial tribunals to asking if the employer acted reasonably in treating the reason given as sufficient grounds for dismissal (s. 57 (3) EPCA). It judges the employer's behaviour against management standards by asking if the behaviour falls within the realm of reasonable responses which can be expected to have been adopted by a reasonable employer at the time of the dismissal (Collins 1993, Blankenburg and Rogowski 1986). An important factor in this assessment is whether the employer followed the procedure established in the company for handling dismissal cases.[22]

The dismissal claim must be filed with the industrial tribunal within three months after the effective date of termination. If the dismissal is judged to have been unfair, the tribunal can call for re-engagement, either in form of reinstatement in the previous job or in the form of employment in an alternative job with the same employer. However, in the vast majority of successful unfair dismissal claims the award is compensation (Dickens *et al.* 1986, ch. 5). In 1990–91 the median award was £1,733.[23] The maximum compensation award at the time of writing (April 1994) was £11,000 (s. 75 EPCA).

In cases of collective redundancies, employers must inform the Secretary of State and are obligated to consult the recognised trade unions. These provisions were first introduced by the Employment Protection Act 1975, which implemented the relevant European Directive, and were recently incorporated into the Trade Union and Labour Relations (Consolidation) Act 1992. In addition, there are separate laws on sex and race discrimination in employment which intend, unlike the unfair dismissal provisions, to change employment practices through judicial intervention of industrial tribunals.

Atypical employment has not received extensive common law or statutory attention. Homeworkers have benefited to some extent from minimum wage law (Lord Wedderburn 1986: 129–32, and Leighton 1986: 509–12). Their contract has been interpreted as a contract of employment if work is conducted on a regular basis (*Nethermere (St. Neots)* v. *Gardiner* [1984] IRLR 240 (Court of Appeal)).

In Britain, temporary or agency work is regulated by the Employment Agencies Act 1973. Unlike in other countries, the aspect of employment protection of agency workers is of minor importance in this Act, which is mainly designed to facilitate the establishment of agencies (Hepple 1993). The Act distinguishes between an employment agency which simply supplies workers and an employment business which supplies workers who are employed by the employment business. Even in the latter case, however, the employment business does not automatically have its workers sign a contract of employment. The case law, which developed before the Act and was then used to interpret it, tends to assume a contract *sui generis* between the employment business and the worker.[24] The agency worker is thus deprived of even basic employment protection measures. However, there are separate regulations which require the employment business to specify the terms and conditions of employment in writing, including whether the worker is employed by the employment business under a contract of service or as a self-employed worker, the kind of work for which the worker will be supplied to users, and the minimum rates of pay (Conduct of Employment Agencies and Employment Business Regulations 1976, SI 1976 no. 715).

The employment business can hire or employ the agency worker on a permanent or a fixed-term basis. In fact, the time period for which the agency worker is hired depends on the nature of the assignment. Nevertheless, even if employed under a contract of employment, the two-year qualifying period deprives agency workers of most of the employment protection rights (Hepple 1993: 265 and 276).

The regulation of fixed-term contracts in the United Kingdom

There are no statutory restrictions in the United Kingdom on entering a fixed-term contract of employment. The employer is not required to justify the use of a fixed-term contract by recourse to a legally prescribed reason and there is no restriction on the length or renewal of the fixed term. The fixed-term contract can therefore take a variety of forms, including a contract for a stated period or until the occurrence of an event which is certain to happen at a definite time. Casual workers who work for relatively short periods in seasonal trades or services are not even considered employees because they are alleged to have the freedom to deny work. Their contract therefore lacks the necessary mutuality of obligations (*O'Kelly* v. *Trusthouse Forte* [1983] ICR 728 (Court of Appeal)). Even if considered to be employees, casual workers often lack the necessary qualifying period of employment to be covered by protective law.

The British approach is to avoid special treatment of fixed-term contracts at the statutory level and to assimilate this type of contract with employment contracts for an indefinite period. The expiry of a fixed term without renewal is included in the definition of dismissal for the purposes of unfair dismissal protection and redundancy payments (s. 55 (2) and 83 (2) EPCA). However, in contrast to the protection offered by permanent contracts, it is possible to exclude from fixed-term contracts the right to complain of unfair dismissal or the right to a redundancy payment through express agreement in writing if the fixed term is one year or more in the case of unfair dismissal, or two years or more in the case of a redundancy payment, and expires without renewal (s. 142 (1) and (2) EPCA).

If the fixed-term contract was concluded for less than one month but in fact lasts three months or more, the law treats the contract as one for an indefinite period for which the employer is obliged to observe the minimum notice period (s. 49 (4) EPCA). This provision is intended to prevent the evasion of the right to notice (Hepple 1993: 261). The fixed-term employee is excluded from guarantee payments and medical suspension payments if the fixed term lasts less than three months, unless the employee has in fact been continuously employed for a period of more than three months (s. 13 (2) and 20 (2) EPCA).

If the fixed-term contract was expressly concluded to replace an employee who is absent because of pregnancy or childbirth, or has been suspended on medical grounds for a certain period, the dismissal based on the return of the previous employee is deemed a valid substantial reason for dismissal. However, the employer must act reasonably according to s. 57 (3) EPCA in carrying out the dismissal. This provision has ceased to have any practical effect since the qualifying period of employment was raised to two years (Selwyn 1993: 48).

In summarising the United Kingdom regulations, it can be said that the two-year qualifying period operates as a functional equivalent for the fixed-term contract and a formal probation period. Employers can freely terminate the employment contract during this period. The British legal situation with respect to employment protection might also explain why the group of fixed-term employees tends to include a large number of relatively well-paid employees who have opted voluntarily to sign a fixed-term contract (Casey 1991).

ATYPICAL EMPLOYMENT AND EUROPEAN LAW

The regulation of atypical employment at the European level forms part of the Social Policy of the European Union. Regulatory attempts under the broad heading of workers' rights and European Social Policy were, in the beginning, centred around the joint concerns of enabling the free movement of workers between Member States (Art. 48 to 51 of the original EEC Treaty) and of over-coming discrimination in employment in the areas of equal pay for equal work and equal treatment between men and women (Art. 117 to 122 of the original EEC Treaty, and in particular Art. 119 and subsequent Directives). During the 1970s, the focus of European Social Policy was gradually expanded. A number of Directives were introduced in the areas of employment protection and health and safety. The employment protection measures included Directives on collective redundancies, employee rights in case of the transfer of an undertaking, and employee rights in case of insolvency of the company. However, these legislative activities were not particularly concerned with regulating new forms of work or atypical employment at the European level.

The initiatives for European regulations in the area of atypical employment started in the 1980s. Draft Directives on atypical workers, i.e. workers employed part-time, on fixed-term contracts and by temporary employment agencies, were first proposed in 1981 and 1982. These attempts were unsuccessful, mainly due to resistance from the United Kingdom (Gold 1993: 24). However, the discussion of whether to introduce regulations on atypical employment became a major concern with the adoption of the Single European Act (SEA), in force since 1987, and the Community Charter of Fundamental Social Rights of Workers (also known as the Social Charter) of 1989. The social provisions of the SEA and the Social Charter led to the 'Action Programme' of the European Commission, which contained forty-seven separate initiatives. As part of this Action Programme, the Commission prepared three draft Directives on atypical employment in 1990 which aimed at ensuring the same level of protection for atypical employees and so-called typical workers. They concerned working conditions, distortion of competition and the health and safety of atypical employees. Only the third Directive on health and safety was subsequently adopted by the European Council on 25 June 1991.

The adopted Directive 91/383 provides that fixed-term employees are afforded the same level of protection with respect to safety and health at the workplace as permanent employees. The fixed-term worker has the right to be informed of the specific risks which he or she faces at the workplace, as well as of any special medical surveillance he or she may be subjected to, or of any special occupational qualifications or skills called for by the job. The atypical worker has the right to receive sufficient training appropriate to the particular characteristics of the job.

The two draft Directives on working conditions and distortion of competition which were not adopted contained a number of specific regulations on fixed-term contracts. These included, for example, the prescription of a maximum fixed term of three years, including renewals, and the requirement of reason which obliges the employer to state in writing 'the grounds for recourse' to an atypical form of employment. Furthermore, fixed-term and other atypical employees were granted the same access to vocational training and to entitlements to annual holidays, dismissal allowances and seniority allowances as full-time employees. In addition, an equitable allowance was demanded in the event of an unjustified break in the employment relationship before the fixed term expires.

These proposals proved to be controversial with respect to both content and procedure. The European Parliament rejected them in October 1990 on the grounds that, in fact, majority voting should apply despite the exclusion of the 'rights and interests of employed persons' from majority voting under Art. 100A Treaty. Furthermore, Member States and employer associations criticised the attempt to address workers' rights issues as a distortion of competition. The United Kingdom objected to regulation in this area in general.

Due to the nature and amount of opposition, the two unsuccessful proposals have been shelved by the Commission. It is uncertain at the moment if new attempts will be initiated in the wake of the Social Protocol and the Social Agreement, which form part of the Annex of the Maastricht Treaty (Treaty on European Union). It seems more likely that some form of special protection for atypical employees, including fixed-term contracts, will be discussed in the attempts to harmonise dismissal protection systems which are currently under investigation.

4

FIXED-TERM EMPLOYMENT PATTERNS IN THE EUROPEAN UNION

Comparative reports on the relationship between labour market regulation and labour market processes face the difficulty of combining both aspects adequately. The analysis of these processes tends to dominate research at the national level. It assumes that the major elements of the institutional background are sufficiently known and, therefore, require no further explanation. Most comparative evaluations of fixed-term employment focus on comparisons of specific features and changes of regulation (Walwei 1991, OECD 1993, 1997, Meulders et al. 1994). Some studies deal almost exclusively with data collection (European Union Foundation for the Improvement of Living and Working Conditions 1992) or try to assemble descriptive information on the socio-economic characteristics of fixed-term and permanent employees (OECD 1993, 1997, Meulders et al. 1994, Delsen 1995). The comparisons are carried out at a high level of abstraction and the analysis of labour market processes frequently lacks the depth which can be achieved at the country level.

The policies of flexibilisation of labour markets through deregulation of fixed-term contracts were the subject of a number of major evaluation studies. However, the evaluations of fixed-term contracts in France (Ministère du Travail et de la Formation Professionnelle 1992, Michon and Ramaux 1993), in Spain (Alba-Ramírez 1991, Segura et al. 1991) and in Germany (Büchtemann and Höland 1989, Infratest 1994) have been single-country studies. They do not refer to experiences in other countries with similar labour market policy instruments, i.e. changing the institutional context within which agents of the labour market act. This may be permissible since changes in one country's legislation is the main subject of these evaluation reports, but there is a risk of underestimating the value of effective functional equivalents which can be learned from other countries. One such functional equivalent of fixed-term contracts is agency work or contracting out labour as 'independent employees'. Legislation on these issues has repercussions on the volume of fixed-term contracts. Additionally, there is a strong case to consider a country's shift in the balance of employment protection and fixed-term employment as a reaction to developments in neighbouring countries or other major competitors on product markets.

Country studies often take for granted that the national employment system and large parts of the institutional background of labour market processes are static. They fail to take into account the fact that legislation changes and that through legislative amendments, collective agreements and judicial interpretation, labour law becomes a dynamic process. The fact that national regulations of fixed-term contracts display country-specific features is illustrated in the previous chapter. We consider five aspects of fixed-term contracts to be crucial for empirical comparisons: (1) the requirement of reason, (2) maximum and/or minimum duration, (3) possibility of renewal, (4) automatic conversion into permanent contract, and (5) the possibility of compensation at the end of the fixed term.

A number of detailed country studies have been published on the evolution of fixed-term employment in most Member States of the Union. However, individual studies have proven to be hard to compare since, in many instances, rather specific country definitions of what constitutes a fixed-term contract, seasonal work, or an apprenticeship contract have been applied. In addition, it is often difficult to make comparisons due to the different sampling techniques and organisation of questionnaires which are applied in country-specific traditions of national labour force surveys in the various data sets.[1]

A study which takes cross-country analyses as its point of departure must define the unit of analysis very carefully. Whereas from a legal perspective there are clearly-defined categories of employment contracts which are classified in each country's employment system, such as fixed-term contracts, the survey data we analyse has to rely on a somehow unified definition of fixed-term employees on the basis of respondents' understanding of their own employment contract. In the data available for this comparative evaluation, the European Union Labour Force Survey, we could not test the possibility of differential interpretation of the same question on the permanency of a job in the various cultural backgrounds of Union Member States. We had to assume that the probability that this item on the questionnaire will be misinterpreted is similar in all Member States.[2] A major advantage of this data set, on the other hand, is its size, which allows detailed multiple cross-tabulations and, at the same time, multivariate analyses based on a harmonised data set within the European Union.

Most countries' questionnaires of the Labour Force Survey deal with the issue of fixed-term employment in a similar way. The issue is introduced with a general question which distinguishes a permanent job from all other types of contracts (Eurostat 1988, 1992). Subsequently, these 'other forms of jobs' are more narrowly identified in the set of questions that follows. The person is asked, for example, whether he or she is employed on a fixed-term contract, as a seasonal worker or whether the job includes apprenticeship-like training. Based on the recoding of national categories into common Eurostat categories, we applied in the following analyses three type of filters: (1) the selection of persons living in private households, (2) persons who did any work for pay or profit during the reference week, (3) excluding those who received any training in the framework of an apprenticeship.

EVIDENCE ON THE EXTENT AND PATTERNS OF FIXED-TERM EMPLOYMENT CONTRACTS

In order to gain a more detailed understanding of country patterns of labour contracts and the extent of fixed-term employment, we consider it necessary to analyse the empirical patterns of employment and fixed-term employment, particularly within industries and occupations. For this reason, we made ample use of the European Union Labour Force Survey. This detailed investigation of employment contracts by industry and occupation – in addition to standard demographic variables such as age, education and family status – allows us to compare in sufficient detail the patterns that have evolved in individual Member States. A more detailed understanding of individual characteristics of employees holding fixed-term contracts as well as knowledge of, for example, occupations and the industrial sector, should enhance our understanding of the reasons for the temporary nature of employment.

In some Member States, legislation or the courts have restricted the use of fixed-term contracts to specific cases. These cases include contracts which offer mainly professional training, those which cover seasonal work, or temporary tasks which last only for a limited period of time. Fixed-term contracts can also be applied in cases where temporary peaks in the workload occur, or in order to replace staff who are temporarily absent (compare Chapter 3).

The validity of these restrictions, whether a task is temporary or not, cannot be analysed based on the survey data available to us for this report. Yet we can compare across countries whether certain occupations or specific industrial sectors typically employ staff using fixed-term contracts. Given the above, it is necessary to collect a great deal of empirical evidence in order to assess the frequently-claimed need for more flexible forms of employment against the increased employment insecurity for employees. We must discuss in this context the insecurity of fixed-term employment, since it is likely to have an impact on subsequent individual careers and employment opportunities.

AGGREGATE TRENDS IN FIXED-TERM EMPLOYMENT

In the Member States of the European Union, 7.23 million people were employed with a fixed-term contract in 1987. This number increased by 62 per cent to 11.5 million in 1996 (compare also Table 4.1 reflecting indices based on

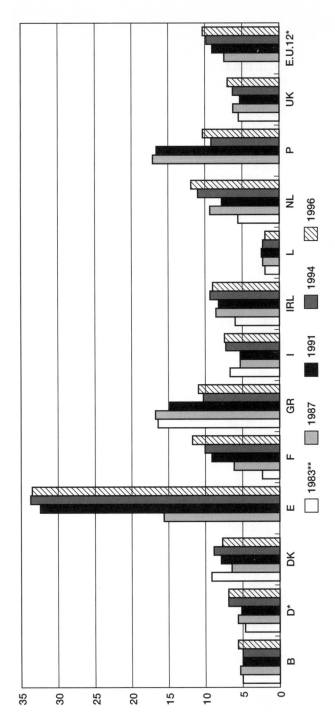

Figure 4.1 Fixed-term employment as a percentage of total dependent employees in the EU

Source: Eurostat European Labour Force Survey; author calculations

Notes: *1994 and 1996 Unified Germany; **Denmark and Germany 1984

the year 1987 and Figure 4.1 showing percentage shares of fixed-term employees among all dependent employees). The annual rate of change of fixed-term employees slowed down from 13 per cent in 1988 to 1 per cent in 1996 in the Union (compare Table 4.5). But there is no general tendency and, moreover, it is a composite of very different trends in the single Member States which have varying influence on the European Union average due to the different sizes of their populations and the degrees of their labour force participation.

Whereas, since 1983, in France and the Netherlands there was a continuous and an extremely steep increase, in Spain a strong increase was followed by stability on a high level, in Portugal an increase was followed by a decrease and in Greece there was a nearly continuous decrease, but there was relatively little movement of percentages of fixed-term employees in the labour force in other Member States. The annual rate of change varies from a sharp increase of 61 per cent in France in 1985 to a decline in fixed-term employment of 35 per cent in Portugal in 1992. In some instances, changes in the legal provisions governing fixed-term contracts can be associated with the rates of change. In France in 1985, far-reaching deregulation caused this surge of fixed-term employees during the same year (Michon and Ramaux 1993), and in Belgium, the Law on Temporary Work (24 July 1987), which limited the use of fixed-term contracts, came into effect and caused a decline of 24 per cent in fixed-term contracting.

Trends in total dependent employment

The variation in the use of fixed-term contracts over time within the Member States is partly dependent on the evolution of total dependent employment (compare Tables 4.2 and 4.3). Labour mobility within the labour market is usually found to be higher in periods of expanding total employment (Emerson 1988, Schettkat 1993). We therefore consider it useful to compare on a descriptive level the changes in the size of the labour force. In Italy the total dependent employment decreased by about 3 per cent between 1983 and 1996. The smallest increase in total dependent employment occurred in France and the United Kingdom, with growth of up to 10 per cent over a period of thirteen years between 1983 and 1996 and in Portugal (10 per cent growth within ten years). The increase of total dependent employment in Belgium (13 per cent), Denmark (14 per cent) and Luxembourg (17 per cent) was just in line with the European Union average rate of job growth for this period (15 per cent). Above average increases in total dependent employment can be found for Greece, Ireland and Luxembourg, enlarging their total dependent employment by more than 20 per cent.

At the top end of the scale of growth in total dependent employment are Spain (22 per cent within the last ten years) and the Netherlands (35 per cent growth within thirteen years). Portugal and Spain show a pattern of a remarkable increase in annual rates of change of total dependent employment up

Table 4.1 Index 1987 of fixed-term employment

	B	D*	DK	E	F	GR	I	IRL	L	NL	P	UK	EUR 12*
1983	93.2	—	—	—	38.4	93.8	123.2	70.6	88.2	51.8	—	84.1	—
1984	103.4	83.4	134.8	—	37.4	108.3	92.3	77.1	93.6	—	—	94.7	—
1985	124.7	94.2	128.7	—	60.2	125.5	89.2	82.0	120.4	69.6	—	108.5	—
1986	131.6	100.1	116.2	—	88.4	112.7	85.0	95.6	111.1	—	84.8	110.2	—
1987	100.0	100.0	100.0	100.0	100.0	100.0	100.0	100.0	100.0	100.0	100.0	100.0	100.0
1988	100.4	101.3	105.4	151.1	112.0	108.8	110.0	108.2	104.0	94.6	113.3	98.9	112.6
1989	94.6	106.6	89.4	190.7	125.2	108.9	119.5	101.1	96.1	94.4	119.0	90.6	121.6
1990	99.6	112.0	109.7	224.3	159.7	108.2	102.1	103.1	98.1	88.5	122.6	88.8	131.4
1991	100.7	106.4	126.1	246.6	158.0	95.2	105.9	102.9	113.6	92.8	110.6	89.1	133.7
1992	98.9	186.5	129.3	250.1	168.2	66.5	140.3	106.9	124.6	119.5	72.3	89.0	150.8
1993	101.1	175.6	121.2	228.3	176.6	69.1	109.8	114.7	107.8	122.4	63.7	93.3	143.7
1994	102.1	176.6	138.6	236.5	176.4	69.8	131.9	123.3	110.7	133.7	59.6	102.3	150.2
1995	106.4	178.7	141.9	255.4	205.0	70.1	129.8	139.6	—	135.5	62.8	113.2	160.4**
1996	117.8	173.8	125.3	253.1	210.9	77.7	135.1	132.7	97.9	152.8	65.7	115.8	162.6

Notes: *1983–91 West Germany, 1992–96 Unified Germany; **without Luxembourg
Source: Eurostat European Labour Force Survey; author calculations

Table 4.2 Index 1987 of total dependent employment

	B	D*	DK	E	F	GR	I	IRL	L	NL	P	UK	EUR 12*
1983	98.3	101.1	89.8	—	99.2	95.5	100.3	101.8	91.8	84.5	—	96.1	—
1984	99.1	98.4	94.4	—	98.8	97.1	97.8	100.4	92.2	—	—	97.2	—
1985	99.3	99.1	97.0	—	99.1	98.6	99.9	97.9	94.3	88.3	—	99.3	—
1986	100.6	99.6	101.1	96.1	100.3	98.8	100.8	100.3	96.4	—	98.2	99.8	—
1987	100.0	100.0	100.0	100.0	100.0	100.0	100.0	100.0	100.0	100.0	100.0	100.0	100.0
1988	101.0	102.3	102.2	105.3	100.5	102.6	102.2	100.6	98.8	101.5	103.8	103.3	102.3
1989	102.6	104.9	100.8	112.0	102.5	105.1	101.3	101.0	99.8	103.9	108.2	105.7	104.5
1990	104.0	111.8	101.8	117.3	102.8	108.7	104.5	104.3	102.3	108.3	111.9	106.7	107.7
1991	108.8	113.5	101.5	119.4	104.7	107.5	105.7	106.6	106.1	112.2	113.9	104.7	108.7
1992	110.9	145.6	103.3	117.3	106.1	109.2	100.7	107.9	108.3	113.9	114.0	102.4	114.9
1993	110.1	143.7	100.5	111.6	106.8	111.6	99.6	107.6	107.1	114.1	112.6	101.8	113.7
1994	110.4	142.2	100.1	110.4	105.9	113.7	98.0	113.7	107.4	114.4	109.7	102.1	113.0
1995	111.5	141.8	102.8	114.6	108.1	116.1	97.2	119.8	105.3	115.6	108.5	103.6	114.1
1996	111.3	140.8	103.8	118.3	109.2	118.4	97.7	126.1	109.3	119.1	107.9	105.3	115.0

Notes: *1983–91 West Germany, 1992–96 Unified Germany
Source: Eurostat European Labour Force Survey; author calculations

Table 4.2 Index 1987 of total dependent employment

	B	D*	DK	E	F	GR	I	IRL	L	NL	P	UK	EUR 12*
1983	98.3	101.1	89.8	—	99.2	95.5	100.3	101.8	91.8	84.5	—	96.1	—
1984	99.1	98.4	94.4	—	98.8	97.1	97.8	100.4	92.2	—	—	97.2	—
1985	99.3	99.1	97.0	—	99.1	98.6	99.9	97.9	94.3	88.3	—	99.3	—
1986	100.6	99.6	101.1	96.1	100.3	98.8	100.8	100.3	96.4	—	98.2	99.8	—
1987	100.0	100.0	100.0	100.0	100.0	100.0	100.0	100.0	100.0	100.0	100.0	100.0	100.0
1988	101.0	102.3	102.2	105.3	100.5	102.6	102.2	100.6	98.8	101.5	103.8	103.3	102.3
1989	102.6	104.9	100.8	112.0	102.5	105.1	101.3	101.0	99.8	103.9	108.2	105.7	104.5
1990	104.0	111.8	101.8	117.3	102.8	108.7	104.5	104.3	102.3	108.3	111.9	106.7	107.7
1991	108.8	113.5	101.5	119.4	104.7	107.5	105.7	106.6	106.1	112.2	113.9	104.7	108.7
1992	110.9	145.6	103.3	117.3	106.1	109.2	100.7	107.9	108.3	113.9	114.0	102.4	114.9
1993	110.1	143.7	100.5	111.6	106.8	111.6	99.6	107.6	107.1	114.1	112.6	101.8	113.7
1994	110.4	142.2	100.1	110.4	105.9	113.7	98.0	113.7	107.4	114.4	109.7	102.1	113.0
1995	111.5	141.8	102.8	114.6	108.1	116.1	97.2	119.8	105.3	115.6	108.5	103.6	114.1
1996	111.3	140.8	103.8	118.3	109.2	118.4	97.7	126.1	109.3	119.1	107.9	105.3	115.0

Notes: *1983–91 West Germany, 1992–96 Unified Germany
Source: Eurostat European Labour Force Survey; author calculations

until 1989, largely due to their joining the European Union common market. This remarkable growth in employment is partly due to higher increases in part-time employment, especially in the Netherlands, Belgium and the United Kingdom (see also the section on fixed-term employment and part-time work).

Because of unification the growth in total dependent employment in Germany (39 per cent) is not directly comparable. But the change in total dependent employment in West Germany between 1984 and 1991 with an increase of 14 per cent and a decrease in unified Germany between 1992 and 1996 of 5 per cent is comparable to the changes in Belgium and Denmark. The annual rates of change increase between 1984 and 1989 up to 3 per cent and, because of the booming economy in the first year after unification to 7 per cent in 1991, with a yearly decrease since 1992 caused by the economic slow-down.

Fixed-term employment and total dependent employment

Despite the differential patterns of job creation within the European Union, the percentages of fixed-term employees on the national level show an interesting evolution over a period of thirteen years. Table 4.4 shows the share of fixed-term employees of all dependent employees between 1983 and 1996. The country-specific differences in patterns range from Luxembourg, with the lowest share of fixed-term contracts (2 per cent of total dependent employment), followed by the United Kingdom, Belgium, Germany and Italy. These countries have up to 7 per cent of total dependent employees working on a fixed-term contract, with a change of less than 3 per cent between 1983 and 1996.

Ireland with a more average use of fixed-term contracts has up to 10 per cent of total dependent employment in fixed-term contracts. This appears to be comparatively few employees in fixed-term contracts considering that Ireland, like the Netherlands (up to 12 per cent of total dependent employment in fixed-term contracts), has no legislation limiting the use of fixed-term contracts. Similarly, Denmark had a temporarily shrinking but average use of up to 9 per cent of total dependent employment. France, on the other hand, has seen its percentage share of fixed-term employees steadily increasing from as low as 2 per cent of the total labour force to rates of around 12 per cent of total dependent employment in 1996.

Southern European Union countries which continue to have a large share of employees in agriculture in general show much higher rates of fixed-term employment, probably due to higher rates of seasonal work. A high-use country like Portugal witnessed a temporary increase in fixed-term employment, with a peak of up to 19 per cent of total dependent employees on fixed-term contracts in 1989. In 1989, however, a new law was introduced

Table 4.4 Fixed-term employment as percentage of total dependent employment

	B	D*	DK	E	F	GR	I	IRL	L	NL	P	UK	EUR 12*
1983	5.1	—	—	—	2.4	16.5	6.6	5.9	2.1	5.7	—	5.5	—
1984	5.6	4.7	9.1	—	2.3	18.7	5.0	6.6	2.3	—	—	6.1	—
1985	6.7	5.3	8.5	—	3.7	21.4	4.8	7.2	2.8	7.3	—	6.8	—
1986	7.0	5.6	7.4	—	5.4	19.2	4.5	8.2	2.6	—	14.7	6.9	—
1987	5.3	5.6	6.4	15.7	6.1	16.8	5.3	8.6	2.2	9.3	17.0	6.3	7.4
1988	5.3	5.5	6.6	22.5	6.8	17.8	5.8	9.2	2.3	8.7	18.6	6.0	8.1
1989	4.9	5.7	5.7	26.7	7.5	17.4	6.3	8.6	2.1	8.5	18.7	5.4	8.6
1990	5.1	5.6	6.9	30.0	9.5	16.7	5.2	8.5	2.1	7.6	18.7	5.2	9.0
1991	4.9	5.2	8.0	32.4	9.2	14.9	5.4	8.3	2.4	7.7	16.5	5.3	9.0
1992	4.8	7.1	8.0	33.5	9.7	10.2	7.4	8.5	2.6	9.8	10.8	5.4	9.7
1993	4.9	6.8	7.7	32.1	10.1	10.4	5.9	9.1	2.2	10.0	9.6	5.7	9.3
1994	4.9	6.9	8.9	33.6	10.2	10.3	7.2	9.3	2.3	10.9	9.2	6.3	9.8
1995	5.1	7.0	8.8	35.0	11.6	10.1	7.1	10.0	—	10.9	9.9	6.8	10.3**
1996	5.7	6.9	7.7	33.6	11.8	11.0	7.4	9.0	2.0	12.0	10.4	6.9	10.4

Notes: *1983–91 West Germany, 1992–96 Unified Germany; **without Luxembourg
Source: Eurostat European Labour Force Survey; author calculations

81

Table 4.5 Annual rates of change in fixed-term employment

	B	D*	DK	E	F	GR	I	IRL	L	NL	P	UK	EUR 12*
1984	10.9	—	—	—	-2.6	15.4	-25.1	9.2	6.2	—	—	12.6	—
1985	20.6	12.9	-4.5	—	61.0	16.0	-3.4	6.3	28.6	—	—	14.6	—
1986	5.5	6.3	-9.8	—	47.0	-10.2	-4.7	16.6	-7.8	—	—	1.5	—
1987	-24.0	-0.1	-13.9	—	13.1	-11.3	17.6	4.6	-10.0	-5.4	17.9	-9.2	—
1988	0.4	1.3	5.4	51.1	12.0	8.8	10.0	8.2	4.0	-0.2	13.3	-1.1	12.6
1989	-5.7	5.2	-15.2	26.2	11.8	0.1	8.6	-6.5	-7.6	-6.2	5.0	-8.5	7.9
1990	5.3	5.0	22.7	17.7	27.6	-0.6	-14.6	1.9	2.1	4.9	3.0	-1.9	8.1
1991	1.1	-5.0	15.0	9.9	-1.0	-12.1	3.7	-0.1	15.8	28.7	-9.8	0.3	1.8
1992	-1.8	—	2.5	1.4	6.4	-30.2	32.4	3.9	9.7	2.4	-34.6	-0.1	—
1993	2.3	-5.8	-6.3	-8.7	5.0	3.9	-21.7	7.2	-13.5	9.3	-11.9	4.8	-4.7
1994	1.0	0.5	14.4	3.6	-0.1	1.0	20.1	7.5	2.7	1.3	-6.5	9.7	4.5
1995	4.2	1.2	2.3	8.0	16.2	0.4	-1.6	13.2	—	5.4	5.4	10.6	6.8**
1996	10.7	-2.7	-11.7	-0.9	2.9	10.9	4.1	-5.0	-11.6	12.8	4.7	2.3	1.4

Notes: *1983–91 West Germany, 1992–96 Unified Germany; **without Luxembourg
Source: Eurostat European Labour Force Survey; author calculations

in Portugal, and since then the use of fixed-term contracts has been curtailed with rates around 10 per cent. Despite the passage of more restrictive legislation in Greece in 1983, the share of fixed-term employees in this country peaked at 21 per cent in 1985, and has since then levelled off at about 11 per cent.

In 1984, Spain introduced new legislation allowing fixed-term employment for specific reasons. Some of these reasons, however, could be interpreted very broadly, so that the law did not, in effect, impose narrow restrictions on the use of fixed-term contracts. The data from Eurostat allow us to trace the increase in fixed-term contracts from 1987 on and, indeed, the increase from 15 per cent in 1987 to 35 per cent in 1995 is the steepest among the Member States of the European Union. The decline in 1996 may be caused by changes in legislation introduced by the new government of Spain (compare also Chapter 6).

After reviewing the trends of fixed-term employment and total dependent employment, and keeping in mind the historical evolution of systems of employment protection and legislation concerning fixed-term contracts, the actual results, as described above, remain puzzling. For example, despite deregulation both in Germany and Spain in nearly the same year, changes concerning the use of fixed-term contracts were very different. A steep increase occurred in Spain, whereas Germany hardly witnessed any change at all over the observed period.

If total dependent employment grows in an industrial sector with less-than-average use of fixed-term contracts for that country, the proportion of the fixed-term employees will decrease (or vice versa). In other words, there may well be evolutions of the shares of fixed-term employees or changes between specific groups in the labour market that cancel each other out, which means the aggregate national figures on the extent of fixed-term employment may lead us to draw simplistic conclusions. In order to understand the processes at work, which may lead to differential growth patterns in fixed-term employment, we need to analyse in more detail cross-tabulations of fixed-term employees by gender, age, education and nationality on the one hand, and breakdowns by occupations and industrial sectors on the other.

IS FIXED-TERM EMPLOYMENT AN ISSUE OF GENDER?

Are women or men more likely to be fixed-term employees? The gender composition of dependent employees in fixed-term employment on the European Union level indicates only little adjustment in the share of women and men over time. Changes range from 53 per cent for men in 1987 to 51 per cent in 1991 and back to 53 per cent in 1996. Because apprentices, military and compulsory services are not included in our data, the percentage distribution of women and men in fixed-term employment differs from OECD publications (OECD 1993).

In the European Union of twelve Member States, women account for about 42 per cent of all dependent employees in 1991. However, close to 50 per cent of all dependent employees on fixed-term contracts were women in that year (compare Figure 4.2). But in most Member States a trend of levelling off this disproportion has taken place in the last years. In 1996 the share of women changed to about 44 per cent of all dependent employees and to about 47 per cent of all dependent employees on fixed-term contracts (compare Figure 4.3). This effect is mainly due to the more rapid growth of labour force participation of women than in fixed-term employment (see also Table 4.6).

In Belgium the difference in overall labour force participation of women and women's share of fixed-term employment is particularly pronounced, while the general share of fixed-term employment is low compared to other Member States. Only Greece and Spain have both low levels of overall participation of women in employment as well as low rates of fixed-term employment in general (compare Figures 4.2 and 4.3).

In Germany, almost half of all fixed-term employees are women. There were only marginal changes of less than 2 per cent over time, swinging from an equal distribution of men and women in fixed-term employment in 1984, to a majority of men (52 per cent) until 1987, and then to a majority of women (51 per cent) in 1990/91. Beside the change in the distribution of fixed-term employment between men and women of about 10 per cent to a majority of men of 56 per cent, the tendency of marginal changes continued after the reunification with less than 3 per cent increase between 1992 and 1996.

France showed an evolution with larger shifts of up to 5 per cent and a general majority of women working under a fixed-term contract (53 per cent in 1996). The Netherlands started in 1983 with 54 per cent women in fixed-term employment, followed by years of an almost equal distribution until 1990. From 1991 there was a large growth of women in fixed-term contracts from 53 per cent to 59 per cent in 1993, and a shrinking until 1995 to 54 per cent swinging back to a 56 per cent female share in fixed-term employment in 1996. In Ireland, patterns shifted from a majority of women (54 per cent) to equal shares of women and men in fixed-term employment in 1988 and back to a majority of women in 1996 (57 per cent).

While we cannot observe a clear evolution over time, Luxembourg had a permanently higher share of women than men in fixed-term employment until 1994. While there are no data available for 1995 the pattern seems to have changed completely in 1996 with only 45 per cent women in fixed-term employment.

This permanently higher share of women than men in fixed-term employment is also present in Denmark, the United Kingdom and Belgium.

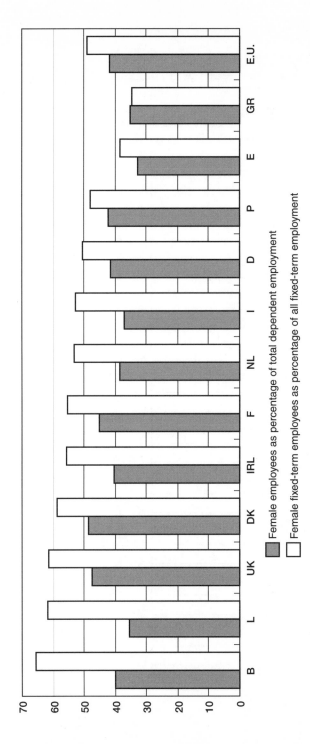

Figure 4.2 Women in fixed-term employment in the EU, 1991

Source: Eurostat European Labour Force Survey; author calculations

85

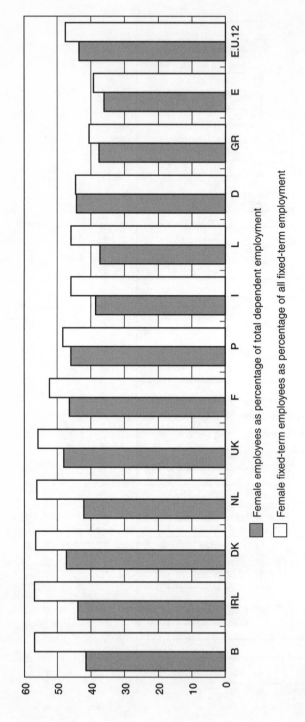

Figure 4.3 Women in fixed-term employment in the EU, 1996

Source: Eurostat European Labour Force Survey; author calculations

Female employees as percentage of total dependent employment

Female fixed-term employees as percentage of all fixed-term employment

In Denmark, the share of women rose from 52 per cent in 1983 to 62 per cent in 1987. By 1990, the share had declined to 56 per cent, but had risen to 61 per cent in 1992 with a level of 57 per cent in 1996. While the share of female fixed-term employees in the United Kingdom shrunk little over a period of three years, from 58 per cent in 1983 to 56 per cent in 1986, the percentage of women rose again to 63 per cent in 1989, and then steadily declined to 54 per cent in 1995, increasing again to 56 per cent in 1996. Belgium registered almost steady growth in the share of women in fixed-term employment between 1983 and 1991, rising from 54 per cent to 65 per cent, and a steady decline until 1996 (57 per cent).

Table 4.6

	Total dependent employment by gender			Fixed-term employment by gender	
B	*Year*	*Male*	*Female*	*Male*	*Female*
	1983	65.61	34.39	44.30	55.70
	1984	65.79	34.21	45.53	54.47
	1985	64.73	35.27	43.46	56.54
	1986	64.10	35.90	40.30	59.70
	1987	63.25	36.75	40.23	59.77
	1988	62.43	37.57	39.97	60.03
	1989	62.05	37.95	35.99	64.01
	1990	61.26	38.74	36.52	63.48
	1991	60.24	39.76	34.69	65.31
	1992	59.88	40.12	36.61	63.39
	1993	59.07	40.93	37.63	62.37
	1994	58.87	41.13	38.24	61.76
	1995	59.17	40.83	41.79	58.21
	1996	58.75	41.25	43.06	56.94
D	*Year*	*Male*	*Female*	*Male*	*Female*
	1983	—	—	—	—
	1984	61.39	38.61	49.33	50.67
	1985	60.64	39.36	51.85	48.15
	1986	60.58	39.42	51.03	48.97
	1987	60.43	39.57	50.59	49.41
	1988	60.46	39.54	49.98	50.02
	1989	60.35	39.65	50.80	49.20
	1990	58.68	41.32	49.00	51.00
	1991	58.48	41.52	49.40	50.60
	1992	57.44	42.56	54.30	45.70
	1993	57.41	42.59	54.24	45.76
	1994	56.97	43.03	53.13	46.87
	1995	56.75	43.25	53.01	46.99
	1996	55.97	44.03	55.53	44.47

Table 4.6 continued

		Total dependent employment by gender		Fixed-term employment by gender	
DK	*Year*	*Male*	*Female*	*Male*	*Female*
	1983	—	—	—	—
	1984	52.62	47.38	47.53	52.47
	1985	52.77	47.23	43.57	56.43
	1986	52.47	47.53	39.60	60.40
	1987	51.75	48.25	37.91	62.09
	1988	51.55	48.45	38.80	61.20
	1989	51.67	48.33	41.72	58.28
	1990	51.22	48.78	44.36	55.64
	1991	51.36	48.64	41.37	58.63
	1992	51.68	48.32	43.34	56.66
	1993	51.17	48.83	39.33	60.67
	1994	52.56	47.44	44.91	55.09
	1995	53.50	46.50	43.71	56.29
	1996	52.90	47.10	43.32	56.68
E	*Year*	*Male*	*Female*	*Male*	*Female*
	1986	71.31	28.69	—	—
	1987	70.98	29.02	65.99	34.01
	1988	69.85	30.15	64.23	35.77
	1989	68.91	31.09	63.72	36.28
	1990	68.00	32.00	63.54	36.46
	1991	67.41	32.59	61.65	38.35
	1992	66.92	33.08	61.39	38.61
	1993	65.93	34.07	60.58	39.42
	1994	65.13	34.87	60.73	39.27
	1995	64.67	35.33	61.38	38.62
	1996	63.94	36.06	60.61	39.39
F	*Year*	*Male*	*Female*	*Male*	*Female*
	1983	58.04	41.96	50.73	49.27
	1984	57.34	42.66	50.85	49.15
	1985	56.89	43.11	54.51	45.49
	1986	56.04	43.96	48.98	51.02
	1987	56.11	43.89	50.22	49.78
	1988	55.67	44.33	49.32	50.68
	1989	55.69	44.31	48.60	51.40
	1990	55.32	44.68	46.89	53.11
	1991	54.88	45.12	44.77	55.23
	1992	55.17	44.83	46.30	53.70
	1993	54.45	45.55	44.92	55.08
	1994	54.02	45.98	46.16	53.84
	1995	54.04	45.96	48.58	51.42
	1996	53.79	46.21	47.68	52.32

	Total dependent employment by gender			Fixed-term employment by gender	
GR	*Year*	*Male*	*Female*	*Male*	*Female*
	1983	69.58	30.42	71.45	28.55
	1984	69.20	30.80	71.83	28.17
	1985	68.03	31.97	70.56	29.44
	1986	67.94	32.06	70.43	29.57
	1987	67.59	32.41	70.98	29.02
	1988	65.82	34.18	69.72	30.28
	1989	65.50	34.50	68.94	31.06
	1990	64.75	35.25	66.34	33.66
	1991	64.97	35.03	65.47	34.53
	1992	64.22	35.78	64.17	35.83
	1993	63.87	36.13	61.45	38.55
	1994	63.67	36.33	62.92	37.08
	1995	62.55	37.45	58.53	41.47
	1996	62.43	37.57	59.38	40.62

	Year	*Male*	*Female*	*Male*	*Female*
I					
	1983	66.84	33.16	53.02	46.98
	1984	66.92	33.08	50.67	49.33
	1985	66.51	33.49	50.70	49.30
	1986	65.99	34.01	51.03	48.97
	1987	65.32	34.68	50.76	49.24
	1988	64.95	35.05	51.40	48.60
	1989	64.04	35.96	49.79	50.21
	1990	63.73	36.27	47.45	52.55
	1991	63.22	36.78	47.18	52.82
	1992	63.01	36.99	52.20	47.80
	1993	62.94	37.06	51.18	48.82
	1994	62.48	37.52	52.18	47.82
	1995	62.08	37.92	51.88	48.12
	1996	61.40	38.60	54.00	46.00

	Year	*Male*	*Female*	*Male*	*Female*
IRL					
	1983	64.07	35.93	47.16	52.84
	1984	63.41	36.59	47.99	52.01
	1985	63.93	36.07	46.79	53.21
	1986	62.84	37.16	48.58	51.42
	1987	61.25	38.75	45.55	54.45
	1988	61.28	38.72	49.81	50.19
	1989	60.46	39.54	45.04	54.96
	1990	60.18	39.82	46.65	53.35
	1991	59.87	40.13	44.34	55.66
	1992	58.33	41.67	43.13	56.87
	1993	57.47	42.53	44.65	55.35
	1994	56.69	43.31	47.25	52.75
	1995	56.33	43.67	47.80	52.20
	1996	56.17	43.83	43.12	56.88

Table 4.6 continued

	Total dependent employment by gender			Fixed-term employment by gender	
L	*Year*	*Male*	*Female*	*Male*	*Female*
	1983	67.70	32.30	34.78	65.22
	1984	67.05	32.95	44.61	55.38
	1985	66.00	34.00	38.58	61.42
	1986	66.07	33.93	35.71	64.29
	1987	65.56	34.44	43.19	56.82
	1988	65.56	34.44	32.24	67.76
	1989	65.12	34.88	40.05	59.95
	1990	65.28	34.72	40.19	59.80
	1991	64.55	35.45	38.26	61.74
	1992	63.03	36.97	48.74	51.26
	1993	63.77	36.23	46.07	53.93
	1994	63.30	36.70	39.22	60.78
	1995	64.29	35.71	—	—
	1996	62.74	37.26	54.01	45.99
NL	*Year*	*Male*	*Female*	*Male*	*Female*
	1983	66.30	33.70	46.33	53.67
	1984	—	—	—	—
	1985	65.12	34.88	50.55	49.45
	1986	—	—	—	—
	1987	64.44	35.56	49.27	50.73
	1988	62.90	37.10	49.25	50.75
	1989	62.68	37.32	49.36	50.64
	1990	62.39	37.61	49.65	50.35
	1991	61.47	38.53	46.82	53.18
	1992	59.82	40.18	42.02	57.98
	1993	59.24	40.76	40.84	59.16
	1994	58.48	41.52	42.36	57.64
	1995	58.54	41.46	46.01	53.99
	1996	57.93	42.07	43.70	56.30
P	*Year*	*Male*	*Female*	*Male*	*Female*
	1986	61.46	38.54	57.81	42.19
	1987	60.82	39.18	59.76	40.24
	1988	59.65	40.35	55.23	44.77
	1989	59.05	40.95	53.76	46.24
	1990	58.48	41.52	53.63	46.37
	1991	57.83	42.17	52.34	47.66
	1992	55.09	44.91	48.47	51.53
	1993	55.26	44.74	49.98	50.02
	1994	54.60	45.40	49.37	50.63
	1995	53.97	46.03	48.80	51.20
	1996	54.04	45.96	51.73	48.27

		Total dependent employment by gender		Fixed-term employment by gender	
UK	Year	Male	Female	Male	Female
	1983	56.41	43.59	42.07	57.93
	1984	55.66	44.34	43.04	56.96
	1985	55.53	44.47	44.12	55.88
	1986	55.00	45.00	43.70	56.30
	1987	54.36	45.64	42.52	57.48
	1988	54.25	45.75	42.88	57.12
	1989	53.28	46.72	36.52	63.48
	1990	53.18	46.82	37.66	62.34
	1991	52.75	47.25	38.55	61.45
	1992	52.44	47.56	42.47	57.53
	1993	51.97	48.03	43.91	56.09
	1994	52.04	47.96	43.83	56.17
	1995	52.21	47.79	46.18	53.82
	1996	52.16	47.84	44.20	55.80
EU 12	Year	Male	Female	Male	Female
	1986	—	—	—	—
	1987	60.16	39.84	52.56	47.44
	1988	59.77	40.23	52.84	47.16
	1989	59.29	40.71	52.22	47.78
	1990	58.70	41.30	51.92	48.08
	1991	58.31	41.69	51.01	48.99
	1992	57.73	42.27	52.34	47.66
	1993	57.32	42.68	51.48	48.52
	1994	56.96	43.04	51.75	48.25
	1995	56.84	43.16	52.69	47.31
	1996	56.38	43.62	52.53	47.47

Source: Eurostat European Labour Force Survey; author calculations

In Portugal, Spain, Italy and Greece, the patterns are completely different from the other European Commission countries. There the share of men in fixed-term employment is mainly more than 50 per cent. As we will see later when the data is broken down by industry sectors, this is a reflection of the more male-dominated seasonal work in agriculture and other services. In all these four southern Member States the share of women increased at least until the early 1990s: in Greece from 29 per cent in 1983 to 40 per cent in 1996; in Spain from 34 per cent in 1987 to 39 per cent in 1993, staying on this level until 1996; in Italy from 47 per cent in 1983 to 53 per cent in 1992, decreasing then to 46 per cent in 1996; and in Portugal from 42 per cent in 1986 to 52 per cent in 1992 followed by a three-year period of staying above 50 per cent and a decrease to 48 per cent in 1996.

This result does not, however, take into account the different participation of women in the labour force across Member States of the European Union. As reported by the European Commission (1993), the increase in activity rates among women was the primary source of job growth of the Union's labour force during the 1980s. For 1996, the Member States can be divided into three groups:

- Denmark, France, Portugal and the United Kingdom with shares of women in the labour force that exceed the European Commission average (46–48 per cent),
- Germany, Belgium, Ireland and the Netherlands with approximately average shares (41–44 per cent),
- Luxembourg, Italy, Greece and Spain with lower-than-average shares (36–38 per cent).

These figures reflect the fact that in all Member States of the European Union, participation of women in the labour market increased, while the countries which have already achieved a higher level of female labour force participation had subsequently smaller increases.

Bringing together this trend of labour force participation with the trends in fixed-term employment, we find that this gender-specific growth in total dependent employment is not reflected in a proportional way in the trends of fixed-term employment (for detailed data see Table 4.6). This finding refers to comparisons analysing annual rates of change in the share of total dependent and fixed-term employment.

Countries with above-average labour force participation such as Denmark, France, Portugal and the United Kingdom had, for the most part, similarly high shares of women in fixed-term employment. Whereas the share of women in the total dependent labour force is comparatively high in the United Kingdom, the share of women holding fixed-term contracts is the second highest in the European Union (compare Table 4.6 and OECD 1993: 24, which uses a slightly different definition, but leading to very similar results). It is noteworthy that in the case of France, female labour force participation had risen to 45 per cent in 1991. However, the female share in fixed-term employment had risen to 55 per cent in 1991. In Portugal the trend in fixed-term employment mirrors the one observed in total dependent employment. Since 1986 there were around 5 per cent more women in fixed-term employment than men. Denmark belongs to the same group of countries with high labour force participation. The Danish example shows a consistently high level of female labour force participation, while female fixed-term employment increased from 1984 to a level of up to 61 per cent in 1993.

In Germany, Belgium, Ireland and the Netherlands, the percentage of women in the labour force was about 42 per cent in 1996. The respective shares of women in fixed-term employment in these countries vary, however, from 45 per cent in Germany and 56 per cent in the Netherlands to 57 per cent in Ireland and Belgium. Whereas in Ireland and the Netherlands the overall percentage of women in fixed-term employment remained at a constant level of about 50 per cent, for Germany this was also the case during the 1980s, while after the reunification, due to the lower share in East Germany, the share varied between 44 per cent and 47 per cent. In Belgium the female share in this type of employment relationship increased substantially until 1991 (65 per cent) and continuously decreased until 1996 (57 per cent).[3] Ireland is also relying to a larger extent on more 'flexible' female fixed-term employment. There, too, we can observe a difference between the overall participation of women in the labour force (44 per cent) and the female share in fixed-term employment (57 per cent in 1996).

Luxembourg, Italy, Greece and Spain have below-average rates of labour force participation of women. In Luxembourg there have been very few changes during the observed period, but generally the share of women in fixed-term employment (62 per cent in 1991) is high compared to 35 per cent of overall female labour force participation.[4] Similarly, included in the trend but at a lower level, Italy has 38 per cent women in the labour force. Since 1983 (47 per cent), however, the share of women in fixed-term employment in Italy increased, reaching 53 per cent in 1991, but dropped down again to 46 per cent in 1996.

In Greece the number of working women grew every year to 37 per cent of the labour force in 1996, with a little more rapid growth in the share of female fixed-term employees (41 per cent). Similarly, in Spain the total female dependent labour force grew to a level of 36 per cent in 1996 due to the general growth of the labour force. Thus we can observe a corresponding increase in the female share in fixed-term employment in Spain, reaching a level of 39 per cent in 1996.

A comparison of the share of women employed under a fixed-term contract to all employed women and the share of men employed under a fixed-term contract to all employed men reveals very different patterns for the Member States. In the European Union as a whole, 6 to 10 per cent of all men were holding a fixed-term contract, while the corresponding share of women was 9 to 11 per cent (compare Table 4.7). Only in Greece until 1992 the proportion of men employed under a fixed-term contract was higher than the proportion of women. In all other Member States of the European Union, women are more likely to be fixed-term employees than men with respect to their own gender reference group.

As a conclusion to this section, we can derive a gendered cluster of the use of fixed-term employment in the European Union in 1991 (compare Figure 4.2 and Table 4.6). The southern Member States of the Union (Greece, Portugal and Spain), who were recent entrants into the Union at that time, showed relatively low rates of female labour force participation compared to the other Member States. However, the female share in fixed-term employment was also relatively low. The difference between female labour force participation (below 40 per cent) and the female share in fixed-term employment (40 per cent) in 1991 suggest a close relationship.

Table 4.7 Fixed-term employees as percentage of total dependent labour force by gender

	Year	Total	Male	Female		Year	Total	Male	Female
B	1983	5.1	3.4	8.2	E	1983	—	—	—
	1984	5.6	3.9	8.9		1984	—	—	—
	1985	6.7	4.5	10.8		1985	—	—	—
	1986	7.0	4.4	11.6		1986	—	—	—
	1987	5.3	3.4	8.7		1987	15.7	14.6	18.4
	1988	5.3	3.4	8.5		1988	22.5	20.7	26.7
	1989	4.9	2.9	8.3		1989	26.7	24.7	31.2
	1990	5.1	3.1	8.4		1990	30.0	28.1	34.2
	1991	4.9	2.8	8.1		1991	32.4	29.7	38.2
	1992	4.8	2.9	7.5		1992	33.5	30.7	39.1
	1993	4.9	3.1	7.5		1993	32.1	29.5	37.2
	1994	4.9	3.2	7.4		1994	33.6	31.4	37.9
	1995	5.1	3.6	7.3		1995	35.0	33.2	38.3
	1996	5.7	4.1	7.8		1996	33.6	31.8	36.7

	Year	Total	Male	Female		Year	Total	Male	Female
D	1983	—	—	—	F	1983	2.4	2.1	2.8
	1984	4.7	3.8	6.2		1984	2.3	2.1	2.7
	1985	5.3	4.5	6.5		1985	3.7	3.6	3.9
	1986	5.6	4.7	7.0		1986	5.4	4.7	6.3
	1987	5.6	4.7	7.0		1987	6.1	5.5	6.9
	1988	5.5	4.6	7.0		1988	6.8	6.0	7.8
	1989	5.7	4.8	7.0		1989	7.5	6.5	8.7
	1990	5.6	4.7	6.9		1990	9.5	8.0	11.3
	1991	5.2	4.4	6.4		1991	9.2	7.5	11.3
	1992	7.1	6.8	7.7		1992	9.7	8.1	11.6
	1993	6.8	6.4	7.3		1993	10.1	8.3	12.2
	1994	6.9	6.5	7.5		1994	10.2	8.7	11.9
	1995	7.0	6.6	7.6		1995	11.6	10.4	13.0
	1996	6.9	6.8	7.0		1996	11.8	10.5	13.4

	Year	Total	Male	Female		Year	Total	Male	Female
DK	1983	—	—	—	GR	1983	16.5	16.9	15.5
	1984	9.1	8.3	10.1		1984	18.7	19.4	17.1
	1985	8.5	7.0	10.2		1985	21.4	22.2	19.7
	1986	7.4	5.5	9.3		1986	19.2	19.9	17.7
	1987	6.4	4.7	8.2		1987	16.8	17.6	15.0
	1988	6.6	5.0	8.3		1988	17.8	18.9	15.8
	1989	5.7	4.6	6.8		1989	17.4	18.3	15.7
	1990	6.9	6.0	7.9		1990	16.7	17.1	16.0
	1991	8.0	6.4	9.6		1991	14.9	15.0	14.7
	1992	8.0	6.7	9.4		1992	10.2	10.2	10.2
	1993	7.7	5.9	9.6		1993	10.4	10.0	11.1
	1994	8.9	7.6	10.3		1994	10.3	10.2	10.5
	1995	8.8	7.2	10.7		1995	10.1	9.5	11.2
	1996	7.7	6.3	9.3		1996	11.0	10.5	11.9

	Year	Total	Male	Female		Year	Total	Male	Female
I	1983	6.6	5.2	9.3	NL	1983	5.7	4.0	9.1
	1984	5.0	3.8	7.5		1984	—	—	—
	1985	4.8	3.6	7.0		1985	7.3	5.7	10.4
	1986	4.5	3.5	6.5		1986	—	—	—
	1987	5.3	4.2	7.6		1987	9.3	7.1	13.3
	1988	5.8	4.6	8.0		1988	8.7	6.8	11.9
	1989	6.3	4.9	8.8		1989	8.5	6.7	11.5
	1990	5.2	3.9	7.6		1990	7.6	6.1	10.2
	1991	5.4	4.0	7.7		1991	7.7	5.9	10.6
	1992	7.4	6.2	9.6		1992	9.8	6.9	14.1
	1993	9.1	7.1	11.9		1993	10.0	6.9	14.5
	1994	9.3	7.7	11.3		1994	10.9	7.9	15.1
	1995	7.1	6.0	9.1		1995	10.9	8.6	14.2
	1996	7.4	6.5	8.8		1996	12.0	9.0	16.0

	Year	Total	Male	Female		Year	Total	Male	Female
IRL	1983	5.9	4.4	8.7	P	1983	—	—	—
	1984	6.6	5.0	9.3		1984	—	—	—
	1985	7.2	5.2	10.6		1985	—	—	—
	1986	8.2	6.3	11.3		1986	14.7	13.8	16.1
	1987	8.6	6.4	12.0		1987	17.0	16.7	17.5
	1988	9.2	7.5	11.9		1988	18.6	17.2	20.6
	1989	8.6	6.4	11.9		1989	18.7	17.1	21.2
	1990	8.5	6.6	11.3		1990	18.7	17.1	20.9
	1991	8.3	6.1	11.5		1991	16.5	15.0	18.7
	1992	8.5	6.3	11.6		1992	10.8	9.5	12.4
	1993	9.1	7.1	11.9		1993	9.6	8.7	10.8
	1994	9.3	7.7	11.3		1994	9.2	8.4	10.3
	1995	10.0	8.5	11.9		1995	9.9	8.9	11.0
	1996	9.0	6.9	11.7		1996	10.4	9.9	10.9

	Year	Total	Male	Female		Year	Total	Male	Female
L	1983	2.1	1.1	4.3	UK	1983	5.5	4.1	7.3
	1984	2.3	1.5	3.8		1984	6.1	4.7	7.8
	1985	2.8	1.7	5.1		1985	6.8	5.4	8.6
	1986	2.6	1.4	4.9		1986	6.9	5.5	8.6
	1987	2.2	1.5	3.7		1987	6.3	4.9	7.9
	1988	2.3	1.2	4.6		1988	6.0	4.7	7.5
	1989	2.1	1.3	3.7		1989	5.4	3.7	7.3
	1990	2.1	1.3	3.7		1990	5.2	3.7	6.9
	1991	2.4	1.4	4.2		1991	5.3	3.9	6.9
	1992	2.6	2.0	3.6		1992	5.4	4.4	6.6
	1993	2.2	1.6	3.3		1993	5.7	4.8	6.7
	1994	2.3	1.4	3.8		1994	6.3	5.3	7.3
	1995	—	—	—		1995	6.8	6.1	7.7
	1996	2.0	1.7	2.5		1996	6.9	5.8	8.0

Table 4.7 continued

	Year	Total	Male	Female
EUR	1986	—	—	—
12	1987	7.4	6.4	8.8
	1988	8.1	7.2	9.5
	1989	8.6	7.5	10.0
	1990	9.0	7.9	10.5
	1991	9.0	7.9	10.6
	1992	9.7	8.8	10.9
	1993	9.3	8.4	10.6
	1994	9.8	8.9	11.0
	1995	10.3	9.6	11.3
	1996	10.4	9.7	11.3

Source: Eurostat European Labour Force Survey;
author calculations

Secondly, we can identify a group of countries which have medium to high levels of female labour force participation, with an approximately 10 per cent higher share of women among fixed-term employees (Germany 42 per cent, 51 per cent; France 45 per cent, 55 per cent; and Denmark 49 per cent, 59 per cent). In a third group of Member States including Ireland, Italy, the Netherlands and the United Kingdom, we can observe even larger differences between female labour force participation and the female share in fixed-term employment. In these countries in 1991, the gap was around 15 percentage points. Fourthly, in Belgium and Luxembourg, this difference constitutes 25 percentage points.

These patterns have changed in 1996 (compare Figure 4.3 and Table 4.6). While the differences between female labour force participation and the female share in fixed-term employment seem to be more equalised in general, the country clustering has changed. Female labour force participation ranges between 36 per cent in Spain and 48 per cent in the United Kingdom; the female share in fixed-term employment ranges from 39 per cent in Spain to 57 per cent in Belgium, Ireland and Denmark.

Grouping the Member States by the differences between these two shares, we can identify the unified Germany now presenting both a level of 44 per cent in female labour force participation and the female share in fixed-term employment. In Portugal the share of women increased only in labour force participation since 1991. Due to this the difference to the share in fixed-term employment decreased to only 2 per cent in 1996. Spain (36 per cent) and Greece (38 per cent) still have the lowest shares of female labour force participation paired with the low female share in fixed-term employment (39 per cent, 41 per cent). Luxembourg (37 per cent) and Italy (39 per cent) have also relatively few women in dependent employment, but the share of women in fixed-term employment is higher (7 per cent, 9 per cent). With a very

Table 4.8 Annual change in gender in (a) permanent employment (b) fixed-term employment

		(a) Permanent employment		(b) Fixed-term employment	
	Year	*Male*	*Female*	*Male*	*Female*
B	1984	1.16	0.33	14.02	8.47
	1985	−1.45	3.30	15.15	25.24
	1986	0.36	3.12	−2.15	11.43
	1987	−1.94	1.73	−24.16	−23.96
	1988	−0.36	3.21	−0.28	0.80
	1989	1.01	2.65	−15.11	0.54
	1990	0.04	3.44	6.82	4.40
	1991	2.91	7.43	−4.01	3.99
	1992	1.32	2.85	3.67	−4.69
	1993	−2.07	1.26	5.10	0.64
	1994	−0.01	0.81	2.61	−0.01
	1995	1.43	0.21	13.87	−1.80
	1996	−0.88	0.84	14.11	8.33
D	*Year*	*Male*	*Female*	*Male*	*Female*
	1984	−3.33	−1.71	—	—
	1985	−0.52	2.63	18.62	7.24
	1986	0.46	0.71	4.59	8.11
	1987	0.12	0.75	−0.94	0.81
	1988	2.31	2.20	0.08	2.56
	1989	2.36	2.84	6.97	3.52
	1990	3.64	11.07	1.30	8.86
	1991	1.19	2.07	−4.21	−5.75
	1992	—	—	—	—
	1993	−1.38	−1.26	−5.94	−5.71
	1994	−1.83	−0.05	−1.53	2.97
	1995	−0.61	0.29	1.00	1.51
	1996	−2.07	1.06	1.88	−7.97
DK	*Year*	*Male*	*Female*	*Male*	*Female*
	1984	6.94	3.29	—	—
	1985	3.00	2.39	−12.43	2.75
	1986	3.70	4.95	−17.99	−3.42
	1987	−2.49	0.38	−17.58	−11.52
	1988	1.83	2.63	7.89	3.94
	1989	−1.15	−1.61	−8.77	−19.22
	1990	0.05	1.87	30.43	17.12
	1991	0.01	−0.54	7.20	21.14
	1992	2.38	1.08	7.40	−0.94
	1993	−3.60	−1.60	−14.97	0.36
	1994	2.29	−3.25	30.62	3.88
	1995	4.50	0.62	−0.40	4.55
	1996	−0.19	2.23	−12.46	−11.06

Table 4.8 continued

		(a) Permanent employment		(b) Fixed-term employment	
	Year	*Male*	*Female*	*Male*	*Female*
E	1987	3.53	5.21	—	—
	1988	3.59	9.40	47.03	58.93
	1989	4.93	9.64	25.20	27.99
	1990	3.40	7.89	17.33	18.22
	1991	0.88	3.61	6.64	15.62
	1992	−2.49	−0.27	1.00	2.10
	1993	−6.25	−2.02	−9.91	−6.76
	1994	−2.24	1.28	3.84	3.18
	1995	3.08	5.19	9.14	6.20
	1996	2.06	5.36	−2.12	1.10
	Year	*Male*	*Female*	*Male*	*Female*
F	1984	−1.70	1.18	−2.31	−2.80
	1985	−0.40	1.43	72.54	48.97
	1986	−0.38	3.14	32.07	64.85
	1987	−0.15	−0.42	15.92	10.31
	1988	−0.27	1.52	10.00	14.03
	1989	2.03	1.91	10.13	13.34
	1990	−0.36	1.15	23.06	31.80
	1991	1.05	2.86	−5.50	2.93
	1992	1.88	0.72	10.07	3.49
	1993	−0.70	2.24	1.87	7.69
	1994	−1.63	0.08	2.64	−2.36
	1995	2.17	2.06	22.30	11.00
	1996	0.53	1.56	1.01	4.68
	Year	*Male*	*Female*	*Male*	*Female*
GR	1984	1.10	2.94	16.01	13.85
	1985	−0.20	5.36	13.92	21.20
	1986	0.06	0.48	−10.37	−9.78
	1987	0.70	2.33	−10.61	−12.96
	1988	−0.06	8.23	6.90	13.53
	1989	1.93	3.39	−1.05	2.66
	1990	2.20	5.61	−4.38	7.70
	1991	−0.75	−1.70	−13.21	−9.77
	1992	0.40	3.75	−31.55	−27.56
	1993	1.69	3.26	−0.47	11.85
	1994	1.57	2.43	3.42	−2.85
	1995	0.29	5.25	−6.56	12.32
	1996	1.80	2.32	12.53	8.66

		(a) Permanent employment		(b) Fixed-term employment	
I	*Year*	*Male*	*Female*	*Male*	*Female*
	1984	−2.35	−2.69	−28.38	−21.33
	1985	1.58	3.44	−3.37	−3.47
	1986	0.03	2.40	−4.03	−5.28
	1987	−1.76	1.21	16.99	18.23
	1988	1.60	3.26	11.42	8.60
	1989	−2.23	1.74	5.23	12.25
	1990	2.63	4.02	−18.60	−10.59
	1991	0.40	2.60	3.15	4.24
	1992	−5.07	−4.20	46.53	19.87
	1993	−1.24	−0.92	−23.25	−20.05
	1994	−2.34	−0.42	22.44	17.64
	1995	−1.44	0.24	−2.15	−0.98
	1996	−0.56	2.34	8.35	−0.48

IRL	*Year*	*Male*	*Female*	*Male*	*Female*
	1984	−2.43	0.40	11.14	7.53
	1985	−1.67	−3.85	3.67	8.78
	1986	0.70	5.54	21.11	12.72
	1987	−2.85	3.96	−1.93	10.75
	1988	0.64	0.50	18.29	−0.27
	1989	−0.93	2.54	−15.46	2.35
	1990	2.80	4.02	5.56	−1.07
	1991	1.67	2.97	−5.09	4.18
	1992	−1.36	5.14	1.07	6.17
	1993	−1.73	1.80	11.02	4.37
	1994	4.19	7.58	13.78	2.46
	1995	4.73	6.28	14.54	12.06
	1996	4.95	5.61	−14.29	3.55

L	*Year*	*Male*	*Female*	*Male*	*Female*
	1984	−0.63	2.37	36.26	−9.81
	1985	0.79	5.63	11.22	42.66
	1986	2.32	2.00	−14.66	−3.48
	1987	2.89	5.26	8.91	−20.42
	1988	−1.17	−1.19	−22.36	24.03
	1989	0.35	2.32	14.77	−18.26
	1990	2.68	1.99	2.50	1.89
	1991	2.56	5.88	10.18	19.50
	1992	−0.28	6.51	39.76	−8.90
	1993	0.06	−3.10	−18.24	−9.03
	1994	−0.47	1.59	−12.53	15.80
	1995	−0.45	−4.60	—	—
	1996	1.33	8.31	—	—

Table 4.8 continued

		(a) Permanent employment		(b) Fixed-term employment	
NL	*Year*	*Male*	*Female*	*Male*	*Female*
	1988	−0.96	5.83	−5.50	−5.40
	1989	2.08	3.06	0.03	−0.42
	1990	3.68	4.96	−5.68	−6.78
	1991	2.10	6.18	−1.06	10.82
	1992	−1.18	5.88	15.55	40.37
	1993	−0.81	1.64	−0.48	4.48
	1994	−1.05	2.08	13.31	6.46
	1995	1.17	0.92	10.06	−5.10
	1996	1.94	4.56	7.14	17.63
P	*Year*	*Male*	*Female*	*Male*	*Female*
	1987	0.78	3.54	21.87	12.49
	1988	1.84	6.95	4.74	26.04
	1989	3.11	5.69	2.22	8.50
	1990	2.44	4.87	2.76	3.29
	1991	0.72	3.47	−11.92	−7.26
	1992	−4.69	6.54	−39.46	−29.33
	1993	−0.96	−1.62	−9.14	−14.44
	1994	−3.68	−1.09	−7.68	−5.41
	1995	−2.25	0.26	4.14	6.56
	1996	−0.46	−0.75	10.95	−1.33
UK	*Year*	*Male*	*Female*	*Male*	*Female*
	1984	−0.22	2.90	15.15	10.68
	1985	1.92	2.43	17.48	12.45
	1986	−0.52	1.65	0.54	2.28
	1987	−0.92	1.66	−11.68	−7.33
	1988	3.04	3.51	−0.24	−1.72
	1989	0.56	4.57	−22.03	1.75
	1990	0.69	1.09	1.15	−3.66
	1991	−2.61	−0.90	2.66	−1.13
	1992	−2.80	−1.60	10.02	−6.50
	1993	−1.52	0.37	8.38	2.20
	1994	0.47	0.19	9.55	9.88
	1995	1.81	1.10	16.57	6.02
	1996	1.56	1.76	−2.10	6.06

		(a) Permanent employment		(b) Fixed-term employment	
EUR 12	*Year*	*Male*	*Female*	*Male*	*Female*
	1987	—	—	—	—
	1988	1.68	3.36	13.25	11.98
	1989	1.32	3.34	6.65	9.34
	1990	1.98	4.53	7.48	8.80
	1991	0.31	1.93	−0.01	3.68
	1992	4.58	7.10	15.71	9.72
	1993	−1.69	−0.03	−6.26	−2.99
	1994	−1.28	0.19	5.04	3.92
	1995	0.73	1.24	8.71	4.69
	1996	0.05	1.93	1.10	1.75

Source: Eurostat European Labour Force Survey; author calculations

similar difference, France (6 per cent) and the United Kingdom (8 per cent) have a higher level of both women in the labour force (46 per cent, 48 per cent) and in fixed-term employment (52 per cent, 56 per cent). With the same level in the share of women in fixed-term employment (56 per cent to 57 per cent) female labour force participation in Denmark (47 per cent), Ireland (44 per cent), the Netherlands (42 per cent) and Belgium (41 per cent) leads to a difference between the shares of 10 per cent to 16 per cent. Although a positive trend towards more equal opportunities in the labour market can be stated, the gender composition still calls for some readjustment of the gendered use of fixed-term contracts in most Member States of the European Union.

THE AGE STRUCTURE OF FIXED-TERM EMPLOYMENT

Data on fixed-term employment by age from 1991 and the earliest year available throughout the Labour Force Data (see Table 4.9 for information about the age structure of all dependent employees and Table 4.10 for the age structure of fixed-term employees) indicate that most employees holding a fixed-term contract come from the youngest age groups. In nearly all countries (compare Figure 4.4) we find a hump-shaped pattern with its peak in the age group of 20–24 years (Denmark and Netherlands 14–19 years and 20–24 years, United Kingdom and Portugal 14–19 years) and a downward slope for older age groups of workers. This differs from the age structure of the dependent labour force as a whole, which has also a humped shape but flattens much less for middle-aged employees (compare Figure 4.5).

A closer scrutiny of the share of fixed-term employment in total dependent employment within age groups indicates that the probability of fixed-term employment is higher the younger the employee. This supports the hypothesis that young people entering the labour market for the first time are most likely to start their individual job career with a fixed-term contract. Changes in the use of fixed-term employment over time also affected younger age groups disproportionally (compare Figures 4.6 and 4.7).

The issue of whether introducing or deregulating fixed-term employment can create additional job opportunities has been of particular interest to many policy-makers interested in facilitating the transition of the young from full-time education to the labour market. An analysis of the age structure and changes therein must be related to changes in total dependent employment. The growth of the total dependent labour force has not taken place in the age groups which, as shown above, have the highest risk of being employed on a fixed-term basis. The patterns of age structures do not match. Changes in total dependent employment are mainly found in the middle age groups, a fact that can be related to the growth of the participation of women in the labour market. We cannot, of course, exclude indirect job creation for the young through general labour market mobility, but, apparently, direct job creation through the facilitation of fixed-term employment plays a minor role in processes of labour force adjustment in the European Union. Since labour mobility is known to decrease with age, this implies to some extent that older or middle-aged workers are less likely to hold fixed-term contracts. Facilitating hirings on the basis of a fixed-term contract might even have negative effects on job mobility rates of older employees since they are unlikely to accept a fixed-term contract if they have previously held an indefinite appointment.

In comparing the age distribution of total employment across age groups within the European Union with the age distribution of fixed-term employment across age groups, it becomes clear that in all countries the share of fixed-term employment is especially concentrated among the younger age groups, mainly those aged between 15 and 29 years of age. This highlights the prevailing 'step-by-step' (or marginal) integration into the labour market.

We can observe that fixed-term contracts tend to be used as a sort of prolonged probationary period and 'port of entry' into the labour market which most young people must pass through, despite the fact that standard work contracts also allow quite extensive probationary periods in most cases. The willingness to accept a fixed-term contract is also higher among young employees, not only because of their greater mobility, but also because they run a higher risk of becoming unemployed.

The share of younger fixed-term employees almost doubled in France and Spain between 1983 and 1991. In France, this concentration of 'precarious' employment among young labour market entrants has led to a re-regulation of fixed-term contracts to curb its rapid increase. Similarly, in Spain, legislation has been introduced that would allow fixed-term contracts to run for longer duration (see inforMISEP 46) in order to prevent further increases in youth

Table 4.9 Total dependent employment by age

Age group	B 1983	B 1991	D 1983	D 1991	DK 1983	DK 1991	E 1983	E 1991	F 1983	F 1991	GR 1983	GR 1991
Total	100.0	100.0	100.0	100.0	100.0	100.0	100.0	100.0	100.0	100.0	100.0	100.0
14–19	2.8	1.2	3.6	1.8	8.5	7.6	5.2	4.9	2.8	1.2	5.3	3.0
20–24	13.8	11.2	12.9	11.1	11.6	9.7	13.2	13.9	13.1	10.7	10.7	10.8
25–29	17.3	17.8	12.5	15.0	12.6	13.3	14.6	15.5	16.0	16.0	14.2	14.5
30–34	16.4	17.0	12.2	13.5	13.8	12.7	13.3	14.6	16.8	15.6	14.6	15.3
35–39	12.4	15.9	11.0	12.3	15.2	12.6	12.1	12.3	13.8	15.6	13.9	15.0
40–44	11.0	14.0	13.8	12.4	11.3	13.1	11.2	11.1	10.3	15.6	11.7	13.7
45–49	10.4	10.1	13.8	11.1	8.7	12.9	8.6	9.2	10.3	10.2	11.3	10.1
50–54	8.8	7.7	10.0	12.6	7.6	8.1	9.5	7.5	9.4	8.3	9.2	8.9
55–59	5.7	4.2	7.9	7.7	6.4	6.0	7.8	6.7	5.6	5.4	6.2	6.1
60–64	1.2	0.8	2.1	2.2	3.1	2.8	4.1	3.8	1.5	1.1	2.2	2.1
65–69	0.1	0.1	0.1	0.2	1.0	1.1	0.4	0.4	0.2	0.2	0.5	0.4
> 70	0.1	0.0	0.2	0.1	0.3	0.2	0.1	0.1	0.2	0.1	0.3	0.1

Table 4.9 continued

Age group	I 1983	I 1991	IRL 1983	IRL 1991	L 1983	L 1991	NL 1983	NL 1991	P 1983	P 1991	UK 1983	UK 1991	EU12 1991
Total	100.0	100.0	100.0	100.0	100.0	100.0	100.0	100.0	100.0	100.0	100.0	100.0	100.0
14–19	5.2	3.9	9.6	6.5	6.8	3.2	4.2	6.2	10.2	9.1	7.0	6.5	3.9
20–24	11.1	12.1	21.4	17.8	15.7	13.3	15.8	14.2	11.4	12.3	13.1	12.4	11.9
25–29	13.2	15.0	16.7	15.9	16.1	17.8	15.8	16.3	13.3	13.4	11.2	13.9	15.0
30–34	15.0	13.7	12.3	14.5	15.1	15.9	15.0	14.4	14.1	13.5	11.1	12.2	13.9
35–39	13.7	13.5	9.8	12.4	12.1	14.2	14.4	14.1	12.8	13.1	12.5	11.2	13.1
40–44	12.5	13.7	8.1	10.7	10.9	12.5	10.8	13.1	10.7	11.6	10.6	12.7	13.2
45–49	10.8	10.4	6.9	8.0	9.9	9.9	8.8	9.6	9.5	9.7	10.2	10.5	10.4
50–54	9.6	9.3	5.9	6.6	8.3	7.8	7.3	6.5	8.2	7.6	9.8	8.5	9.3
55–59	6.4	5.5	4.9	4.2	3.9	4.2	5.4	4.2	5.3	5.3	8.3	6.9	6.3
60–64	2.1	2.3	3.3	2.6	1.0	1.1	2.2	1.0	3.3	3.1	4.7	3.8	2.4
65–69	0.3	0.4	0.7	0.5	0.2	0.2	0.2	0.2	0.9	1.0	0.9	0.9	0.4
> 70	0.2	0.2	0.4	0.3	0.1	0.0	0.1	0.2	0.3	0.3	0.6	0.5	0.2

Source: Eurostat European Labour Force Survey; author calculations

Table 4.10 Fixed-term employment by age

Age group	B 1983	B 1991	D 1983	D 1991	DK 1983	DK 1991	E 1983	E 1991	F 1983	F 1991	GR 1983	GR 1991
Total	100.0	100.0	100.0	100.0	100.0	100.0	100.0	100.0	100.0	100.0	100.0	100.0
14–19	12.6	6.7	19.4	9.8	21.4	19.6	15.8	12.3	16.7	7.1	11.0	7.4
20–24	34.6	26.6	23.4	20.4	22.5	17.2	26.6	28.5	31.8	31.6	16.9	18.0
25–29	18.7	24.8	1.7	20.1	14.9	18.9	17.5	21.2	16.5	22.5	15.5	16.9
30–34	12.2	15.3	10.7	14.5	10.6	10.4	9.9	12.2	11.0	12.5	13.0	12.7
35–39	6.5	10.5	7.6	9.0	9.2	10.4	7.8	7.7	7.5	9.9	11.3	10.8
40–44	4.3	6.9	6.9	7.6	6.1	7.3	6.5	6.0	5.8	7.5	9.9	9.9
45–49	4.7	4.7	6.3	6.3	4.1	4.6	5.2	4.7	5.4	3.8	8.0	8.4
50–54	3.4	2.7	3.9	6.6	3.8	4.2	4.9	3.4	3.1	2.5	7.2	7.9
55–59	2.6	1.4	3.0	3.4	3.4	3.1	3.8	2.7	1.6	1.9	4.7	5.6
60–64	0.4	0.3	1.0	1.7	2.4	2.7	1.8	1.2	0.4	0.5	1.8	1.9
65–69	0.0	0.2	0.4	0.5	1.1	1.4	0.1	0.1	0.1	0.2	0.3	0.5
> 70	0.1	0.0	0.4	0.1	0.4	0.3	0.0	0.0	0.1	0.1	0.5	0.1

Table 4.10 continued

Age group	I 1983	I 1991	IRL 1983	IRL 1991	L 1983	L 1991	NL 1983	NL 1991	P 1983	P 1991	UK 1983	UK 1991	EU12 1991
Total	100.0	100.0	100.0	100.0	100.0	100.0	100.0	100.0	100.0	100.0	100.0	100.0	100.0
14–19	11.5	10.0	28.7	16.4	24.1	13.7	13.6	17.0	28.2	23.5	29.4	22.8	12.9
20–24	17.3	22.8	25.2	21.5	17.9	22.8	26.8	28.2	2.2	25.2	13.6	13.9	24.9
25–29	14.4	21.1	13.9	12.8	11.8	16.9	19.4	18.1	15.4	18.6	10.3	10.0	19.4
30–34	10.8	11.6	7.3	11.7	18.9	14.9	12.5	12.9	9.6	10.4	10.1	10.4	12.2
35–39	8.9	9.0	6.2	10.5	9.4	12.1	11.0	9.1	6.7	7.2	10.2	9.6	8.8
40–44	9.2	6.5	5.6	10.1	8.8	8.1	5.8	7.4	5.0	5.0	6.2	8.6	7.0
45–49	8.7	4.5	4.3	6.7	2.9	5.6	3.7	3.3	4.4	3.3	5.2	6.3	4.9
50–54	9.5	6.0	3.1	5.2	3.6	2.6	2.9	2.0	3.9	3.0	4.5	4.9	4.2
55–59	6.7	4.4	2.7	2.6	0.9	1.7	1.4	1.2	2.2	1.9	3.5	4.6	0.3
60–64	2.2	2.6	1.3	1.7	1.2	1.2	1.7	0.3	1.8	1.1	3.2	3.8	1.6
65–69	0.5	0.9	1.1	0.5	0.0	0.5	0.7	0.3	0.6	0.5	2.3	3.5	0.7
> 70	0.3	0.7	0.5	0.3	0.5	0.0	0.4	0.3	0.4	0.2	1.6	1.7	0.3

Source: Eurostat European Labour Force Survey; author calculations

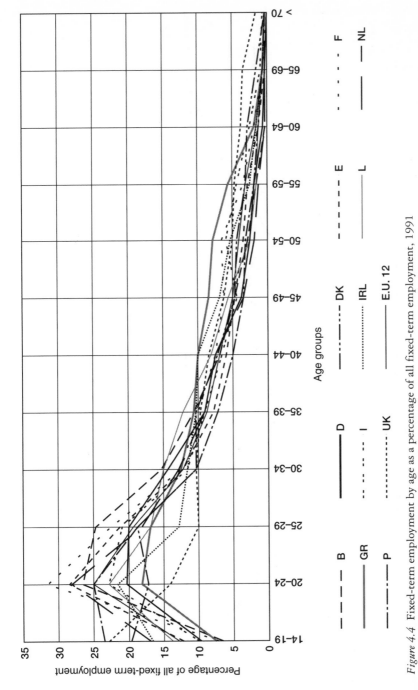

Figure 4.4 Fixed-term employment by age as a percentage of all fixed-term employment, 1991

Source: Eurostat European Labour Force Survey; author calculations

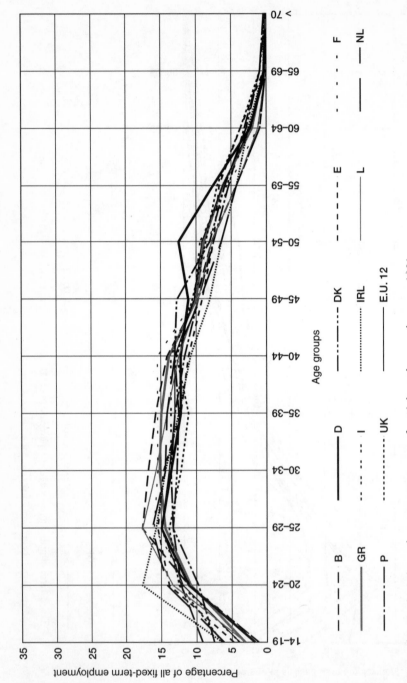

Figure 4.5 Total employees by age as percentage of total dependent employment, 1991

Source: Eurostat European Labour Force Survey; author calculations

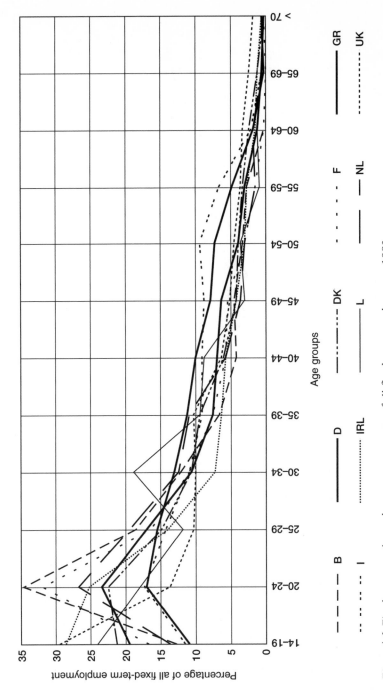

Figure 4.6 Fixed-term employees by age as percentage of all fixed-term employment, 1983

Source: Eurostat European Labour Force Survey; author calculations

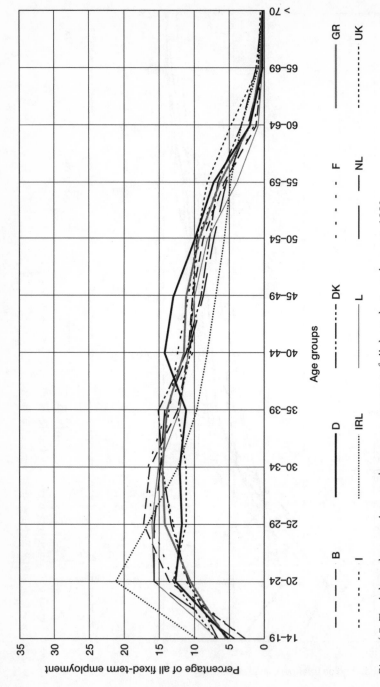

Figure 4.7 Total dependent employment by age as percentage of all dependent employment, 1983

Source: Eurostat European Labour Force Survey; author calculations

unemployment due to numerous fixed-term contracts reaching their dates of expiration (Alba-Ramírez 1991).

WORKING FIXED-TERM AND PART-TIME: ACCUMULATING RISKS OR JUST WHAT YOU WANTED?

As shown above, in most Member States of the European Union women are more likely than men to be employed on a fixed-term contract. Since a higher share of women work part-time, we also expect a higher share of female part-time employees in fixed-term employment. Analysing the share of part-time work in total dependent employment in 1991, we derive three groups of Member States of the European Union (compare Figure 4.8):

• Italy, Luxembourg, Ireland, Greece, Portugal and Spain with less than 10 per cent,
• Germany, France and Belgium with more than 10 and less than 20 per cent, and
• Denmark, the Netherlands and the United Kingdom with more than 20 per cent of the work force employed on a part-time basis.

Grouping countries by shares of part-time workers among all fixed-term employees, we derive the following divisions:

• Portugal and Spain with less than 10 per cent and Greece 12 per cent,
• Germany and France with less than 30 per cent and Belgium with 33 per cent,
• Denmark, Italy, Luxembourg and Ireland with between 40 per cent and 50 per cent,
• the Netherlands with 53 per cent and the United Kingdom with 66 per cent of all fixed-term employees working part-time (compare Figure 4.8 and Table 4.11).

While Greece, Portugal and Spain registered a slow decrease, all other countries showed an increase in the share of part-time work, corresponding to the increasing participation of women in the labour market, in both total dependent and fixed-term employment. It is reasonable to conclude that fixed-term employment often goes together with part-time employment. Similarly, in the majority of cases, part-time jobs are an involuntary restriction of working time to a lower number of hours than are usual for full-time work. Employees in some Member States, however, are much more likely to seek a full-time job than in others. While in the United Kingdom in 1991 only 11 per cent of part-time employees said they could not find a full-time job, in Italy as many as 64 per cent of

111

Table 4.11 Fixed-term employees as percentage of total dependent employment by full-time/part-time

B	Year	Total	Full-time job	Part-time job	Full-time job not found	Full-time job not wanted
	1983	5.1	3.9	18.3	37.9	8.9
	1984	5.6	4.4	18.1	35.0	5.8
	1985	6.7	5.1	22.3	40.3	6.5
	1986	7.0	5.5	19.9	36.6	6.2
	1987	5.3	3.9	17.0	32.6	3.6
	1988	5.3	4.0	16.0	30.1	4.9
	1989	4.9	3.7	14.0	26.9	3.4
	1990	5.1	3.7	14.6	28.5	9.4
	1991	4.9	3.7	13.1	25.0	7.0

D	Year	Total	Full-time job	Part-time job	Full-time job not found	Full-time job not wanted
	1984	4.7	4.0	10.1	26.4	5.0
	1985	5.3	4.9	8.3	22.1	5.2
	1986	5.6	5.0	9.4	21.2	5.6
	1987	5.6	5.1	8.4	21.3	5.3
	1988	5.5	4.9	9.2	23.7	5.5
	1989	5.7	5.1	9.3	21.6	5.7
	1990	5.6	4.7	10.1	24.6	6.0
	1991	5.2	4.5	8.9	21.0	5.6

DK	Year	Total	Full-time job	Part-time job	Full-time job not found	Full-time job not wanted
	1984	9.1	7.9	13.4	22.6	7.3
	1985	8.5	7.5	11.2	21.5	5.9
	1986	7.4	5.6	12.2	22.3	6.6
	1987	6.4	5.0	10.2	25.8	5.4
	1988	6.6	5.0	11.1	25.8	4.9
	1989	5.7	4.5	9.0	17.3	3.8
	1990	6.9	5.3	11.4	23.8	5.6
	1991	8.0	6.1	13.4	26.2	5.8

E	Year	Total	Full-time job	Part-time job	Full-time job not found	Full-time job not wanted
	1987	15.7	14.3	43.9	53.8	23.6
	1988	22.5	21.3	48.2	59.8	37.6
	1989	26.7	25.6	53.4	64.5	51.8
	1990	30.0	28.9	56.6	67.8	47.9
	1991	32.4	31.4	57.2	68.3	51.3

F

Year	Total	Full-time job	Part-time job
1983	2.4	2.3	3.1
1984	2.3	2.2	3.3
1985	3.7	3.2	7.8
1986	5.4	4.3	14.1
1987	6.1	5.0	14.7
1988	6.8	5.7	15.0
1989	7.5	6.4	15.0
1990	9.5	8.1	19.2
1991	9.2	7.7	19.7

GR

Year	Total	Full-time job	Part-time job	Full-time job not found	Full-time job not wanted
1983	16.5	14.1	62.6	86.0	53.4
1984	18.7	16.7	64.4	89.0	54.4
1985	21.4	19.5	62.6	89.0	61.5
1986	19.2	17.2	62.8	89.9	63.4
1987	16.8	15.1	58.0	89.9	56.8
1988	17.8	15.9	63.6	89.0	64.1
1989	17.4	15.6	63.9	85.2	59.1
1990	16.7	15.0	68.2	87.9	56.5
1991	14.9	13.3	68.5	84.3	57.0

I

Year	Total	Full-time job	Part-time job	Full-time job not found	Full-time job not wanted
1983	6.6	4.8	54.0	74.5	42.1
1984	5.0	2.6	61.3	75.7	41.9
1985	4.8	2.2	57.2	75.5	30.0
1986	4.5	2.3	56.1	74.1	28.6
1987	5.3	2.6	58.2	74.7	31.7
1988	5.8	3.1	55.5	73.6	28.2
1989	6.3	3.7	52.0	72.7	24.2
1990	5.2	2.9	51.3	71.5	26.1
1991	5.4	2.9	49.9	72.9	24.8

IRL

Year	Total	Full-time job	Part-time job	Full-time job not found	Full-time job not wanted
1983	5.9	3.2	49.0	66.3	33.4
1984	6.6	4.2	46.4	63.5	30.2
1985	7.2	4.7	46.1	63.1	30.2
1986	8.2	5.0	54.3	72.6	37.8
1987	8.6	5.4	47.9	62.2	31.9
1988	9.2	5.6	48.5	67.6	28.0
1989	8.6	5.3	45.8	62.3	30.6
1990	8.5	5.3	41.2	60.2	24.9
1991	8.3	4.6	45.0	63.9	30.7

Table 4.11 continued

L	Year	Total	Full-time job	Part-time job	Full-time job not found	Full-time job not wanted
	1983	2.1	1.5	11.4	17.5	10.5
	1984	2.3	1.6	14.0	30.6	12.1
	1985	2.8	1.7	23.3	41.4	16.8
	1986	2.6	1.6	18.8	29.7	14.4
	1987	2.2	1.5	14.3	31.3	9.8
	1988	2.3	1.5	18.3	36.7	14.8
	1989	2.1	1.3	16.4	41.7	12.0
	1990	2.1	1.3	16.2	41.5	11.9
	1991	2.4	1.5	14.5	42.2	8.0

NL	Year	Total	Full-time job	Part-time job	Full-time job not found	Full-time job not wanted
	1983	5.7	3.7	13.2	19.0	6.9
	1985	7.3	5.2	14.5	29.4	9.9
	1987	9.3	5.9	17.6	26.5	8.2
	1988	8.7	5.6	15.7	23.6	8.2
	1989	8.5	5.7	14.4	22.2	7.3
	1990	7.6	5.3	12.6	20.1	6.6
	1991	7.7	5.2	12.9	19.2	7.1

P	Year	Total	Full-time job	Part-time job	Full-time job not found	Full-time job not wanted
	1986	14.7	13.9	35.3	41.0	19.5
	1987	17.0	16.2	35.3	40.7	25.2
	1988	18.6	17.9	34.0	40.0	21.3
	1989	18.7	18.0	37.9	42.6	24.0
	1990	18.7	17.9	38.0	44.8	27.9
	1991	16.5	15.8	35.7	42.3	20.2

UK	Year	Total	Full-time job	Part-time job	Full-time job not found	Full-time job not wanted
	1983	5.5	3.0	15.1	29.7	8.8
	1984	6.1	3.6	15.1	31.3	9.6
	1985	6.8	2.9	15.7	30.5	10.3
	1986	6.9	2.9	16.2	33.9	10.5
	1987	6.3	3.0	17.0	39.5	10.1
	1988	6.0	2.9	16.2	35.5	10.2
	1989	5.4	2.6	14.9	23.9	10.6
	1990	5.2	2.6	14.3	20.9	9.7
	1991	5.3	2.4	14.9	25.0	10.0

Source: Eurostat European Labour Force Survey; author calculations

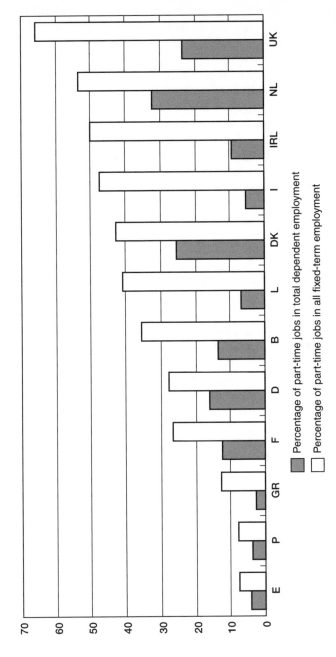

Figure 4.8 Percentage of part-time employment in fixed-term and total employment in the EU, 1991
Source: Eurostat European Labour Force Survey; author calculations

■ Percentage of part-time jobs in total dependent employment

□ Percentage of part-time jobs in all fixed-term employment

part-time employees reported that they were unable to find a full-time job. In general, the percentages of those working part-time who could not find a full-time job is higher among the fixed-term employees (compare Table 4.11).

Figure 4.8 reflects the share of part-time workers engaged in total dependent employment as one of the columns (left) and compares the percentage of part-time employees in fixed-term employment to these overall shares, leading us to conclude that there are more part-timers working on a fixed-term basis.

The two components of flexibility, part-time work and reduced job security, are frequently 'joint' phenomena in Member States and might even constitute, to some extent, functional equivalents in some countries. It is, therefore, no surprise that early attempts at regulation on the national as well as on the European Union level have tried to address these complementary issues simultaneously. The European Union Directive on 'temporary work' and the debate in the mid-1980s had a lasting impact on the legal regulation of this issue.[5] Our analysis, however, favours the separation of these two issues since working time patterns and regulations thereof cannot be dealt with in the same depth within the context of this study.

DOES HIGHER EDUCATION WORK AS INSURANCE AGAINST FIXED-TERM EMPLOYMENT?

Unfortunately, the administrators of the European Union Labour Force Survey (a standardised set of data consisting of recodes of national questionnaires into a common terminology) have had ongoing difficulties in achieving common definitions when it comes to classifying educational qualifications. Data dealing with the educational structure of dependent employees based on data from the European Union Labour Force Survey must be cross-checked with national data due to ELFS's problems in having to apply one classification to different educational systems and its high share of missing answers.

The European Union Labour Force Survey summarises three categories of educational attainment.[6] According to the ISCED classification of educational systems, the levels 'no qualification', 'primary level' and 'second level/first stage' were all regrouped into one category which reflects (1) the legal minimum number of years to be spent in the education system. The two higher levels of education are (2) 'second level/second stage', which usually equals university entry levels and (3) 'third level', which indicates university or polytechnical studies.

By analysing the share of fixed-term employees within these specific educational groups in 1991, we can derive groups of countries. The difference between the highest and lowest share of fixed-term employees within a given educational group in nearly all Member States of the European Union varies very slightly by up to 3 percentage points. By contrast, in Greece, Portugal and Spain, the countries with the highest share of fixed-term employees in total, there seems to be a more differentiated educational structure in the use of fixed-term contracts (11–15 percentage point differences). Overall, the legal changes do not appear to have influenced the process of selection according to the breakdown in educational levels of fixed-term employees (compare Tables 4.12 and 4.13).

In Belgium and the United Kingdom, the shares of fixed-term employees in the third educational category are above average. In Denmark, Germany and the Netherlands, the shares of fixed-term employees in the second level/second stage category are below national averages, which indicates that those with either a low level or a high level of education are more likely to accept fixed-term employment than those with a mid-level education. In Ireland, Italy and Greece, the least-educated employees have a higher share of fixed-term employment, while employees belonging to the third group are overrepresented in fixed-term employment in Portugal and Spain.

By focusing on the level of education, we can identify which educational level is most likely to lead to fixed-term employment (Table 4.14). In Denmark and Germany, the highest share of fixed-term employees attained a second level/second stage education. In all other countries the highest share of fixed-term employees had either no qualifications or a second stage/first level education, which equals the compulsory minimum education. This varies from 37 per cent in the Netherlands to 86 per cent in Portugal. In Germany, France, Belgium, and the United Kingdom, this low education selectivity is accompanied by the second-highest percentage of those holding university-level educational qualifications.

This mixed pattern might be due to the different industrial or occupational distribution of employees in the European Union. At the same time, because of a general shift in the emphasis of the educational structure towards higher educational qualifications in all Member States between 1988 and 1991, we can also observe this trend towards 'educational upgrading' among fixed-term employees.

IMPLICATIONS OF A CHANGING OCCUPATIONAL STRUCTURE ON FIXED-TERM EMPLOYMENT

By comparing the shares of occupational groups in the total dependent labour force with the percentages of fixed-term employment by occupation, we are able to trace the co-evolution of these two structures. Unfortunately, the occupational classification which we can use at the Eurostat level for the 1980s data is an abridged version of the one-digit ISCO classification of occupations. Yet even given these broad categories and taking into account the 'caution' which Eurostat (1988) demands of users, this enables us to gain an overview of some aspects of a country's 'internal' structure of the use of fixed-term employment (compare Tables 4.15 to 4.17).

Table 4.12 Fixed-term employees as percentage of total dependent employment by level of education attained

	Year	2nd level 1st stage or lower	2nd level 2nd stage	Third level
B	1988	4.4	6.1	6.3
	1989	3.9	5.4	6.6
	1990	4.4	5.4	6.2
	1991	4.4	4.7	6.2
D	1988	6.3	4.3	7.6
	1989	7.2	4.2	7.9
	1990	6.8	4.6	6.9
	1991	6.2	3.7	6.6
DK	1988	7.5	5.8	7.2
	1989	6.2	5.5	5.5
	1990	7.9	6.2	7.2
	1991	8.3	7.3	7.9
E	1988	24.2	23.4	12.6
	1989	28.9	27.9	14.8
	1990	32.6	31.0	16.7
	1991	35.1	33.1	19.5
F	1988	6.8	6.8	4.9
	1989	7.6	7.6	4.9
	1990	n.a.	n.a.	n.a
	1991	n.a.	n.a.	n.a
GR	1988	24.8	10.5	8.8
	1989	23.9	11.7	8.4
	1990	22.6	11.7	9.0
	1991	20.3	11.5	7.8
I	1988	6.7	4.2	3.4
	1989	7.1	5.1	4.1
	1990	5.8	4.5	3.3
	1991	6.1	4.2	3.4
IRL	1988	9.9	8.5	9.0
	1989	9.0	8.2	8.4
	1990	9.2	7.3	8.9
	1991	8.9	7.7	8.0
L	1988	2.4	1.7	2.7
	1989	2.1	1.4	3.9
	1990	2.1	1.4	3.9
	1991	2.2	2.8	3.4

	Year	2nd level 1st stage or lower	2nd level 2nd stage	Third level
NL	1988	n.a.	n.a.	n.a.
	1989	n.a.	n.a.	n.a.
	1990	8.1	6.6	8.7
	1991	7.9	7.0	8.9
P	1988	19.6	18.7	7.6
	1989	20.0	17.8	7.8
	1990	19.9	18.9	6.9
	1991	17.4	18.1	7.8
UK	1988	5.6	5.0	6.4
	1989	4.6	5.0	6.4
	1990	4.4	4.5	6.6
	1991	4.5	4.8	6.5

Source: Eurostat European Labour Force Survey, calculated on the basis
of valid cases

Table 4.13 Total dependent employment by level of education attained

	Year	2nd level 1st stage or lower	2nd level 2nd stage	Third level
B	1988	49.4	26.5	24.1
	1989	49.0	27.1	23.9
	1990	46.8	28.4	24.8
	1991	43.5	29.9	26.6
D	1988	29.1	46.8	15.4
	1989	22.2	54.4	17.5
	1990	22.2	50.3	16.0
	1991	14.9	58.3	17.8
DK	1988	30.1	49.2	20.7
	1989	28.7	49.9	20.0
	1990	28.5	49.9	21.6
	1991	26.7	48.6	22.0
E	1988	70.5	16.3	13.2
	1989	67.8	18.1	14.0
	1990	66.8	19.0	14.2
	1991	66.0	19.5	14.5
F	1988	71.8	9.0	16.2
	1989	71.5	9.0	16.4
	1990	n.a.	n.a.	n.a.
	1991	n.a.	n.a.	n.a.

Table 4.13 continued

	Year	2nd level 1st stage or lower	2nd level 2nd stage	Third level
GR	1988	45.7	24.5	24.9
	1989	44.5	25.9	24.8
	1990	43.0	27.5	25.4
	1991	41.1	29.8	25.1
I	1988	65.5	27.2	7.4
	1989	64.3	28.1	7.6
	1990	63.6	28.7	7.8
	1991	62.2	30.0	7.7
IRL	1988	44.1	34.6	21.1
	1989	43.6	34.2	22.0
	1990	42.4	34.5	22.9
	1991	42.6	34.0	23.2
L	1988	73.4	11.8	14.7
	1989	75.6	14.8	9.6
	1990	75.6	14.7	9.7
	1991	75.6	14.6	9.7
NL	1988	n.a.	n.a.	n.a.
	1989	n.a.	n.a.	n.a.
	1990	38.9	40.0	21.1
	1991	36.8	41.3	21.7
P	1988	85.7	5.7	8.2
	1989	83.3	6.9	9.3
	1990	82.6	8.1	9.0
	1991	81.5	8.4	9.8
UK	1988	62.2	17.3	15.8
	1989	61.2	18.0	15.9
	1990	59.3	19.2	16.7
	1991	58.9	19.2	17.2

Source: Eurostat European Labour Force Survey, calculated on the basis of valid cases

Table 4.14 Fixed-term employees by level of education attained

	Year	2nd level 1st stage or lower	2nd level 2nd stage	Third level
B	1988	41.3	30.2	28.5
	1989	38.5	29.7	31.9
	1990	40.1	29.8	30.1
	1991	38.3	28.1	33.6
D	1988	33.4	36.3	21.1
	1989	28.3	40.4	24.4
	1990	27.0	41.3	19.8
	1991	17.7	41.4	22.4
DK	1988	34.3	43.3	22.5
	1989	31.1	48.8	19.4
	1990	32.5	45.2	22.4
	1991	27.8	44.8	21.9
E	1988	75.7	16.9	7.4
	1989	73.3	18.9	7.8
	1990	72.5	19.6	7.9
	1991	71.4	19.9	8.7
F	1988	71.9	9.0	11.7
	1989	72.8	9.2	10.7
	1990	n.a	n.a	n.a
	1991	n.a	n.a	n.a
GR	1988	63.8	14.4	12.3
	1989	61.2	17.5	11.9
	1990	58.1	19.2	13.7
	1991	56.1	23.1	13.2
I	1988	75.6	20.0	4.4
	1989	72.1	22.9	5.0
	1990	70.4	24.7	4.9
	1991	71.2	23.8	4.9
IRL	1988	47.5	31.9	20.6
	1989	45.6	32.7	21.5
	1990	46.0	29.9	24.0
	1991	45.9	31.7	22.4
L	1988	74.6	8.4	17.0
	1989	72.8	9.7	17.4
	1990	72.7	9.7	17.6
	1991	68.5	17.4	14.1

Table 4.14 continued

	Year	2nd level 1st stage or lower	2nd level 2nd stage	Third level
NL	1988	n.a	n.a	n.a
	1989	n.a	n.a	n.a
	1990	41.1	34.7	24.1
	1991	37.6	37.3	25.0
P	1988	90.4	5.7	3.3
	1989	88.9	6.6	3.9
	1990	88.1	8.2	3.3
	1991	85.9	9.2	4.6
UK	1988	58.4	14.5	17.0
	1989	52.6	16.7	18.9
	1990	50.1	16.8	21.1
	1991	49.7	17.1	20.9

Source: Eurostat European Labour Force Survey, calculated on the basis of valid cases

In all Member States of the European Union[7] we can confirm the widely-documented decline in production-oriented occupations in total employment. During the 1980s and up until 1991, this group of occupations represented the largest share of all employees, with the Netherlands having the lowest share at 25 per cent, and Portugal the highest at 43 per cent in 1991. In fixed-term employment, production-oriented occupations had the highest shares in five Member States. This was the case in Ireland (26 per cent), France (29 per cent), Spain (46 per cent), Portugal (47 per cent) and Greece (54 per cent). As Figure 4.9 (a and b) illustrates, Greece, Spain and Portugal all have very similar occupational structures in terms of fixed-term employment.

In Germany, the Netherlands, Belgium and Denmark the highest shares (28 per cent to 39 per cent) of all fixed-term employees are in the professional occupations, followed by the production-oriented occupations with shares of 20 per cent in the Netherlands and up to 27 per cent in Denmark. In the United Kingdom, professionals (24 per cent) are followed by clerical occupations (22 per cent), sales personnel (22 per cent) and production-oriented occupations (16 per cent). Fixed-term employees in Luxembourg are represented in equal shares of around 23 per cent in production-oriented occupations, professional, clerical and service occupations which resembles statistically a largely randomised distribution across the major occupational groups.

The smallest occupational group in both total dependent and fixed-term employment in France, Greece, Portugal and Spain is administration, and in Belgium, Denmark and Germany agricultural occupations. In Ireland and the

Table 4.15 Total employees by occupational status

Occupation	B 1983	B 1991	D 1984	D 1991	DK 1984	DK 1991	E 1986	E 1991	F 1983	F 1991	GR 1983	GR 1991
Professional	20.5	23.9	15.9	18.2	21.7	28.5	11.2	13.5	18.4	20.2	16.5	18.8
Administrative	2.4	2.3	3.7	3.1	4.1	4.0	1.3	1.3	0.2	0.2	2.3	1.4
Clerical	23.0	23.9	21.5	22.7	17.5	17.1	16.3	17.2	23.9	24.5	18.1	21.4
Sales	5.0	5.8	8.1	7.9	7.1	7.8	6.4	7.2	6.4	7.2	4.7	6.5
Service	9.6	10.2	9.8	9.5	15.5	10.0	16.4	14.5	13.8	14.7	11.6	11.5
Agricultural	0.6	0.5	1.3	1.2	2.6	2.0	6.9	5.1	1.8	1.7	2.6	1.8
Production	38.8	33.4	38.3	34.9	31.4	30.5	41.6	41.1	35.5	31.5	44.1	38.5

Occupation	IRL 1983	IRL 1991	L 1983	L 1991	NL 1983	NL 1991	P 1986	P 1991	UK 1983	UK 1991
Professional	18.1	18.7	12.2	13.0	22.2	25.0	10.3	12.2	16.3	18.0
Administrative	3.9	4.6	0.9	1.1	3.1	4.5	0.5	0.9	6.6	5.2
Clerical	21.3	20.2	25.4	29.1	21.2	20.5	19.0	18.9	20.4	20.8
Sales	9.1	9.6	6.1	5.8	8.9	9.9	5.6	6.1	9.7	9.7
Service	10.1	12.8	12.5	13.5	12.2	12.4	13.7	14.4	13.8	13.8
Agricultural	2.9	3.0	1.0	1.3	2.3	2.0	5.7	4.1	1.7	1.4
Production	34.4	30.9	40.8	36.2	29.7	25.3	45.3	43.4	31.2	25.6

Source: Eurostat European Labour Force Survey; author calculations. Italy: no data available

Table 4.16 Fixed-term employees by occupational status

Occupation	B 1983	B 1991	D 1984	D 1991	DK 1984	DK 1991	E 1987	E 1991	F 1983	F 1991	GR 1983	GR 1991
Professional	31.5	32.8	28.0	28.4	33.9	38.8	7.7	8.8	15.6	22.4	9.0	12.2
Administrative	0.5	1.1	3.6	2.7	1.2	1.8	0.2	0.2	—	0.0	0.2	0.2
Clerical	22.4	25.1	15.3	17.9	9.8	11.4	9.2	12.4	23.4	21.8	7.2	9.4
Sales	4.8	5.0	7.2	7.0	6.3	5.9	5.8	7.7	4.8	4.4	4.6	6.5
Service	15.4	16.9	12.7	10.1	13.3	13.7	16.5	16.0	11.2	20.1	12.0	13.4
Agricultural	1.1	0.9	2.8	2.2	4.0	1.8	16.7	8.6	2.2	2.5	8.1	4.7
Production	24.4	18.2	27.0	25.4	31.6	26.6	43.8	46.2	42.7	28.9	58.7	53.6

Occupation	IRL 1983	IRL 1991	L 1983	L 1991	NL 1983	NL 1991	P 1986	P 1991	UK 1983	UK 1991
Professional	21.1	22.0	21.5	21.6	36.6	31.2	5.6	8.5	19.0	23.7
Administrative	0.3	0.5	—	2.3	1.4	0.9	0.1	0.1	1.1	1.3
Clerical	16.2	17.9	17.0	23.6	18.3	20.4	8.9	13.6	17.2	22.2
Sales	8.9	9.7	8.0	4.4	6.9	7.6	6.2	7.1	14.4	11.4
Service	19.6	18.8	30.1	22.8	14.1	15.6	15.9	16.8	20.5	21.8
Agricultural	4.1	4.0	0.6	1.8	3.6	2.6	12.2	6.8	4.1	2.1
Production	28.8	26.1	22.8	23.5	18.3	20.4	51.1	47.1	23.1	15.7

Source: Eurostat European Labour Force Survey; author calculations. Italy: no data available

Table 4.17 Fixed-term employees as percentage of total dependent employment by occupational status

Occupation	B 1983	B 1991	D 1984	D 1991	DK 1984	DK 1991	E 1987	E 1991	F 1983	F 1991	GR 1983	GR 1991
Total	5.1	4.9	4.7	5.2	8.5	8.0	15.7	32.4	2.4	9.2	16.5	14.9
Professional	7.8	6.8	8.3	8.2	10.8	10.8	10.1	21.2	2.0	10.2	9.0	9.6
Administrative	1.0	2.3	4.5	4.7	3.4	3.6	2.5	5.4	—	1.6	1.5	1.9
Clerical	4.9	5.2	3.4	4.1	4.9	5.3	9.1	23.4	2.3	8.2	6.6	6.5
Sales	4.8	4.3	4.2	4.6	7.4	6.0	14.3	34.6	1.8	5.6	16.1	14.9
Service	8.1	8.2	6.1	5.6	10.3	10.9	16.8	35.8	1.9	12.6	17.1	17.3
Agricultural	9.0	8.3	10.1	9.6	15.3	7.1	39.1	54.8	3.0	13.6	50.2	38.0
Production	3.2	2.7	3.3	3.8	8.1	7.0	16.3	36.5	2.8	8.5	21.9	20.7

Occupation	IRL 1983	IRL 1991	L 1983	L 1991	NL 1983	NL 1991	P 1986	P 1991	UK 1983	UK 1991
Total	5.9	8.3	2.1	2.4	5.7	7.7	14.7	16.5	5.5	5.3
Professional	6.9	9.7	3.8	4.0	9.5	9.6	8.0	11.5	6.4	7.0
Administrative	0.4	0.9	—	5.1	2.7	1.5	2.1	2.1	0.9	1.3
Clerical	4.5	7.3	1.4	1.9	5.0	7.7	6.9	11.9	4.6	5.7
Sales	5.8	8.4	2.8	1.8	4.5	5.9	16.3	19.3	8.2	6.3
Service	11.5	12.1	5.1	4.0	6.6	9.7	17.1	19.3	8.1	8.4
Agricultural	8.4	11.0	1.2	3.2	8.9	10.0	31.7	27.4	13.0	8.1
Production	5.0	7.0	1.2	1.5	3.5	6.2	16.6	17.9	4.1	3.3

Source: Eurostat European Labour Force Survey; author calculations. Italy: no data available

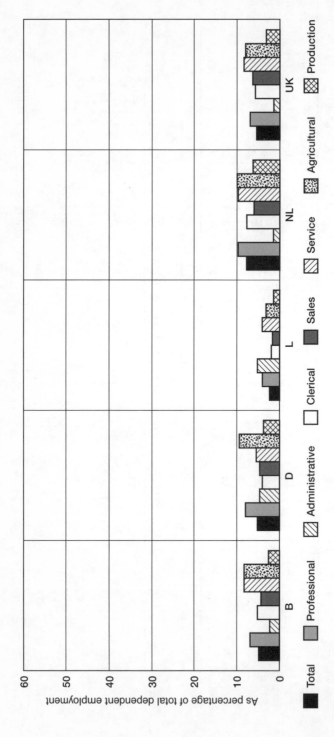

Figure 4.9a Fixed-term employees as percentage of total dependent employment by occupation in selected EU Member States, 1991
Source: Eurostat European Labour Force Survey; author calculations

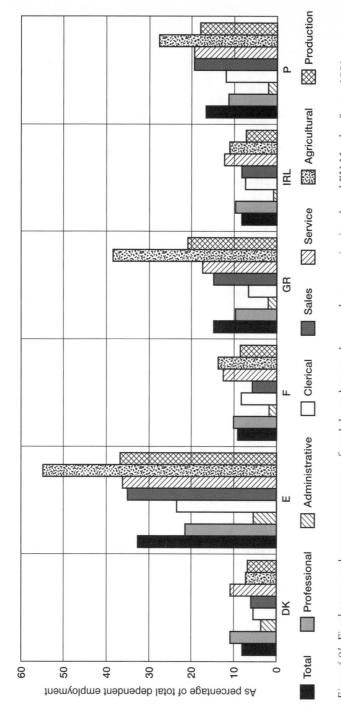

Figure 4.9b Fixed-term employees as percentage of total dependent employment by occupation in selected EU Member States, 1991
Source: Eurostat European Labour Force Survey; author calculations

United Kingdom, agricultural occupations make up the smallest share of total dependent employment, and administrative occupations the smallest share in fixed-term employment.

Obviously, changes over time in fixed-term employment which did not correspond directly to the trends in total dependent employment occurred in France in the service occupations, with an increase from 11 per cent to 20 per cent between 1983 and 1991 (only 14 per cent to 15 per cent in total dependent employment) and in the United Kingdom in the clerical occupations with an increase of 5 per cent (0.5 per cent in total dependent employment).

Next we will analyse the share of fixed-term contract holders within a specific occupational group, which represents the individual risk of being employed on a fixed-term basis. In seven Member States of the European Union, the highest percentage of fixed-term employees is found in the agricultural occupations (up to 55 per cent in Spain, 38 per cent in Greece, 27 per cent in Portugal, 14 per cent in France and 8 per cent in Belgium). In the United Kingdom, the highest proportional use of fixed-term contracts is in services and agriculture (both 8 per cent). Germany, the Netherlands, Ireland and Denmark have their highest shares in professional occupations.

When countries are compared, there appears to be very little movement in shares of fixed-term employees in occupational groups which can be related to changes in the legal systems. At best, the change in legislation (re-regulation) in Belgium in 1987 had an impact on the production-oriented occupations, which decreased their share of all fixed-term employees from 24 per cent in 1987 to 18 per cent in 1991. Deregulation in Spain, France and Germany during the 1980s led to increases in fixed-term employment among all occupational groups, despite the general European Union trend away from production-oriented occupations.

INDUSTRIAL SECTOR DIFFERENCES

When fixed-term employees are compared across industrial sectors in the European Union, differences in the industrial structure and in employment practices become apparent. Although in Spain and Portugal fixed-term employees are numerous in all industries, their shares are highest in construction and agriculture. These two sectors are also among those with the highest shares of fixed-term employees in Greece. In most other Member States, many fixed-term contracts are in the service sector and in agriculture (compare Table 4.18 for 1991 data).

The reasons for the low percentages of fixed-term employees in the mining and chemical industries, as well as in manufacturing industries, include not only the nature of the work, i.e. reliance upon more highly-skilled workers, but also the fact that collective agreements limit the use of this form of 'precarious' employment in some countries. In Germany, for example, agreements

Table 4.18 Fixed-term employment as percentage of total dependent labour force by industrial sectors in the EU in 1991

Country	Agriculture	Public administration	Other services	Distributive trades	Banking & finance	Construction	Manufacturing	Mining & chemical	Transport & communication	Energy & water
B	6.2	8.8	8.3	4.8	3.5	2.7	2.1	2.5	2.9	3.5
D	16.5	13.5	13.4	10.7	8.7	7.9	7.1	6.1	5.8	5.5
DK	14.9	12	14.7	15	6.4	18.2	8.5	4.7	7.1	1.6
E	54.4	15.7	27.8	38.9	26.3	55.7	28.5	22.9	19.3	9.9
F	13.9	10	14.8	10.2	7.5	10.1	8.5	5.5	6.1	4.2
GR	40.2	2.7	12.1	17.2	9.4	50	12.9	7.9	9.6	5.4
I	24.4	2.2	6.5	6.3	3.3	7.5	2.9	1.8	2	1
IRE	10.6	6.4	13.7	9.4	7.2	10.5	3.8	4.8	3.5	4
L	3.9	2.5	5.7	4.5	2.8	2.2	2.3	1.3	1.6	1
NL	11.5	6.2	10.4	8	7.4	3.8	6.3	3.5	5.1	4.4
P	29.1	8.5	14.8	21.5	15.1	23.5	16.5	12.9	10.8	6.8
UK	6.8	4	8.1	7.8	4.3	3.6	2.7	1.9	2.6	3.6

Source: Eurostat European Labour Force Survey; author calculations

in the metal industries limit the maximum duration of fixed-term contracts in some regions to three months – well below the maximum duration of eighteen months defined by labour law (see Chapter 3 for more details).

There is additional concern in the coal, mining and chemical industries about short-duration fixed-term contracts when fixed-term employees are assigned to particularly hazardous working environments. However, we found few explicit restrictions regarding the use of fixed-term contracts in such instances in the legislation of Member States, despite the existence of a European Union Directive Nr.91/383 which introduced the same level of protection for health and safety regulations for employees on fixed-term contracts (see Chapter 3).

Technically-advanced industrial sectors such as energy and water supply, which are often organised as public enterprises, have the lowest or second lowest share of fixed-term employees in almost all Member States. These characteristics of the distribution of fixed-term employees across industrial sectors reflect different employment practices within countries with regard to the reliance on internal versus external flexibility (European Foundation 1992).

The patterns of fixed-term employment in the industrial sector are influenced by the development of industrial structures of the countries and their procedures of collective bargaining. The role of legislation in this context varies greatly between countries. Deregulation of fixed-term contracts in Spain has led to an across-the-board increase in the use of fixed-term contracts, whereas similar changes in the legal regulations in Germany did not lead to more fixed-term employment in all industrial sectors. In France, deregulation in 1984 had its strongest impact on employment practices in 'other services' and in public administration, where the number of fixed-term contracts increased rapidly until the re-regulation in 1991. These effects are confirmed by multivariate logistic regression results (see Chapter 5).

LABOUR MARKET DYNAMICS

The European Union Labour Force Survey includes a set of questions in which respondents are asked to provide information concerning their employment status one year prior to the survey. Unfortunately, this rudimentary retrospective information does not allow us to analyse multiple changes at different points in time (for example, transition between unemployment and fixed-term employment). Nonetheless, a crude comparison of two points in time is possible.

In comparing the shares of fixed-term and more permanent employees with reference to their employment status one year earlier, we find that, in general, very few unemployed workers return to the labour market on a permanent contract. Only between 1 per cent and 2 per cent of all employees holding a permanent contract in 1991 were thus formerly unemployed (Table 4.19,

Table 4.19 Current employees with a permanent or fixed-term contract by selected labour force status one year earlier

Percentages

Country	Unemployed with a permanent job one year later			Inactives with a permanent job one year later			Unemployed with a fixed-term contract one year later			Inactives with a fixed-term contract one year later		
	1985	1988	1991	1985	1988	1991	1985	1988	1991	1985	1988	1991
B	1.80	1.87	0.86	2.29	2.18	2.87	18.01	17.84	8.40	23.10	17.24	19.56
DK	2.55	1.82	1.81	3.23	3.74	3.04	13.45	9.63	11.77	18.14	21.29	20.10
D	0.83	0.75	0.75	1.44	1.22	1.99	3.46	3.24	2.53	15.12	13.33	15.97
GR	2.18	1.87	1.08	2.86	2.76	2.45	9.23	8.34	6.04	11.21	12.31	11.50
E	n.a.	3.72	2.09	n.a.	2.17	1.91	n.a.	32.96	22.30	n.a.	12.18	12.09
F	2.35	2.64	n.a.	3.14	2.88	n.a.	19.46	23.58	n.a.	31.39	26.79	n.a.
IRL	2.50	2.43	1.76	2.87	3.06	3.52	19.34	21.80	16.34	29.88	24.67	27.29
I	n.a.	n.a.	n.a.	n.a.	n.a.	n.a.	n.a.	n.a.	n.a.	n.a.	n.a.	n.a.
L	1.25	0.77	0.78	3.21	3.03	3.16	3.74	4.81	6.24	27.42	28.81	28.03
NL	1.42	0.72	0.74	3.02	11.65	14.21	12.69	6.54	4.70	24.55	49.88	49.64
P	n.a.	1.38	1.04	n.a.	1.57	1.44	n.a.	15.36	10.58	n.a.	9.67	11.89
UK	2.55	2.64	1.59	4.81	5.26	4.49	14.31	17.23	5.10	42.82	28.43	28.62

Source: Eurostat European Labour Force Survey; author calculations

131

column 3). In addition, between 1985 and 1991 the percentage of unemployed leaving unemployment for permanent employment decreased in all Member States, possibly due to the recession.

Only a few of the previously unemployed were recruited while holding a fixed-term contract and their share has not increased over time. With the exception of Luxembourg, where fixed-term contracts make up only 2 per cent of total employment, the hiring chances of the unemployed on a fixed-term contract have decreased over time (Table 4.19, columns 7 to 9). Much larger shares of fixed-term employees are recruited from among previously inactive people (last three columns in Table 4.19) and especially from the previously employed (either fixed-term or permanent). Of those holding a fixed-term contract in 1991, between 56 per cent in Ireland and 81 per cent in Germany and Greece were unemployed one year earlier. These figures cast doubt on the success of policies which advocate fixed-term contracts as a labour market policy instrument to create additional jobs and especially to reduce unemployment.

5

MULTIVARIATE ANALYSIS OF COUNTRY PATTERNS

In the previous section, we presented the results from cross-tabulations of fixed-term employees by other socio-economic factors based on the European Labour Force Survey 1983–96. The goal of this section is to test the hypotheses developed in Chapter 2 using multivariate analyses on data from 1988 to 1991. Since results proved very stable we report only estimates from 1991; other results can be obtained from the authors on request. The phenomenon in question is: who is likely to hold a job without specification of the date of expiration, i.e. a 'standard' work contract? Obviously, the opposite value determines the probability of holding a fixed-term contract.

Multivariate analyses allow us to test in a more comprehensive way hypotheses and adjustment of estimated effects of each variable included in the model for differences in the distribution of other independent variables. While keeping the levels of other independent variables constant, multivariate estimates make it possible to estimate effects of independent variables on holding a fixed or permanent appointment when other intervening variables are kept constant. This means, estimated coefficients of the logistic regression model compare individuals who differ only in the characteristic of interest (for example age, gender, or prior labour force status) and hold the values of all other variables constant (for example industrial sectors). We have chosen a logistic regression model since it allows a binary (0,1) dependent variable, i.e. the value 1 for having a standard work contract and the value 0 for a fixed-term contract (see Appendix for detailed results by country of the estimation and Table 5.1 for an abbreviated summary[1] of all estimated coefficients).

The likelihood ratio tests for the significance of the estimated equations were all significant at the 1 per cent level. Due to the large number of cases available at Eurostat for carrying out these calculations, the number of complete information cases (individuals, not households) varies between 9,000 persons in Luxembourg and 90,000 in West Germany due to the original country size and the basic filters on employment status applied.[2] We applied as filters the selection of (1) persons living in private households and (2) who did any form of work for pay or profit during the reference week, but (3) did not receive any training in the framework of an apprenticeship. For the years used in the multivariate analysis, more detailed information on sampling and definitions of variables can be found in the regular Eurostat (1988, 1992) publications theme 3 series E.

GENDER DIFFERENCES

Table 5.1 presents a summary of effects concerning the *gender distributions, marital status and household structures* in the twelve Member States of the European Union in 1991. In almost all Member States, the probability of women holding a fixed-term contract is significantly higher than for men. Exceptions to this rule are Denmark, West Germany and the United Kingdom, where the effect is not statistically significant, which means that the differences are relatively small in size after controlling for all other independent variables. Alternatively, other variables in the estimated equations are statistically more important such as the household structure in the Netherlands and West Germany.

In the latter three countries, the variable which statistically is more important than gender is marital status. Relative to married people, those who are single have a higher probability of having a fixed-term contract. This is a very general pattern across Europe, excepting Ireland. Similarly, persons who are widowed, divorced or legally separated are, in all countries except for Ireland, more likely to be in a fixed-term employment situation than married people, but significant levels are not reached in half of the cases. In Belgium, France, Greece, Italy, the Netherlands, Portugal, and Spain, both women and singles are most likely to be engaged in fixed-term employment. In the remaining European Union countries, it is either women or singles who have a statistically higher probability of holding a fixed-term contract.

In addition to gender and marital status, we included two measures of household structure in the multivariate analysis. If a person is the head of a household, he or she is more likely in West Germany and the Netherlands to enter into a fixed-term contract. In France, Italy, Spain and the United Kingdom, a head of a household is less likely to hold a fixed-term contract. Hence, we can conclude that fixed-term employees are more likely to be female, single, widowed, divorced, or separated people. Status as head of a household increases the risk of fixed-term employment in West Germany and the Netherlands but decreases the risk in France, Italy, Spain and the United Kingdom.

AGE STRUCTURE

One of the major variables determining the probability of engagement in fixed-term employment is age and the distribution of non-standard forms of

Table 5.1 Summary table of estimated coefficients for fixed-term employment in the EU in 1991

	Belgium	Denmark	France	Germany W.	Greece	Ireland
Female	+	(+)	+	(−)	+	+
Single	+	+	+	+	+	(−)
Widowed, divorced, separated	(+)	(+)	+	+	+	(−)
Head of household	(−)	(+)	−	+	(−)	(−)
Spouse of head of hh.	(+)	+	(−)	+	(+)	(+)

	Italy	Luxembourg	Netherlands	Portugal	Spain	United Kingdom
Female	+	+	+	+	+	(+)
Single	+	(+)	+	(+)	+	+
Widowed, divorced, separated	(+)	+	+	(−)	+	(+)
Head of household	−	(−)	+	(−)	−	−
Spouse of head of hh.	(+)	+	+	(+)	(+)	(+)

	Belgium	Denmark	France	Germany W.	Greece	Ireland
Age	+ 4\	+ 3\	+ 4\	+ 4\	+ 3\	+ 2\
EC-national	(+)	(+)	(−)	(−)	(+)	(+)
No EC-national	(+)	+	+	+	+	+
Compulsory education	(+)	(+)	no info	−	+	+
A-levels/BAC/ABI	(−)	(+)	no info	−	(−)	(−)

Table 5.1 continued

	Italy	Luxembourg	Netherlands	Portugal	Spain	United Kingdom
Age	+ 4 \	+ 1 ~	+ 4 \	+ 4 \	+ 4 \	+ 1 ~
EC-national	no info	(+)	+	(−)	(+)	+
No EC-national	no info	+	+	(+)	(+)	+
Compulsory education	+	(−)	−	+	+	−
A-levels/BAC/ABI	(+)	(+)	−	+	(+)	−

Previous employment status one year ago	Belgium	Denmark	France	Germany W.	Greece	Ireland
Unemployed	+	+	+	+	+	+
In education	+	+	+	+	+	+
Inactive	+	+	(−)	+	+	+
Self-employed	(−)	(+)	(+)	(+)	(+)	+

Previous employment status one year ago	Italy	Luxembourg	Netherlands	Portugal	Spain	United Kingdom
Unemployed	no info	+	+	+	+	+
In education	no info	+	+	+	+	+
Inactive	no info	+	+	+	+	+
Self-employed	no info	(+)	+	+	+	+

	Belgium	Denmark	France	Germany W.	Greece	Ireland
Other services	(+)	+	+	+	+	+
Public sector	+	(+)	+	+	−	(+)
Banking/insurance	(−)	(−)	(−)	(+)	+	(−)
Transport/communication	(−)	(−)	(+)	(+)	+	−
Distributive trade/hotels	(−)	(−)	(−)	+	+	(−)
Building	−	−	(−)	(+)	+	(+)
Other manufacturing	−	(−)	(−)	+	+	−
Manufacturing	−	(−)	(−)	(+)	(−)	−
Mining/chemicals	(−)	(−)	(−)	(+)	(+)	−
Agriculture	(−)	(+)	(+)	(+)	+	(−)

	Italy	Luxembourg	Netherlands	Portugal	Spain	United Kingdom
Other services	+	(+)	−	(+)	+	(+)
Public sector	+	(+)	−	(+)	+	(−)
Banking/insurance	(+)	(+)	−	(+)	+	−
Transport/communication	(+)	(+)	−	(+)	+	−
Distributive trade/hotels	+	(+)	−	+	+	(+)
Building	+	(−)	−	+	+	(−)
Other manufacturing	(+)	(−)	−	(−)	+	−
Manufacturing	(+)	(−)	−	(+)	+	−
Mining/chemicals	(+)	(−)	−	(+)	+	−
Agriculture	+	(+)	(−)	+	+	(−)

Table 5.1 continued

	Belgium	Denmark	France	Germany W.	Greece	Ireland
Professional	+	(+)	(+)	–	+	+
Agricultural	+	(–)	(+)	(–)	+	+
Clerical	+	(–)	(+)	–	(+)	(+)
Sales	(+)	(–)	(+)	–	+	(+)
Services	+	(–)	(+)	–	+	+
Production	(+)	(+)	(+)	–	+	+

	Italy	Luxembourg	Netherlands	Portugal	Spain	United Kingdom
Professional	no info	–	+	+	+	+
Agricultural	no info	(–)	(–)	+	+	+
Clerical	no info	–	(+)	(+)	+	+
Sales	no info	–	–	(+)	+	+
Services	no info	–	(–)	+	+	+
Production	no info	(–)	+	+	+	+

Source: Eurostat European Labour Force Survey 1991; author calculations

employment across age groups. The most clear-cut pattern common to all Member States is the significantly higher probability of younger employees to hold a fixed-term contract.[3] For theoretical and historical reasons, this pattern is hardly surprising since some Member States first began facilitating the issuing of fixed-term contracts in the mid-1980s. Considering that mostly new labour market entrants will receive such wage contracts and possibly, but to a lesser extent, people changing jobs, it is expected that mainly the young labour market entrants will have to carry most of the adjustment of the legal framework concerning more flexible employment contracts. Employees who lost their jobs due to involuntary separations are potentially equally affected by this, but apparently some seniority status prevents them from being commonly employed on a fixed-term basis. We will present more detailed information on this issue below.

The estimated logistic regressions show that in seven out of twelve countries, employees between the ages of 15 and 34 are significantly more likely to hold fixed-term contracts. In Denmark, Greece, Ireland, Luxembourg and the United Kingdom, the range of young people holding fixed-term contracts is more narrow, affecting only the very young: up to about 20 years of age in the United Kingdom and Luxembourg; up to 24 years in Ireland; and up to 29 years of age in Greece and Denmark.

There is a marked linear trend of decreasing probability of working on a fixed-term contract with increasing age in all Member States, excepting Luxembourg and the United Kingdom. This is reflected in the size of the co-efficients which have their peaks for the 15–19-year-old age group, and then drop from one age group to the other until the 30–34-year-old age group, which still has a significantly higher risk of holding fixed-term contracts than the reference age group of 35–39-years-olds.

NATIONALITIES

Even after controlling for other variables like age, education, occupation, industrial sector and previous employment status, we found that in most countries, women have a higher probability of being engaged in fixed-term employment. This raises concerns that if a disproportionate number of women are relegated to non-standard employment situations, discriminatory employment practices unfavourable to women may be enhanced by the deregulation of legislative requirements for employment on a fixed-term contract. Similarly, it might be hypothesised that in making it easier to employ on a fixed-term contract without 'objective' reason for the limited period of employment, foreign workers, European Union nationals or not, could be discriminated against by a differential hiring practice.

In order to test for this form of discrimination, we constructed three so-called 'dummy' variables which indicate whether the person is a national of the country he or she is working in, whether a person is a national of a European

Union Member State but is working in another European Union country, or whether the person comes from a non-European Union country. Our results show that, in 1991, with the exception of three countries (Belgium, Portugal and Spain; no data for Italy), non-European Union nationals generally have a higher risk of holding 'only' fixed-term employment contracts within the European Union. This gives further support to a kind of process of restricting longer-term appointments to European Union nationals while workers from outside the European Union provide a higher share of 'flexible' labour.

We also estimated the probability of a European Union national having a fixed-term contract while working in another European Union country. In almost all countries, European Union nationals do not face more job insecurity in terms of a non-standard work contract. We found higher probabilities for European Union nationals holding fixed-term contracts only in the Netherlands (1991 and 1988) and the United Kingdom in 1991 (no data for Italy). Considering the non-discriminatory employment policies of the European Union, there might be reason to monitor these effects more closely in order to ensure equal treatment of women and men and ethnic minorities. Such a monitoring could be pursued on the basis of the European Labour Force Survey or the European Household Panel.

SELECTIVITY BY LEVEL OF EDUCATION

The European Labour Force Survey includes questions about the highest level of education or training completed. This set of questions has only been included in the survey since 1988, and major revisions to cover better the specific features of the educational systems of each country are currently being discussed. Due to the difficulties in precisely classifying some of the branches of an education system, we used, on the advice of the Eurostat office, only three broad categories of educational levels:

1   the first grouping includes all levels up to the second level, first stage according to the ISCED international standard classification of education, which corresponds in all European countries to the level usually reached by following compulsory minimum education measured in duration of years most commonly for nine years of education;
2   second level, second stage education has been grouped as a separate level since reaching this level allows the entry into higher education of universities or polytechnics;
3   the third category regroups all third level education, be it university degrees or professional equivalent certificates.

Results from the logistic regressions show that in Belgium, Denmark and Luxembourg, there are no statistically significant differences in the probability of holding a fixed-term or a permanent work contract with respect to educational level. In most Member States people with the minimum level of education have a higher risk of fixed-term employment. This is the case in Greece, Ireland, Italy, Portugal and Spain. In these five countries, except for Portugal, there is no significant difference between those with completed secondary education and those who hold a university degree in their chances of working on a more permanent appointment. In Portugal, it is only university graduates who are unlikely to work on a fixed-term contract, whereas all other lower educational levels run a higher risk of 'only' holding a fixed-term contract.

The remaining three countries, the Netherlands, West Germany and the United Kingdom, show a very different pattern compared to the other Member States.[4] Both groups, those having no or just compulsory minimum-level O-levels, and those with A-levels, which allow admission to university, have a lower probability of working on a fixed-term contract than university or polytechnic graduates. This fact lends credence to the view that large numbers of university graduates in these three countries and the employment practices of the public sector, which is still the number-one employer for university graduates, have led to the development of a specific policy of fixed-term recruitment for highly-educated young labour market entrants. It is also likely that in the public sector new legislation on fixed-term employment is applied fastest. In the United Kingdom, however, this specification of a fixed duration for an appointment, particularly for graduates, could be interpreted as more favourable treatment of graduates entering the labour market, since normal employment protection starts only after a minimum of two years of employment with the same employer.

Despite the difficulties in properly identifying employees who have no formal education certificate in most countries, the group with medium-level education – this corresponds to second-level, second-stage education, or A-levels – faces the lowest risk of being employed in a fixed-term situation. However, it should be kept in mind that in a growing number of Member States, some of these persons spent a few years in apprenticeship-like occupational training, during which time they received reduced wages for a previously-specified duration of employment. Those who currently hold an apprenticeship-type of contract have been excluded from the analysis in order to distinguish clearly between training contracts and employment contracts.

IMPACT OF EMPLOYMENT STATUS LAST YEAR

The European Labour Force Survey includes a set of questions in which respondents are required to provide information concerning their situation with regard to their economic activity one year prior to the survey. This allows us to test for sequences of unemployment and employment or time spent in education during the previous year, and employment status the following year. We constructed four dummy variables which evaluate the effects of (1) unemployment in the previous year, (2) any kind of education in the previous year, (3) inactivity one year ago, or (4) whether the person was self-employed a year ago.

For all countries it proved to be very important to include this rudimentary retrospective information in the analysis of employment relationships, since a large part of progress on the labour market is, in fact, 'path dependent', meaning that previous durations in unemployment, participation in higher education or spells of inactivity, reflect easily observable characteristics of employees and the unemployed. From a theoretical point of view, the theory of labour market segmentation makes explicit reference to the importance of information contained in previous education and employment histories of workers. Employees with a very unstable education or employment record with frequent interruptions of the work history due to unemployment or inactivity might be considered as potentially unreliable and will find it difficult to obtain more permanent employment opportunities.

Compared to the reference group of people who were employed during the previous year,[5] the unemployed are, in nine out of eleven countries, the most likely to hold a fixed-term contract.[6] Only in the United Kingdom are the previously inactive more likely than the previously unemployed to be hired on a fixed-term contract, and, in West Germany, those who were in education one year prior to the survey year 1991 were more likely than the unemployed to hold a fixed-term appointment in 1991. In most countries the coefficients on unemployment one year ago have the strongest effect of all coefficients, even higher than the first two age groups of the 15–24 years old. Only in France and West Germany is the effect to the age selectivity among the very young stronger than the recruitment of fixed-term employees from the unemployed.

Apparently, those persons with very little or no labour market experience or who have temporarily been out of contact with the labour market due to inactivity or unemployment have to pass through the screening period of fixed-term employment before moving on to 'standard' contracts with unspecified employment duration. However, the data of the ELFS do not allow us to investigate this question further. National longitudinal studies which follow the same individual over a number of years, for example in Spain (Alba-Ramírez 1991), the Netherlands (Vissers and Dirven 1994) and Germany (Schömann and Kruppe 1993), indicate that the unemployed, together with young people without much labour market experience, have substantial difficulties in finding more stable employment than the prevailing fixed-term contracts (OECD 1996: 16–19). Hence it is largely these labour market groups which provide employers with the flexibility to employ workers for short periods or during temporary peaks in production.

In legislation, legally temporary peaks in production have been one of the 'traditional' justifications for fixed-term employment, but the integration of the young and the unemployed or long-term unemployed during times of tight labour markets cannot be achieved by relying on fixed-term contracts. Compared to 1988 both in Germany and in France the effect of recruitment into fixed-term employment among the unemployed has decreased. While France has reintroduced some regulations governing fixed-term contracts, in Germany less regulation did not stimulate recruitment among the unemployed, as the percentage of fixed-term employees remained the same in both countries. Similar results are reported by the OECD (1996) based on data for 1994.

Since employees recruited into fixed-term contracts were either unemployed one year ago, were in education or not in the labour force, we consider fixed-term contracts to have become a 'prolonged' trial period in which employers assess the effective work of new employees on-the-job. In jobs where unobservable or hard-to-certify skills are needed, like communication skills or handling of software, a prolonged period of assessment of the true value of educational credentials appears to be a common hiring practice. Expressed in the framework of the reflexive labour law theory the results on the transition into more permanent employment indicate that research on the effective use of probationary periods is necessary to further enlighten this employment practice. It is likely that regulation of probationary periods as one component of a 'normal' work contract has been interpreted in a very narrow or protective sense by labour courts which has led firms to look for another contractual arrangement (fixed-term contracts) to keep an option of dismissal after a negative evaluation of a probationary period.

Potentially, fixed-term contracts might have become only an alternative to the effective use of probationary periods, whereby employers found it too difficult to obtain permission from works councils or even law courts to justify dismissal of employees on probationary periods. Fixed-term contracts in this case would offer an alternative, ensuring a cost-free separation without legal obligations during this period. Fixed-term contracts would even allow in most countries a longer duration of this trial period than standard work contracts. The exception to this rule is countries with a specific regulation which precludes the use of fixed-term contracts for these purposes, and the United Kingdom, where employment protection is applied after a minimum duration of two years of employment.

Whereas inactivity or education during the previous year might signal a lack of work experience to employers, strong effects of previous unemployment on fixed-term employment support efficiency wage theory considerations which claim that the unemployed and young labour market entrants will exercise a downward pressure on wages in the aggregate. The high level of previously unemployed persons on fixed-term contracts face on average, a wage disadvantage of about 10 per cent compared to standard work contracts (Alba-Ramírez 1991, Vissers and Dirven 1994, Schömann and Kruppe 1993). This means fixed-term employment is not an attractive alternative for experienced employees. Hence, if firms rely on recruitment into new positions on fixed-term contracts overall labour mobility of experienced workers is likely to decrease due to the lack of attractive offers, equally causing wage moderation of older employees following the rationale of efficiency wage theory.

INDUSTRIAL SECTOR EFFECTS

Industrial structures still vary a lot across the Member States of the European Union. Simple descriptive statistics do not allow us to disentangle the combination of effects, which might be due to a restructuring of an industry or the increase in importance of services in an economy. Only the inclusion of dummy variables for industrial sector effects allows us to control the remaining differences of industrial structures in Member States. Furthermore, these dummy variables (see Appendix) allow us to some extent to estimate institutional effects on employment in industrial sectors, like trade union strength and the wage bargaining process. These institutional factors have a likely influence on the occurrence of a sectoral collective agreement on employment protection or fixed-term employment. We introduced ten dummy variables based on the NACE 1-digit[7] level of classification of industries into industrial sectors. We have chosen the energy and water sector as the reference sector against which we interpret the estimates, since it can reasonably be assumed that this sector has a similar structure across Member States due to the high technology and security standards applied throughout the Union. Coal, gas, oil and nuclear power industries are included in this reference sector, as well as the generation of electricity and water distribution and purification.

The results from the logistic regressions show that, at least with respect to industrial sectors, the southern countries – Greece, Italy, Portugal and Spain – have a very similar spread of fixed-term employees across industrial sectors. In these four countries, the building and construction sector and agricultural production are the two sectors with the highest and statistically significant coefficient. This means that after keeping other socio-demographic characteristics, such as age, gender and previous employment status, constant, fixed-term contracts in southern Europe are mainly used in agriculture and the building industries. Other sectors, like trade and the financial sectors, use fixed-term contracts more often than the water and energy industries, but still considerably less than in building and agriculture.

In northern and central Europe, which has a much lower share of employees in agriculture and frequently specific labour laws governing the construction sector, such as bad weather allowances and winter building arrangements, these two sectors 'traditionally' rely heavily on shorter-duration contracts and, therefore, it is no longer in the industrial sector that we would expect to find the largest share of fixed-term employees. In fact, in all other Member States we find insignificant use of fixed-term contracts in agriculture. Due to regulatory features (collective agreements and statutory features) governing the building and construction sector in northern Europe, we find insignificant differences between the use of fixed-term contracts and more permanent contracts in West Germany, France, Ireland and the United Kingdom. Belgium, Denmark and the Netherlands seem to have opted for an institutional arrangement which favours more permanent employment in the construction sector despite the organisational feature that most projects in this industry are of limited duration. More permanent employment could be understood as an institutionalised form of 'compensation' for the otherwise unstable employment patterns in this sector. A more in-depth analysis of sector-specific agreements is necessary to determine at which level this favourable or compensating use of permanent employment is ensured.

A common feature in northern Europe is higher recourse to fixed-term employment in the public sector and other services like health, education, research, cultural affairs, and personal and domestic services. In both France and West Germany these two sectors figure among the two highest positive and significant coefficients in the estimated equations. Similarly, in Belgium (public sector), Denmark (other services), Ireland (public sector) and Italy (both sectors) we find higher probabilities of fixed-term employment compared to the reference category of the energy and water sector.

In the United Kingdom in 1988 this pattern of more fixed-term employment in public administration and other services compared to energy and water was also similar to other European countries, but since then the rate of fixed-term employment has equalised between sectors.[8] No significant differences between industrial sectors were found in Luxembourg, whereas relative to the reference sectors, almost all other sectors in the Netherlands had a lower rate of fixed-term employment.

Another general pattern appears to be that fixed-term employment is less prevalent in the manufacturing industries, such as mechanical and electrical engineering and motor vehicles and accessories. This holds true for Belgium, Denmark, Ireland, the Netherlands and the United Kingdom. In other countries there are only minor differences between this sector and the reference sector after controlling for differences in age, gender and educational levels. In Belgium and Ireland, fixed-term employment is also less likely in the other manufacturing industries, such as textile, wood, food and paper industries. In the Netherlands and the United Kingdom, employees in the mineral extraction and chemical industries are less likely to hold fixed-term contracts.

While the extent of fixed-term employment in the individual countries of the European Union in 1991 was to some degree comparable, differences in patterns between northern and southern countries reflect prevailing differences in industrial structures between countries. Whereas in the southern countries fixed-term contracts are found mostly in agriculture and building industries, in northern countries public administration and other services such as health, education and research have higher rates of fixed-term employment than the reference sectors. Countries with more restrictive legislation on fixed-term contracts all permit fixed-term employment for seasonal tasks. This is still the case in countries where the share of employees in these two sectors has decreased considerably over the last decades.

The northern countries, which have evolved to a larger extent in the direction of service economies, have also experienced higher rates of fixed-term employment in the service industries, but this growth in fixed-term employment seems to be limited to a few sectors like public administration where this form of labour contract can be seen as an outcome of attempts to reduce government budget deficits by means of 'lean' management of public employees.

In the public sector this evolution can be understood as a legislative reaction to the perceived 'favoured' status of civil servants. Following the rationale of the efficiency wage theory, unemployment is no longer a plausible threat to civil servants, therefore there is a risk of upward wage pressure. Fixed-term employment at entry into this sector contributes to slow down wage increases due to seniority. A similar argument can be advanced for other service sectors since the sector comprising health, education, research, cultural affairs, and personal and domestic services is still dominated by public funding. Due to the allocation of public funds for only fixed durations, employment in the form of fixed-term labour contracts is also likely for organisational reasons in small organisations with limited potential for horizontal job mobility.

A common feature which adds a market-oriented perspective to the analysis of fixed-term employment is the fact that in the manufacturing industries, in mineral extraction and the chemical industries we find few fixed-term employees. Industries that rely predominantly on skilled employees seem to prefer longer-term work contracts. This is a finding which supports the interpretation according to the efficiency wage theory (errors by employees will be very costly to the firm), human capital theory (investment in knowledge of firm-specific security standards is being compensated by employment protection) as well as segmentation theories (high productivity in this sector is shared with employees also in terms of employment protection). In order to test these statements with more rigour within our multi-layered approach, we would have to carry out a detailed study of collective agreements in these industries. For example in Germany, the metal workers' trade union (IG-Metall) and the employers' federation (Gesamtmetall) have restricted the use of fixed-term contracts to a maximum duration of three months, well below the maximum duration according to the legislation. There is reason to believe that similar clauses can be found in other industrial sectors' agreements for occupational groups and in other countries within the European Union.

Scarcity or abundance of employees with specific skills determines bargaining positions on the labour market just as trade union influence does. These factors have proved to be important determinants of fixed-term employment within the Member States. Even if the regulation of fixed-term employment has been, to a large extent, relaxed, as in West Germany, there is no automatic mechanism which ensures that the social partners will make use of such employment practices. By means of collective bargaining, the range of durations or the percentage of employees concerned might be determined as an outcome of negotiations rather than being introduced just after a change in legislation. This applies more to industries with a high amount of regulation being determined by collective agreements and to industries with larger firm size. More precarious employment is frequently prevalent in small firms and employees in these firms are equally less likely to be covered by collective agreements.

OCCUPATIONAL SEGREGATION

Due to the effect coding necessary in multivariate analyses of categorical data, we have to choose a reference category against which the other effects are evaluated. This choice is particularly hard to make in the case of multi-level country comparisons, since a reference occupational group in one country may not be suitable to another country's occupational structure. Therefore, including seven major occupational groups according to the ISCO-classification mainly has the function of controlling for occupational differences between countries when estimating effects for age, gender, or previous employment status.

There are, however, a number of interesting effects which are worth mentioning explicitly. As reference category we chose administrative occupations, since we assume that administrative tasks follow fairly standardised routines throughout the Union, as comparable levels of office automation among Member States have been reached by 1991 (for example, personal computer facilities). Despite high shares of fixed-term employees in public administration and other services in the industrial grouping discussed in the previous section, we find even higher shares in agricultural occupations in most countries, although some of these differences are not statistically significant.

In West Germany, Luxembourg and the Netherlands, sales-related occupations have a significantly lower probability of employing on a fixed-term basis. This might be explained by the fact that labour contracts for these occupations frequently include 'sales turnover targets' which employees have to achieve to receive the full wage. If sales personnel fall behind these targets they run the risk of incurring substantial 'wage penalties'. In this sense, these immediate effects on wages of sales personnel constitute another 'functional equivalent' to job insecurity. However, it needs to be investigated in more detail to what extent such labour contracts include some guaranteed minimum income based on longer-run sales figures and contacts with clients.

The occupational group of professionals includes occupations whose major tasks are expected to require a relatively high level of professional knowledge and experience in fields such as natural and social sciences or the humanities. Teaching and health-related professionals fall into this group. In Belgium, Denmark, Ireland, the Netherlands, Portugal, Spain and the United Kingdom, professionals in this group run a higher risk of being employed on a fixed-term basis compared to those in administrative occupations.

6

FIXED-TERM CONTRACTS AND THEIR RELATIONSHIP TO MACRO-ECONOMIC CONDITIONS

It can be expected that the level of economic activity will also influence the amount of fixed-term contracts concluded in a country or an industrial sector. However, there is still little research on this aspect of cyclical variation with regard to kinds of employment contracts or growth and productivity effects due to more or less job security. It appears to be an underresearched question whether firms make more use of fixed-term contracts in periods of slack or strong demand for their products. Despite the fact that most legislation on employment protection and fixed-term employment has been enacted promising more jobs in the aggregate to the electorate, economic theories predict that in periods when few new employees are hired the facilitation of fixed-term employment is unlikely to have pervasive effects. In periods with strong labour demand firms tend to employ additional labour to a larger extent but it is unclear whether the legal potential to employ only for a fixed-term contract is really adequate to attract new labour in a booming phase.

From a theoretical point of view fixed-term contracts have been considered as a possible remedy to low demand for labour at times of slow economic growth. However, in periods of economic recovery firms might find it difficult to recruit a sufficient number of well-qualified employees willing to accept fixed-term contracts in highly demanded occupations. Macro-economic studies either use data on the national level or, more frequently, tend to carry out analyses of a disaggregated nature for a specific industrial sector only. In the latter case, the unit of analysis for efficiency or productivity changes is one industrial sector or a number of different sectors in comparison. Alternatively, firm-level data can be used and combined to yield nationally representative information about inflows and outflows of employment.

THE EXAMPLE OF SPAIN

The Spanish case is of particular interest in this respect since several studies estimated macro-economic employment effects of the deregulation of fixed-term employment during the 1980s. The percentage share of fixed-term employees in comparison with the total number of employees rose from 10 per cent in 1984 to above 30 per cent in 1991 and remained largely at this level until 1996. In 1991 the Spanish government realised that the amount of fixed-term contracts in the Spanish economy indicated an overshooting of the amount of flexibility provided to firms above its original intention. It commissioned evaluations of the practice of fixed-term employment which were carried out by Alba-Ramírez (1991), Bentolila and Saint-Paul (1991), Jimeno and Toharia (1991) and by a group of experts (Segura *et al.* 1991).

The report by Bentolila and Saint-Paul (1991) takes a macro-economic perspective of fixed-term employment. On the basis of a labour demand model of the Spanish economy, which is based on Bertola (1990), they introduce labour endogeneity in the form of two types of labour who, assumingly, differ in respect to productivity, wages and firing costs. A type one worker ('rigid' labour) holds a permanent work contract and has considerable firing costs, a type two worker ('flexible' labour) on a fixed-term contract has no firing costs. Wages and productivity of both types of workers are also assumed to be equal following efficiency-wage type of arguments whereby fixed-term employees will be less costly in terms of wages but subject to higher monitoring costs due to shirking.

Three policy regimes are distinguished: (1) one in which fixed-term contracts are not permitted, (2) such contracts can readily be applied, and (3) a transition from the employment system without fixed-term contracts to one which allows lower cost dismissal. The application to Spanish data of this model takes a short-run perspective since data from 1985–88 are the basis for the estimates. A sample of 1,214 manufacturing non-energy private firms is the basis for the empirical analysis. Data on employment, balance sheets for capital stock and sales are applied using panel data estimation techniques (Bentolila and Saint-Paul 1991). Results confirm the hypotheses of the theoretical model that in the employment regime with fixed-term contracts both wage elasticity for fixed-term employees and the elasticity of flexible labour to an exogenous shock to the economy is higher for fixed-term employees than more permanent employees. In the case of Spain the introduction of fixed-term employment has introduced a more procyclical reaction of labour demand, i.e. more rapid expansion in booms and faster discharging of employees by private firms during recessions. However, the effect of the introduction of fixed-term contracts had caused only a one and a half percentage point increase in the elasticity of labour demand during the observed period, mainly a booming period in Spain. During a recession more severe loss of jobs can be expected, accompanying an additional drop in sales due to fast job loss. Evidence presented in the *Employment Outlook* (1996) indicates that, indeed, more contracting flexibility means faster dismissal or expiry of a fixed-term contract at times of slack labour demand in the case of Spain.

Jimeno and Toharia (1991) simultaneously carried out an evaluation of the

Spanish evolution of fixed-term employment for the late 1980s. Their approach incorporates an interesting example of a successful combination of micro- and macro-level results starting with a description of personal characteristics of fixed-term and permanent employees. The most important change of the many parts of legislative changes in 1984 was the discontinuation of the 'causality principle' which made it necessary to provide a specific reason for fixed-term employment and allowing a maximum term of three years. In making use of two sets of data, the Spanish labour force survey and the Bank of Spain Survey on Firms' Balance Sheets which includes information on a firm's employees, they find that both sources suggest the most intense use of fixed-term contracts in small and newly created firms. Among the sectors which employ more than 30 per cent of all employees on fixed-term contracts are agriculture, construction, shoe and leather production as well as hotels and restaurants. The age structure of fixed-term employees is highly skewed in the sense that two-thirds of young persons aged between 20 and 24 years are fixed-term employees.

In their multivariate assessment of the probability of having a permanent job after entering employment during the previous twelve months, they estimate for two points in time this probability of finding a permanent job after unemployment one year ago. Results based on the Labour Force Survey confirm the age-selectivity of fixed-term employment and the industrial sector selectivity. Additionally most fixed-term employees have entered the labour market from the status of not being a member of the labour force rather than from unemployment. Based on a theoretical model the authors suggest that the introduction of fixed-term employment gives rise to co-operation and efficiency effects due to the fact that the distribution of permanent workers and fixed-term employees in a firm will have an impact on average productivity levels in the firms and for the economy as a whole.

For the evaluation of legal systems and systems of employment protection in general, Jimeno and Toharia (1991) propose to estimate wage effects of fixed-term employment. Although, de jure, there is no possibility for different wages to be paid for two groups of employees. Spanish labour law actually forbids collective bargaining agreements to specify different wage rates for permanent and fixed-term employees as is the case for male and female wage rates. Any form of wage discrimination apparently is excluded ex ante. However, the evaluation of legal systems is dealing with just this kind of proclaimed functioning of the labour market. The multivariate empirical evidence for Spain regarding wage effects based on a special survey of the Spanish Statistical Office in 1990 shows that hourly wage rates were, on average, 11 per cent lower than wage rates of permanent employees with the same characteristics such as age, sex, industrial sector of job, and level of educational attainment.

In addition to this individual-level evidence of wage effects, Jimeno and Toharia (1991) made cross-section estimates for various industrial sectors for a number of years using as a dependent variable the growth in labour productivity computed from the industrial production index. With and without controlling for personal characteristics and the composition of the staff (percentage fixed-term/permanent employees), there appears to be a negative correlation between the share of fixed-term employment and labour productivity, although decreasing over time. On the industry level, Jimeno and Toharia (1991) find no evidence in support of a lower wage push effect of Spanish trade unions since the introduction of more fixed-term employees in most industries and firms, allowing for the differential impact of firm-level wage bargaining. Another major outcome of the analysis was that wage rates and the percentage of fixed-term employees seem to be determined endogenously, which means one operates largely independent of the other (Segura *et al.* 1991, Jimeno and Toharia 1993: 320–1).

In Spain, regulations to achieve the goal of job creation, or even to lower unemployment, were in some instances contradictory to the goal of lowering fixed-term employment. Most fixed-term contracts which, after the maximum duration of three years, were about to expire in 1993 and thus would cause an additional rise of the already high level of unemployment, were allowed to be extended by between six and twelve months. In addition, employers received a subsidy of PTA 250,000 if they converted the temporary employment contract into a permanent one after the fourth year. In 1993 and 1994 changes were made for apprenticeship contracts, the spread of part-time working contracts (permanent or temporary) and the (practical) training contracts were reformed. Permanent contracts with discontinuous working periods were abolished. Labour promotion contracts with a maximum duration of three years and expiring during 1994 were allowed to be extended for one additional period of up to eighteen months. To stop the dualisation of the labour market, based on excessive use of flexible employment, collective bargaining was strengthened. One of the main changes was a reform of the regulation of dismissals in 1994. Organisational and technical reasons related to production were now introduced as a satisfying condition for dismissals in the standard work contracts. Redundancies affecting less than 10 per cent of the workforce in firms with less than 300 employees (or less than 30 employees in firms with more than 300 employees) were no longer treated as mass redundancies. In 1994 the legal basis for activities of temporary employment agencies came into effect. All these legal responses underscore the reflexivity between branches of regulation. Most macro-economic evaluations, however, singled out just one dimension – notably fixed-term employment – in their evaluation attempts, neglecting other functional equivalents to fixed-term employment.

Using stock data for Spain (see Table 6.1) we find nearly constant shares of permanent and fixed-term employment between 1992 and 1995. In absolute numbers almost twice as many male as female employees were working on a fixed-term contract. Compared to all male or female employees, calculated as a percentage of the specific group, women were more likely to have that kind of contract than men. The decomposition of the share of temporary employment by sectors (see Tables 6.2 and 6.3) reveals that in total this type of contract is mainly used in the service sector. But between 58 and 63 per cent of the employees in the construction sector and between 55 and 60 per cent of the agricultural sector were hired under a fixed-term contract.

Table 6.1 Dependent employment by duration of contracts and gender as percentage of all dependent employees

Employment duration	1992	1993	1994	1995
permanent	66.5	67.7	66.2	65.1
fixed-term	33.5	32.3	33.8	34.9
male fixed-term	30.8	29.8	31.8	33.2
female fixed-term	38.9	37.1	37.5	38

Source: Instituto Nacional de Estadistica; Encuesta de la poblacion activa; author calculations

Table 6.2 Dependent employment by duration of contracts and sectors as percentage of all dependent employees

Employment duration	1992	1993	1994	1995
permanent	66.5	67.7	66.2	65.1
fixed-term	33.5	32.3	33.8	34.9
Agriculture	2.5	2.3	2.4	2.4
Industry	7.5	6.4	6.6	7.0
Construction	5.9	5.4	5.5	6.1
Services	17.6	18.1	19.2	19.3

Source: Instituto Nacional de Estadistica; Encuesta de la poblacion activa; author calculations

Table 6.3 Dependent employment by duration of contracts and sectors as percentage of all dependent employees of the specific sector

Sectors	1992	1993	1994	1995
Agriculture				
permanent	42.8	45.2	42.4	40.2
fixed-term	57.2	54.8	57.6	59.8
Industry				
permanent	71.9	74.5	72.9	70.5
fixed-term	28.1	25.5	27.1	29.5
Construction				
permanent	41	42.1	40.1	36.7
fixed-term	59.0	57.9	59.9	63.3
Services				
permanent	70.2	70.3	69.1	69.1
fixed-term	29.8	29.7	30.9	30.9

Source: Instituto Nacional de Estadistica; Encuesta de la poblacion activa; author calculations

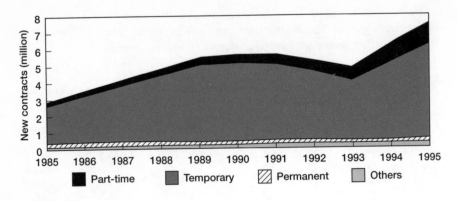

Figure 6.1 Flows into new contracts, Spain 1985–95

Source: Instituto Nacional de Estadistica; Encuesta de la poblacion activa

To identify labour market segmentation, we analysed data from 1985 to 1995 of the composition of labour market flows into new contracts (Figure 6.1). Besides a small constant recruitment of permanent employment, the portion of new contracts with a limited duration rises rapidly over time following relatively closely the evolution of aggregate labour demand. In February 1997,[1] 96 per cent of a total of 711,178 new hirings were on fixed-term contracts and only 4 per cent on permanent contracts. Only a share of 8.7 per cent of the 4 per cent of contracts were converted from temporary to permanent. The main reasons for a fixed-term contract were: 36.3 per cent (*contratos eventuales por circunstancias de la production*) to 'meet circumstantial market developments, a backlog of work or a surge in orders, even in the ordinary course of the employer's business' and 28.3 per cent (*contratos de obra o servicio determinado*) with the purpose 'to carry out works or render services which have some independence and substance of their own within the employer's business, but are limited in time and are to be carried out or rendered for a term that cannot be fixed in advance'.[2]

As a result of these developments, and now as a process of collective bargaining, in April 1997 a tripartite commission of the social partners made the following agreement,[3] which was framed into legislation in August 1997:

- A new type of training contract (*contrato de formación*) replaces the already existing type of fixed-term contract (*contrato de aprendizaje*) to further the integration of youth into the labour market by optimising the theoretical and practical training of the youth with the possibility of obtaining an occupational certificate at the end. There is a reduction in duration to a maximum of two years and age of entry to 21 but also a rise of income to the interprofessional minimum wage and in social security.

- Definitions and reasons for fixed-term contracts are now more precise; the reason for fixed-term contracts associated with the start-up of new activities for a firm no longer exist.
- A new type of permanent contract for youth, long-term unemployed, elderly and discouraged workers as well as for those under fixed-term contracts is introduced allowing lower costs in the case of dismissals compared to standard employment contracts. There is also a reduction in social security contributions of 40 to 90 per cent for this new type of permanent contract.
- Reasons for dismissals and procedures have been restated with more precision and are now also a possible issue in collective agreements.

In conclusion it seems that these reforms of the Spanish labour market have not delivered the effects intended by the government and suggested by many economists (OECD 1993). With both the highest unemployment rate and the highest rate of precarious employment in form of fixed-term contracts in the European Union in 1996 (Eurostat 1997), this way of flexibilisation is not promising in the fight against unemployment. This is at least circumstantial evidence that a massive increase in fixed-term employment is not enhancing labour market efficiency taking a longer run perspective. On the grounds of the equity and efficiency trade-off discussed in Chapter 2 there is no indication that those who enter the labour market with the disadvantage of job insecurity and lower wages are in some other way compensated for this. Hence, the policy changes do not appear to have been a Pareto-efficient improvement of the labour market.

COMPARATIVE ASPECTS OF MACRO-PERFORMANCE

A similar macro-level evaluation of employment effects was performed for West Germany. A multivariate estimation of the effects of fixed-term employment on firm-level employment practices was carried out by Kraft (1993). His analysis of the speed of employment adjustment in West Germany between the years 1970 and 1987 was based on data of twenty-one West German manufacturing industries. The study used as a dependent variable the change in employment within the industry and a proxy for product demand and nominal wages. He supplemented his analysis with information on the level of unionisation. The presence of a particular union (IG Metall) was used as a dummy variable which was supposed to capture the impact of the Employment Promotion Act in a spline function of the time trend variable. However, contrary to the findings in his other studies (Kraft 1994), he reports a slowdown in employment adjustment since the introduction of deregulation in German manufacturing industries, particularly in industries dominated by collective bargaining by the IG Metall.

Based on a disaggregate analysis of monthly data from 202 industries over the period from January 1977 to December 1992, Hunt (1993) estimated a similar model to Kraft (1993) and the Spanish evaluation attempts. The information on employment adjustment, wages and sales is used in separate models of employment adjustments for blue-collar and white-collar employees. The rather surprising finding by Kraft (1993) was confirmed, that employment adjustment slowed down after the introduction of the Employment Promotion Act in 1985.

A weakness in the macro-evaluations of fixed-term employment in Germany consists in the focus of evaluations on a single change in legislation, notably the Employment Promotion Act of 1985. The problem arises since the deregulation of fixed-term contracts by legal provisions was counteracted in collective agreements in some industries, mainly the manufacturing industries, which reduced the maximum length of fixed-term contract to cover six months instead of eighteen months as specified in the law (Adamy 1988, Linne and Voswinkel 1989). Most studies, particularly those focusing on the manufacturing industries, therefore have found counterintuitive results due to an inadequate measurement of the various components of a country's system of employment protection and labour law in general.

In France no multivariate estimation of wage reducing effects of fixed-term contracts are available. However, results of a survey in 1984 suggested a 20 per cent lower wage cost incurred by agency workers mainly due to the fact that seniority status is not honoured for non-standard employees (Henry and Guergoat 1987). French analysts have emphasised research on what type of firms have an extended use of fixed-term or agency work. Based on surveys among firms and descriptive statistics over ten years Guergoat and Hocquaux (1991) concluded that firm size is a differentiating category in the use of non-standard employment. Fewer small firms use fixed-term contracts, but those that do use them show a tendency to use them extensively. It was found that between 1977 and 1987 the increase of non-standard employment originated in the fact that more firms used fixed-term contracts rather than the same firms employing more fixed-term employees. Unfortunately no estimates of productivity effects are available to our knowledge.

In comparative perspective, and keeping in mind the difficulty of assessing the impact of legal changes on aggregate measures of labour market outcomes (Michon and Ramaux 1993: 96, Kraft 1997), the link or correlation between degree of flexibility introduced by legal reforms and the extent of recourse to non-standard employment appears closely related in France in comparison to the German labour market. In Spain the speed of adjustment is fastest among the countries for which macro-level evaluations have been carried out. The effects of deregulation of employment protection and fixed-term employment on the overall performance of an economy in terms of productivity and labour market efficiency, however, remains an unresolved issue unless more comprehensive models which allow for various feedback effects between legislation and employment practice, including collective agreements, and better comparable data can be used in such analyses.

7

CONCLUSIONS

We can conclude our study with some general remarks on its approach and findings. Firstly, we found strong evidence of path-dependency of national systems of regulation. The importance of nationally-specific factors requires in our view an in-depth analysis of each country's legal and socio-economic evolution. Secondly, the comparative analysis of legal regulation and economic development of atypical employment suggests the need to use a comprehensive research design which incorporates economic, sociological and legal theories as well as a broad set of socio-legal and socio-economic indicators (Rogowski 1997). This allows us to move beyond the mere description of employment systems of the Member States and the European Union as a whole and thus to overcome shortcomings of previous research in this field.[1] Thirdly, an interdisciplinary approach implies a shift of the analytical perspective from flexibility to efficiency in studying the impact of employment security and fixed-term contract regulation on labour markets in the European Union.

The third point can be illustrated with respect to developments in evaluation research of employment security and fixed-term employment. During the 1980s and the early 1990s theoretical debates centred on the concepts of deregulation (Büchtemann 1993) and in particular flexibility (OECD 1986, 1990, Pollert 1991, Jessop et al. 1991). The originally narrow concept which focused on internal flexibility (within the firm) versus external flexibility (of the whole labour market) was then enlarged by distinguishing between numerical flexibility and functional flexibility (Mosley 1994). The theoretical debate of flexibility was further developed by the idea of strategic choice of flexibility policies within firms (Lutz 1993), and by the concept of coordinated flexibility which emphasises the potential complementarity of employment security and flexibility within the wider labour market context; it stresses the importance of institutional set-ups and socio-economic environments of firms and households (Schmid 1993).

In the debates on flexibility and flexibilisation of the labour market, the focus gradually shifted to a discussion of the efficiency of the labour market. Our study is a contribution to this discussion. The concept of economic efficiency refers in general to the maximisation of wealth within a society and, applied to the labour market, of maximising the number of 'legal' jobs in an economy.[2] Our understanding of efficiency is thereby based on an economic notion of Pareto-efficiency and we assume that policy changes aim foremost at improving labour market efficiency.

There are a number of attempts to combine normative and analytical aspects in the discussion of efficiency. Thurow, for example, asks: 'To be efficient at the macro-level is to be unfair at the micro-level. Where is the balance to be drawn?' (Thurow 1979: 30). He sees a real dilemma in modern economies between fairness and efficiency. Unemployment experienced by an individual (for example after expiration of a fixed-term contract) is perceived as unfair, but on the aggregate level of the analysis unemployment causes wage restraint which can get more people back into employment (ceteris paribus, as in most statements in economics).

Schmid (1994) is concerned with tensions between efficiency and equity. He extends Ouchi's concept of comparative efficiency of institutions such as markets, bureaucracies and networks, by adding a fourth category of civil rights as coordinating factor of the labour market, which incorporates the element of solidarity into the equity and efficiency discussion. Schmid's political economy perspective does not deny the normative aspect in the search for the potential of equity cum efficiency solutions of policy changes in the domain of labour market policies. His suggestion of a policy of 'consistent application of efficiency-enhancing equity standards' (Schmid 1994: 263) aims at legal standards which need to be controlled with respect to efficiency losses in the pursuit of balancing efficiency and equity.

Our own solution transcends to some extent the normative legal and economic views. It opts for a socio-legal and socio-economic perspective which reconstructs legal and economic views as descriptions of dimensions of the complex process of regulation. In this way, we can combine the different views in a multi-layered concept, which provides the basis for neither legal nor economic but sociological hypotheses.

A sociological analysis of regulation acknowledges the relative autonomy of economic, legal and political processes. Each system has capacities to regulate itself. Furthermore, it assumes specific relations between the political and the legal system. In Chapter 3, we present both a comprehensive description of national regulations and an empirical and theoretical analysis of the history of current labour regulations governing fixed-term contracts in the twelve Member States, prior to the recent enlargement of the European Union. In addition, we discuss regulation attempts of the Commission of the European Communities in the area of atypical employment, including the successful regulation so far, i.e. the Council Directive 91/383 of 25 June 1991.

The national labour law systems display a rich diversity of approaches in regulating fixed-term contracts, as illustrated in Chapter 3 and summarised in Table 7.1. This diversity reflects fundamental differences in legal views of fixed-term contracts as well as traditions of industrial relations. It shows the

Table 7.1 Regulations of fixed-term contracts in the EU

	Belgium	Denmark	France	Germany	Greece	Ireland
Statutory Sources	Law on Employment Contracts of 3 July 1978; Law on Temporary Work of 24 July 1987	Provisions in the Act on White-Collar Employees; Act on the Placing of Workers and Insurance against Unemployment, as amended in 1990	L 122-1 (and the following provisions) of the Labour Code, as amended by the Law of 12 July 1990	Sec. 620 of the Civil Code; Employment Promotion Act of 1985; Act on Fixed-term Employment in Universities and Research Institutes of 1985	Sec. 669 to 671 of the Civil Code; Act 1359 of 1945 (amended 1983); Act 2081 of 1952 on seasonal work	Provisions in the Redundancy Payments Act of 1967; Unfair Dismissal Act of 1977; Maternity Protection of Employees Act
Requirement of Reason	No	No	Ten reasons, including seasonal work, replacement, and temporary nature of work	Seven categories of reasons under case law, including seasonal work, replacement, and temporary nature of work	Four reasons, including temporary nature of work	No
Duration	Maximum duration of 2 years for replacement contracts	No maximum or minimum duration	Maximum duration varies between 9 months and 2 years according to reason for fixed term	Statutory maximum for fixed-term contracts under the Employment Promotion Act is normally 18 months, in exceptional cases 24 months	No maximum or minimum duration	No maximum or minimum duration

	Belgium	Denmark	France	Germany	Greece	Ireland
Renewal	In a limited number of industries and under particular circumstances like temporary increase in workload	Unlimited	Once, up to the maximum fixed term	In general only up to the maximum fixed term; four months interruption before a new contract can be concluded under the Employment Promotion Act	Twice	Unlimited
Automatic Conversion into Permanent Contract	Yes, if continued after the contractual or maximum fixed term and in case of illegality	Yes, if found to be illegal	Yes, if continued after the contractual or maximum fixed term	Yes, if continued after the contractual or maximum fixed term and in case of illegality of the fixed-term contract	Yes, if continued after the contractual or maximum fixed term	No
Compensation at the End of the Fixed Term	No. Employer pays twice the normal rate of compensation if dismissal before the expiry of the fixed term was unlawful	No	Yes. 6% of gross salary, except in cases of seasonal work.	No	No	No
National Regulatory Features			Close resemblance of regulations on fixed-term contracts and temporary or agency work	The requirement of reason for the use of fixed-term contracts was established by the Federal Labour Court		

Table 7.1 continued

	Italy	Luxembourg	Netherlands	Portugal	Spain	United Kingdom
Statutory Sources	Sec. 2094 (and following) of the Civil Code; Workers' Statute of 1970; Law 230 of 1960; Law 876 of 10977; Law 79 of 1983.	Law of 24 May 1989; Grandducal Regulation of 11 July 1989	Sec. 1639 e to g of the Civil Code	Decree-Law 781 of 28 October 1976; Decree-Law 64A of 27 February 1989	Workers' Statute of 1970; Law 32 of 2 August 1984; Law 18 of 3 December 1993	Sec. 13 (2), 20 (2), 49 (4), 55 (2), 83 (2), 142 (1) (2) Employment Protection (Consolidation) Act of 1978
Requirement of Reason	Nine reasons, including seasonal work, replacement, and temporary and occasional character of work	Ten reasons, including seasonal work, replacement, and temporary and occasional character of work	No	No, unless the fixed term is for less than 6 months. In this case the work must be temporary in nature	Eleven reasons, including specific purposes, but excluding seasonal work	No
Duration	Maximum fixed term 6 months; in case of training contracts 24 months	Maximum fixed term 2 years	No maximum or minimum duration	Maximum duration 6 years (maximum fixed term is 3 years with the possibility of renewal for a further 3 years)	Maximum fixed term 3 years	No maximum or minimum duration
Renewal	Once for the same duration as the previous contract	Twice, up to the maximum fixed term	Unlimited	Up to the maximum fixed term	Up to the maximum fixed term	Unlimited

	Italy	Luxembourg	Netherlands	Portugal	Spain	United Kingdom
Automatic Conversion into Permanent Contract	Yes, if continued after the contractual or maximum fixed term	Yes, if continued after the contractual or maximum fixed term	No, instead, automatic renewal for a maximum of 1 year if continued for the first time after the expiry of the fixed term. But conversion into a permanent contract, if continued beyond the extra year without express renewal	Yes, if continued after the maximum fixed term	Yes, if continued after the contractual or maximum fixed term	Yes, if the fixed-term contract is concluded for less than a month and is continued beyond three months of employment
Compensation at the End of the Fixed Term	No	No	No	Yes, two days' basic remuneration for each month of service	Yes, twelve days per year of service	No
National Regulatory Features	Restrictive judicial interpretation of regulations on fixed-term contracts				The use of fixed-term contracts is induced by strict dismissal protection regulations	Common law rules on contract apply in the case of performance of a particular task

163

extent to which policies of regulation and deregulation were influenced by national labour market policies and, above all, by features of national legal cultures. Attempts to use employment protection reforms for purposes of labour market flexibility or efficiency are largely limited by existing labour laws. The lesson of attempts at deregulation so far seem to be that regulations of fixed-term contracts are closely linked to dismissal protection. In the majority of Member States, the regulation of fixed-term contracts is still narrowly defined and predominantly concerned with limiting the possibilities to circumvent dismissal protection regulations. The reform of one part of the employment protection system has repercussions for other parts, which then tends to invalidate incremental reforms of flexibilising institutional structures of the labour market.

Deregulation often meant in fact further regulation by adding a labour market policy perspective to the existing understanding of employment law. Furthermore, deregulation affects mainly employees who are exempted from regular employment protection. No Member State of the European Union, with the exception of some procedural changes in the United Kingdom in which the qualifying period for employment protection was raised to two years (Dickens 1994), changed the general dismissal protection system as such. However, there are attempts to introduce large loopholes in the employment protection legislation through actively supporting a broad use of fixed-term employment which amount in fact to a substantial change of the whole employment protection system (Standing 1993). For example, in Spain 90 per cent of new employment contracts are only concluded for a fixed term since 1984.

The evidence presented in Chapter 3 suggests a correlation between changes in the political system, in particular a victory of free-market policies over social-democratic welfare policies, and a regulatory change affecting the balance between fixed-term employment and standard employment. Similarly, since there are different political opinions when the critical point is reached at which efficiency losses become too large in the pursuit of equity, we were able to trace the evolution of each Member State's balance between employment protection legislation in general and legislation on fixed-term contracts.

The comparisons in Chapters 4 and 5 focus on processes and the testing of theoretical hypotheses outlined and discussed in Chapter 2. The empirical analysis uses data from the European Labour Force Survey and data from some national longitudinal surveys. The findings can be summarised as follows. Labour market segmentation and the segregation of women into less attractive occupational careers has frequently led to structural disadvantages for women in the European Union.[3] Fixed-term contracts function as 'ports of entry' to labour markets. They do not overcome segmentation or segregation of labour markets, but rather perpetuate structural deficiencies in most Member States (see also Michon and Ramaux 1993). The overrepresentation of women in fixed-term employment in nearly all Member States is, in fact, one of the major mechanisms with which labour market segmentation is upheld and even new forms of discriminatory practices are made possible.

Multivariate longitudinal analyses of earnings differentials between fixed-term employees and permanent employees show that in Spain (Alba-Ramírez 1991), the Netherlands (Vissers and Dirven 1994) and Germany (Schömann and Kruppe 1993), fixed-term employees earn about 10 per cent less than employees with 'standard' employment contracts, even after controlling for other effects such as age, gender and educational differences. Major differences in the use of fixed-term contracts can be explained by analysing the distribution of fixed-term employees across industrial sectors. The industrial sectors with the highest productivity increases in the recent past also have the lowest shares of fixed-term employees in most Member States of the European Union.

The large share of young fixed-term employees (see Chapters 4 and 5, Eurostat 1997: 10–11) indicates that fixed-term contracts serve as prolonged probation periods. The standard probation periods, foreseen by legislation or collective agreements, are thereby enlarged for the group of new labour market entrants. This practice in consequence turns into a 'last in, first out' employment strategy of firms, particularly in periods of economic recession. Indeed, among the reasons for unemployment, the expiry of a fixed-term contract has become increasingly significant in many countries (Mosley and Kruppe 1993). The rising share of fixed-term employees among the young can thus lead to increasing youth unemployment at times of overall slack demand for labour, as witnessed in most European countries.

We have shown that both the legal development and the growth of atypical forms of employment are dependent on an array of factors such as the business cycle, the sectoral distribution of employment, changes in individual preferences and the country-specific system of employment, employment protection and industrial relations practices. However, it remains largely undetermined, whether a lowering of standards of employment protection is directly efficiency-enhancing or desirable for other economic reasons. Franz (1994), following Coase (1984), argues that a reduction of dismissal protection might in fact lead to an increase in transaction costs as a result of rapid labour turnover, which would have negative consequences on labour market efficiency and overall employment prospects. The reviews of industry and occupation distributions (Chapters 4 and 5) and macro-economic evidence (Chapter 6) indeed indicate such negative effects on productivity, at least in industrial sectors with rapid growth and high productivity.

In examining the regulation and empirical evidence on fixed-term and standard employment contracts, and its implications for labour market efficiency, it becomes apparent that each Member State has chosen a specific mix of deregulation policies (Rogowski and Schmid 1997). Some countries preferred to privatise whole industrial sectors or monopolies while at the same time preserving standard employment relationships for employees within these industries (France, Germany, the Netherlands), whereas other countries opted for a widespread deregulation of employment relationships by means of facilitating fixed-term contracts rather than abolishing monopolies or applying large-scale privatisation (mainly Spain). The United Kingdom used both ways simultaneously and earlier than most other Member States of the European Union.[4] Shifting whole firms from the public to the private sector means that the long-term commitment of the public sector to its employees vanishes. Furthermore deregulation as privatisation also has negative implications for the employment protection of the (remaining) public employees. The public sector adopts management practices similar to private enterprises'. These include engaging self-employed persons on functions which have been previously carried out by internal employees, or out-sourcing of whole units of production as new firms. These practices are likely to reduce employment protection of employees in these units, in particular when new agreements, involving another trade union, or union-free agreements are concluded.

Employment protection and fixed-term employment will continue to be an important component of policies to influence the efficiency of European labour markets. The impact of regulatory changes on employment, unemployment and labour market efficiency differs greatly between Member States. A number of varying legal practices as well as economic consequences can be observed in the European Union which affect the efficiency of fixed-term employment. Examples include periods of notice before the expiry of a fixed-term contract, probationary periods as part of fixed-term contracts, or the form of compensation at the end of a fixed-term contract and its impact on continuation of the employment relationship. Furthermore, the regulation of employment protection and fixed-term contracts is in these days an attractive instrument for policy-makers because regulatory changes in this area involve little or no cost for the political decision-maker aiming to fulfil the Maastricht budget deficit criteria.

With respect to future efforts to regulate atypical employment we recommend the adoption of a differentiated view.[5] The three main forms of atypical employment – fixed-term employment, agency work and part-time work – should be treated differently. They do not display similar characteristics which would enable the introduction of comprehensive laws for all forms of atypical employment. Instead national and supranational protection should treat them in separate regulations. However, before legislation is introduced, an 'implicit' agreement on the critical point in the balance of equity and efficiency on the labour market has to be reached.[6]

Labour market policy, be it at the national or European level, can facilitate transitions from fixed-term into open-ended or standard employment relationships. The concept of transitional labour markets (Schmid 1995) emphasises the importance of transitions between household work and labour force participation, from school to work, or of transitions from work into retirement. Fixed-term contracts could play an important role in organising such transitions, balancing efficiency and equity concerns.

The multi-layered concept of a socio-legal and socio-economic analysis indicates that compensating wage differentials are more likely to occur along the lines of wage differentials between occupations or industries. However, official legal compensation for wage differentials exists only in France and Portugal (see Table 7.1) where a specific compensation is granted to fixed-term employment independent of occupation or industry or the job at the end of the contract. In all other Member States the evidence suggests that earnings of fixed-term employees are lower than those of employees with a more permanent employment contract. In our view the introduction of a lump sum compensation at the end of a fixed-term contract which compensates for job insecurity appears to be a suitable policy option to avoid misuse of fixed-term contracts. It is also a measure against tendencies to reduce wages for employees with only a marginal attachment to the firm and thus against an increase in income inequality.

APPENDIX

ESTIMATES OF THE PROBABILITY TO HOLD A
FIXED-TERM CONTRACT IN COMPARISON WITH A
PERMANENT APPOINTMENT (BY COUNTRY)

YEAR OF SURVEY = 1991   COUNTRY = Belgium

Number of Observations: 21857

	Value	FIXED	Count
	1	0	20767
	2	1	1090

Criteria for Assessing Model Fit

Criterion	Intercept Only	Intercept and Covariates	Chi-Square for Covariates
AIC	8663.104	7174.588	—
SC	8671.096	7494.279	—
−2 LOG L	8661.104	7094.588	1566.516 with 39 DF (p = 0.0001)
Score	—	—	2137.760 with 39 DF (p = 0.0001)

Analysis of Maximum Likelihood Estimates

Variable	DF	Parameter Estimate	Standard Error	Wald Chi-Square	Pr > Chi-Square	Standardised Estimate	Odds Ratio
INTERCPT	1	4.6090	0.9015	26.1361	0.0001	—	100.382
FEMALE	1	−0.5429	0.1004	29.2232	0.0001	−0.146522	0.581
HEAD	1	0.0726	0.1135	0.4091	0.5224	0.019763	1.075
SPOUSE	1	−0.2061	0.1573	1.7157	0.1902	−0.049369	0.814
AGE1	1	−1.9347	0.2124	82.9293	0.0001	−0.117386	0.144
AGE2	1	−1.0662	0.1375	60.0939	0.0001	−0.180524	0.344
AGE3	1	−0.7826	0.1210	41.8233	0.0001	−0.158455	0.457
AGE4	1	−0.3358	0.1250	7.2130	0.0072	−0.068939	0.715
AGE6	1	0.3083	0.1507	4.1870	0.0407	0.060232	1.361
AGE7	1	0.1996	0.1671	1.4269	0.2323	0.033858	1.221
AGE8	1	0.6001	0.2122	8.0001	0.0047	0.090843	1.822
AGE9	1	0.6618	0.2658	6.1987	0.0128	0.077675	1.938
AGE10	1	0.3078	0.4690	0.4307	0.5116	0.017649	1.360
AGE11	1	0.2103	0.7666	0.0752	0.7839	0.004363	1.234
NATIOEC	1	−0.2668	0.1587	2.8287	0.0926	−0.031631	0.766
NONEC	1	−0.2832	0.2531	1.2519	0.2632	−0.020008	0.753
EDUC1	1	−0.2317	0.1100	4.4392	0.0351	−0.063333	0.793
EDUC2	1	0.1676	0.1001	2.8027	0.0941	0.042251	1.182
SINGLE	1	−0.4416	0.1248	12.5220	0.0004	−0.102726	0.643
WIDISEP	1	−0.3464	0.1733	3.9950	0.0456	−0.045527	0.707
UNEMPAGO	1	−2.2407	0.1450	238.8646	0.0001	−0.137942	0.106
EDUCAGO	1	−1.4786	0.1476	100.3349	0.0001	−0.105582	0.228
INACAGO	1	−1.4338	0.1479	93.9614	0.0001	−0.108018	0.238
EMSELF	1	0.3260	1.0270	0.1008	0.7509	0.007488	1.385
OSERV	1	−0.4084	0.3368	1.4699	0.2254	−0.098307	0.665
PUBLIC	1	−1.0163	0.3370	9.0917	0.0026	−0.176701	0.362
BANK	1	0.5498	0.3568	2.3743	0.1233	0.083139	1.733
TRANS	1	0.2418	0.3562	0.4609	0.4972	0.037613	1.274
TRADE	1	0.5452	0.3471	2.4666	0.1163	0.100520	1.725
BUILD	1	1.0192	0.3902	6.8213	0.0090	0.133143	2.771
OMAN	1	1.0322	0.3634	8.0664	0.0045	0.171780	2.807
MANU	1	1.0521	0.3690	8.1305	0.0044	0.173850	2.864
MINC	1	0.5242	0.3801	1.9022	0.1678	0.064841	1.689
AGRIC	1	1.2093	0.7399	2.6713	0.1022	0.042222	3.351
PROF	1	−0.8937	0.3148	8.0587	0.0045	−0.210615	0.409
AGRI	1	−1.4630	0.5510	7.0510	0.0079	−0.058354	0.232
CLER	1	−0.7716	0.3159	5.9647	0.0146	−0.182341	0.462
SALE	1	−0.7754	0.3565	4.7310	0.0296	−0.099421	0.461
SERV	1	−0.8430	0.3215	6.8757	0.0087	−0.141020	0.430
PROD	1	−0.7361	0.3293	4.9971	0.0254	−0.190363	0.479

Association of Predicted Probabilities and Observed Responses

Concordant	=	81.3%	Somers' D	=	0.636
Discordant	=	17.7%	Gamma	=	0.643
Tied	=	1.0%	Tau-a	=	0.060
(22636030 pairs)			c	=	0.818

YEAR OF SURVEY = 1991   COUNTRY = Denmark

Number of Observations: 12538	Value	FIXED	Count
	1	0	11560
	2	1	978

Criteria for Assessing Model Fit

Criterion	Intercept Only	Intercept and Covariates	Chi-Square for Covariates
AIC	6869.423	5734.047	—
SC	6876.860	6031.508	—
−2 LOG L	6867.423	5654.047	1213.376 with 39 DF (p = 0.0001)
Score	—	—	1672.665 with 39 DF (p = 0.0001)

Analysis of Maximum Likelihood Estimates

Variable	DF	Parameter Estimate	Standard Error	Wald Chi-Square	Pr > Chi-Square	Standardised Estimate	Odds Ratio
INTERCPT	1	3.1548	0.5590	31.8499	0.0001	—	23.449
FEMALE	1	−0.1893	0.1014	3.4841	0.0620	−0.052189	0.828
HEAD	1	−0.3859	0.1861	4.2994	0.0381	−0.098653	0.680
SPOUSE	1	−0.6761	0.2375	8.1046	0.0044	−0.164625	0.509
AGE1	1	−1.4078	0.2015	48.8070	0.0001	−0.202999	0.245
AGE2	1	−0.6458	0.1628	15.7464	0.0001	−0.105379	0.524
AGE3	1	−0.5745	0.1447	15.7621	0.0001	−0.107899	0.563
AGE4	1	0.0547	0.1536	0.1269	0.7217	0.010002	1.056
AGE6	1	0.3013	0.1643	3.3646	0.0666	0.056065	1.352
AGE7	1	0.6915	0.1872	13.6422	0.0002	0.127748	1.997
AGE8	1	0.4116	0.1981	4.3164	0.0377	0.061396	1.509
AGE9	1	0.4374	0.2163	4.0905	0.0431	0.058697	1.549
AGE10	1	−0.3693	0.2414	2.3412	0.1260	−0.032930	0.691
AGE11	1	0.8188	0.3346	5.9864	0.0144	0.041331	2.268
NATIOEC	1	−0.2367	0.4487	0.2782	0.5979	−0.009444	0.789
NONEC	1	−0.7394	0.2280	10.5154	0.0012	−0.050573	0.477
EDUC1	1	−0.0445	0.1115	0.1594	0.6897	−0.010863	0.956
EDUC2	1	−0.0129	0.1006	0.0163	0.8983	−0.003544	0.987
SINGLE	1	−0.4359	0.1219	12.7745	0.0004	−0.115651	0.647
WIDISEP	1	−0.3323	0.1548	4.6084	0.0318	−0.051895	0.717
UNEMPAGO	1	−2.4998	0.1235	409.4453	0.0001	−0.232636	0.082
EDUCAGO	1	−1.3708	0.1280	114.6972	0.0001	−0.135675	0.254
INACAGO	1	−1.3151	0.2591	25.7650	0.0001	−0.063201	0.268
EMSELF	1	−0.5153	0.6154	0.7012	0.4024	−0.016802	0.597
OSERV	1	−0.7796	0.3242	5.7819	0.0162	−0.200083	0.459
PUBLIC	1	−0.2520	0.3499	0.5187	0.4714	−0.034470	0.777
BANK	1	0.4326	0.3539	1.4948	0.2215	0.068929	1.541
TRANS	1	0.3396	0.3570	0.9049	0.3415	0.048703	1.404
TRADE	1	0.1396	0.3340	0.1748	0.6759	0.026840	1.150
BUILD	1	0.00306	0.3566	0.0001	0.9932	0.000375	1.003
OMAN	1	0.5950	0.3420	3.0268	0.0819	0.103746	1.813
MANU	1	0.7498	0.3607	4.3197	0.0377	0.113512	2.116
MINC	1	0.9595	0.5283	3.2987	0.0693	0.075673	2.610
AGRIC	1	−0.2620	0.4252	0.3799	0.5377	−0.022681	0.769
PROF	1	−0.1939	0.2694	0.5180	0.4717	−0.048348	0.824
AGRI	1	0.5589	0.4452	1.5765	0.2093	0.042995	1.749
CLER	1	0.0991	0.2807	0.1247	0.7240	0.020630	1.104
SALE	1	0.1385	0.3007	0.2122	0.6450	0.020578	1.149
SERV	1	0.1060	0.2810	0.1422	0.7061	0.017557	1.112
PROD	1	−0.0902	0.2711	0.1106	0.7394	−0.022831	0.914

Association of Predicted Probabilities and Observed Responses

Concordant	=	79.4%	Somers' D	=	0.597
Discordant	=	19.7%	Gamma	=	0.602
Tied	=	0.9%	Tau-a	=	0.086
(11305680 pairs)			c	=	0.798

YEAR OF SURVEY = 1991   COUNTRY = France

Number of Observations: 54704	Value	FIXED	Count
	1	0	49649
	2	1	5055

Criteria for Assessing Model Fit

Criterion	Intercept Only	Intercept and Covariates	Chi-Square for Covariates
AIC	33707.355	27096.423	—
SC	33716.264	27434.991	—
−2 LOG L	33705.355	27020.423	6684.932 with 37 DF (p = 0.0001)
Score	—	—	9209.707 with 37 DF (p = 0.0001)

Analysis of Maximum Likelihood Estimates

Variable	DF	Parameter Estimate	Standard Error	Wald Chi-Square	Pr > Chi-Square	Standardised Estimate	Odds Ratio
INTERCPT	1	3.5353	0.8474	17.4072	0.0001	—	34.307
FEMALE	1	−0.1995	0.0520	14.7410	0.0001	−0.054781	0.819
HEAD	1	0.3267	0.0501	42.5569	0.0001	0.089057	1.386
SPOUSE	1	0.1562	0.0646	5.8523	0.0156	0.040134	1.169
AGE1	1	−2.1372	0.1082	390.1442	0.0001	−0.131779	0.118
AGE2	1	−1.3704	0.0659	432.7285	0.0001	−0.233471	0.254
AGE3	1	−0.7358	0.0608	146.2954	0.0001	−0.148114	0.479
AGE4	1	−0.1903	0.0645	8.6990	0.0032	−0.038104	0.827
AGE6	1	0.2658	0.0721	13.5752	0.0002	0.053053	1.304
AGE7	1	0.4768	0.0884	29.1058	0.0001	0.079465	1.611
AGE8	1	0.7199	0.1023	49.5462	0.0001	0.110829	2.054
AGE9	1	0.5348	0.1132	22.3252	0.0001	0.067762	1.707
AGE10	1	0.4155	0.2125	3.8225	0.0506	0.024113	1.515
AGE11	1	0.3702	0.3561	1.0808	0.2985	0.009185	1.448
NATIOEC	1	0.2338	0.1096	4.5501	0.0329	0.021854	1.263
NONEC	1	−0.2526	0.0905	7.7837	0.0053	−0.023894	0.777
EDUC1	0	0	—	—	—	—	—
EDUC2	0	0	—	—	—	—	—
SINGLE	1	−0.3782	0.0461	67.2469	0.0001	−0.094338	0.685
WIDISEP	1	−0.3352	0.0760	19.4693	0.0001	−0.049804	0.715
UNEMPAGO	1	−1.7872	0.2684	44.3407	0.0001	−0.189709	0.167
EDUCAGO	1	−0.9711	0.2731	12.6411	0.0004	−0.075018	0.379
INACAGO	1	0.2912	0.2644	1.2132	0.2707	0.038733	1.338
EMSELF	1	−2.3296	1.2807	3.3088	0.0689	−0.009511	0.097
OSERV	1	−0.6845	0.1668	16.8391	0.0001	−0.161758	0.504
PUBLIC	1	−0.6699	0.1707	15.3981	0.0001	−0.107915	0.512
BANK	1	0.1782	0.1732	1.0590	0.3035	0.029750	1.195
TRANS	1	−0.00774	0.1786	0.0019	0.9654	−0.001069	0.992
TRADE	1	0.3118	0.1701	3.3623	0.0667	0.062472	1.366
BUILD	1	0.1900	0.1769	1.1531	0.2829	0.026789	1.209
OMAN	1	0.1905	0.1730	1.2133	0.2707	0.030866	1.210
MANU	1	0.1230	0.1721	0.5113	0.4746	0.020907	1.131
MINC	1	0.2828	0.1962	2.0771	0.1495	0.028976	1.327
AGRIC	1	−0.2066	0.2378	0.7548	0.3849	−0.013352	0.813
PROF	1	−1.1712	0.7182	2.6595	0.1029	−0.259050	0.310
AGRI	1	−1.2769	0.7335	3.0306	0.0817	−0.090330	0.279
CLER	1	−0.9397	0.7183	1.7111	0.1908	−0.222795	0.391
SALE	1	−0.7528	0.7219	1.0873	0.2971	−0.107045	0.471
SERV	1	−1.0587	0.7184	2.1714	0.1406	−0.207324	0.347
PROD	1	−1.2169	0.7184	2.8692	0.0903	−0.311546	0.296

Association of Predicted Probabilities and Observed Responses

Concordant	=	80.1%	Somers' D	=	0.610
Discordant	=	19.1%	Gamma	=	0.614
Tied	=	0.8%	Tau-a	=	0.102
(250975695 pairs)			c	=	0.805

YEAR OF SURVEY = 1991   COUNTRY = Germany (West)

Number of Observations: 90147

Value	FIXED	Count
1	0	85284
2	1	4863

Criteria for Assessing Model Fit

Criterion	Intercept Only	Intercept and Covariates	Chi-Square for Covariates
AIC	37858.656	32443.211	—
SC	37868.065	32819.579	—
−2 LOG L	37856.656	32363.211	5493.444 with 39 DF (p = 0.0001)
Score	—	—	8416.004 with 39 DF (p = 0.0001)

Analysis of Maximum Likelihood Estimates

Variable	DF	Parameter Estimate	Standard Error	Wald Chi-Square	Pr > Chi-Square	Standardised Estimate	Odds Ratio
INTERCPT	1	3.6019	0.2995	144.6527	0.0001	—	36.666
FEMALE	1	0.0712	0.0424	2.8233	0.0929	0.019381	1.074
HEAD	1	−0.1942	0.0470	17.0876	0.0001	−0.052586	0.824
SPOUSE	1	−0.6044	0.0747	65.4501	0.0001	−0.142166	0.546
AGE1	1	−2.0660	0.0901	525.5561	0.0001	−0.149284	0.127
AGE2	1	−0.9501	0.0685	192.3551	0.0001	−0.165043	0.387
AGE3	1	−0.5335	0.0633	71.1369	0.0001	−0.105384	0.587
AGE4	1	−0.3693	0.0641	33.1526	0.0001	−0.069714	0.691
AGE6	1	0.1268	0.0739	2.9400	0.0864	0.022865	1.135
AGE7	1	0.2037	0.0783	6.7723	0.0093	0.035229	1.226
AGE8	1	0.2124	0.0770	7.6027	0.0058	0.038898	1.237
AGE9	1	0.3245	0.0942	11.8559	0.0006	0.047583	1.383
AGE10	1	−0.1184	0.1242	0.9083	0.3406	−0.009586	0.888
AGE11	1	0.1819	0.2471	0.5415	0.4618	0.005529	1.199
NATIOEC	1	0.0379	0.1122	0.1143	0.7353	0.003144	1.039
NONEC	1	−0.4274	0.0651	43.1593	0.0001	−0.051502	0.652
EDUC1	1	0.1600	0.0522	9.4152	0.0022	0.030932	1.174
EDUC2	1	0.6831	0.0377	328.8355	0.0001	0.185607	1.980
SINGLE	1	−0.7264	0.0522	193.4931	0.0001	−0.181750	0.484
WIDISEP	1	−0.7098	0.0712	99.3215	0.0001	−0.101320	0.492
UNEMPAGO	1	−1.7620	0.0863	416.9670	0.0001	−0.095728	0.172
EDUCAGO	1	−1.9552	0.0712	753.4054	0.0001	−0.115767	0.142
INACAGO	1	−1.1815	0.0750	248.0087	0.0001	−0.086716	0.307
EMSELF	1	−0.0367	0.1619	0.0515	0.8205	−0.002031	0.964
OSERV	1	−1.2343	0.1697	52.8985	0.0001	−0.262828	0.291
PUBLIC	1	−0.8138	0.1739	21.9010	0.0001	−0.126692	0.443
BANK	1	−0.3843	0.1772	4.7024	0.0301	−0.056869	0.681
TRANS	1	−0.3659	0.1811	4.0809	0.0434	−0.048623	0.694
TRADE	1	−0.6394	0.1717	13.8685	0.0002	−0.126602	0.528
BUILD	1	−0.1738	0.1809	0.9239	0.3365	−0.024067	0.840
OMAN	1	−0.4231	0.1736	5.9428	0.0148	−0.070565	0.655
MANU	1	−0.0476	0.1713	0.0773	0.7810	−0.010146	0.953
MINC	1	−0.3415	0.1818	3.5279	0.0603	−0.043680	0.711
AGRIC	1	−0.4436	0.2393	3.4373	0.0637	−0.024794	0.642
PROF	1	0.2102	0.0650	10.4660	0.0012	0.045169	1.234
AGRI	1	−0.3148	0.1578	3.9806	0.0460	−0.018963	0.730
CLER	1	0.4689	0.0671	48.7873	0.0001	0.108709	1.598
SALE	1	0.4914	0.0861	32.5798	0.0001	0.073126	1.635
SERV	1	0.7174	0.0767	87.4904	0.0001	0.115371	2.049
PROD	1	0.4127 .	0.0674	37.4790	0.0001	0.107841	1.511

Association of Predicted Probabilities and Observed Responses

Concordant	=	76.0%	Somers' D	=	0.532
Discordant	=	22.8%	Gamma	=	0.539
Tied	=	1.3%	Tau-a	=	0.054
(414736092 pairs)			c	=	0.766

YEAR OF SURVEY = 1991   COUNTRY = Greece

Number of Observations: 26520

	Value	FIXED	Count
	1	0	22579
	2	1	3941

Criteria for Assessing Model Fit

Criterion	Intercept Only	Intercept and Covariates	Chi-Square for Covariates
AIC	22293.724	18321.190	—
SC	22301.909	18648.616	—
−2 LOG L	22291.724	18241.190	4050.533 with 39 DF (p = 0.0001)
Score	—	—	4722.818 with 39 DF (p = 0.0001)

Analysis of Maximum Likelihood Estimates

Variable	DF	Parameter Estimate	Standard Error	Wald Chi-Square	Pr > Chi-Square	Standardised Estimate	Odds Ratio
INTERCPT	1	4.0397	0.5176	60.9213	0.0001	—	56.810
FEMALE	1	−0.2862	0.0615	21.6246	0.0001	−0.075268	0.751
HEAD	1	0.0775	0.0700	1.2240	0.2686	0.021273	1.081
SPOUSE	1	−0.0981	0.0997	0.9682	0.3251	−0.021473	0.907
AGE1	1	−0.4971	0.1156	18.4924	0.0001	−0.046847	0.608
AGE2	1	−0.4325	0.0866	24.9343	0.0001	−0.073953	0.649
AGE3	1	−0.3647	0.0774	22.2180	0.0001	−0.070826	0.694
AGE4	1	−0.1443	0.0765	3.5612	0.0591	−0.028600	0.866
AGE6	1	0.0599	0.0803	0.5572	0.4554	0.011371	1.062
AGE7	1	−0.0322	0.0849	0.1437	0.7046	−0.005349	0.968
AGE8	1	−0.0525	0.0873	0.3610	0.5479	−0.008239	0.949
AGE9	1	−0.00054	0.0982	0.0000	0.9956	−0.000070926	0.999
AGE10	1	−0.00657	0.1471	0.0020	0.9644	−0.000524	0.993
AGE11	1	0.4518	0.2944	2.3549	0.1249	0.015191	1.571
NATIOEC	1	−0.0321	0.4461	0.0052	0.9427	−0.000727	0.968
NONEC	1	−0.9117	0.1417	41.3816	0.0001	−0.052985	0.402
EDUC1	1	−0.2214	0.0618	12.8154	0.0003	−0.060067	0.801
EDUC2	1	0.0157	0.0642	0.0597	0.8070	0.003956	1.016
SINGLE	1	−0.3109	0.0735	17.9007	0.0001	−0.077813	0.733
WIDISEP	1	−0.4174	0.1026	16.5416	0.0001	−0.044693	0.659
UNEMPAGO	1	−1.8248	0.1004	330.2102	0.0001	−0.134808	0.161
EDUCAGO	1	−1.5634	0.1280	149.2799	0.0001	−0.094690	0.209
INACAGO	1	−1.3930	0.0892	244.0462	0.0001	−0.121137	0.248
EMSELF	1	−0.6874	0.1716	16.0465	0.0001	−0.033985	0.503
OSERV	1	−0.6161	0.1914	10.3624	0.0013	−0.137055	0.540
PUBLIC	1	0.5582	0.2111	6.9901	0.0082	0.099742	1.747
BANK	1	−0.6614	0.2040	10.5114	0.0012	−0.087653	0.516
TRANS	1	−0.6895	0.1927	12.8087	0.0003	−0.112370	0.502
TRADE	1	−0.8519	0.1891	20.3056	0.0001	−0.170715	0.427
BUILD	1	−2.7045	0.1872	208.7986	0.0001	−0.416572	0.067
OMAN	1	−0.5911	0.1887	9.8153	0.0017	−0.116864	0.554
MANU	1	−0.2756	0.2105	1.7135	0.1905	−0.031058	0.759
MINC	1	−0.2799	0.2154	1.6885	0.1938	−0.030067	0.756
AGRIC	1	−1.2816	0.2831	20.4918	0.0001	−0.088731	0.278
PROF	1	−1.0675	0.3899	7.4971	0.0062	−0.230021	0.344
AGRI	1	−2.3557	0.4389	28.8101	0.0001	−0.174381	0.095
CLER	1	−0.6845	0.3900	3.0811	0.0792	−0.154883	0.504
SALE	1	−1.0076	0.3953	6.4970	0.0108	−0.137407	0.365
SERV	1	−1.7060	0.3908	19.0590	0.0001	−0.300155	0.182
PROD	1	−1.3534	0.3897	12.0608	0.0005	−0.363093	0.258

Association of Predicted Probabilities and Observed Responses

Concordant	=	79.2%	Somers' D	=	0.590
Discordant	=	20.2%	Gamma	=	0.593
Tied	=	0.6%	Tau-a	=	0.149
(88983839 pairs)			c	=	0.795

YEAR OF SURVEY = 1991   COUNTRY = Ireland

Number of Observations: 35587

	Value	FIXED	Count
	1	0	32620
	2	1	2967

Criteria for Assessing Model Fit

Criterion	Intercept Only	Intercept and Covariates	Chi-Square for Covariates
AIC	20424.058	16463.326	—
SC	20432.537	16802.516	—
−2 LOG L	20422.058	16383.326	4038.731 with 39 DF (p = 0.0001)
Score	—	—	6001.132 with 39 DF (p = 0.0001)

Analysis of Maximum Likelihood Estimates

Variable	DF	Parameter Estimate	Standard Error	Wald Chi-Square	Pr > Chi-Square	Standardised Estimate	Odds Ratio
INTERCPT	1	3.8406	0.3546	117.2724	0.0001	—	46.553
FEMALE	1	−0.4501	0.0575	61.1835	0.0001	−0.121821	0.638
HEAD	1	0.1973	0.0839	5.5305	0.0187	0.054187	1.218
SPOUSE	1	−0.0599	0.1069	0.3139	0.5753	−0.013329	0.942
AGE1	1	−0.6793	0.1157	34.4820	0.0001	−0.091979	0.507
AGE2	1	−0.4339	0.0971	19.9562	0.0001	−0.089525	0.648
AGE3	1	−0.0940	0.0902	1.0868	0.2972	−0.018915	0.910
AGE4	1	0.00193	0.0882	0.0005	0.9825	0.000377	1.002
AGE6	1	−0.0578	0.0917	0.3984	0.5279	−0.009978	0.944
AGE7	1	0.0391	0.1011	0.1500	0.6985	0.006056	1.040
AGE8	1	0.0359	0.1111	0.1042	0.7469	0.004868	1.037
AGE9	1	0.3482	0.1394	6.2381	0.0125	0.039396	1.416
AGE10	1	0.1376	0.1683	0.6683	0.4136	0.011886	1.148
AGE11	1	0.0631	0.2715	0.0541	0.8161	0.002722	1.065
NATIOEC	1	−0.0906	0.1414	0.4106	0.5217	−0.007264	0.913
NONEC	1	−0.8699	0.2138	16.5617	0.0001	−0.035942	0.419
EDUC1	1	−0.3648	0.0764	22.7941	0.0001	−0.099622	0.694
EDUC2	1	−0.1126	0.0704	2.5584	0.1097	−0.029359	0.894
SINGLE	1	0.0285	0.0886	0.1032	0.7480	0.007729	1.029
WIDISEP	1	0.1565	0.1790	0.7643	0.3820	0.011536	1.169
UNEMPAGO	1	−2.7227	0.0705	1493.4554	0.0001	−0.257628	0.066
EDUCAGO	1	−2.0278	0.0848	571.6042	0.0001	−0.196623	0.132
INACAGO	1	−2.5774	0.0850	919.5911	0.0001	−0.208843	0.076
EMSELF	1	−1.0850	0.2603	17.3720	0.0001	−0.036503	0.338
OSERV	1	−0.4689	0.1658	7.9956	0.0047	−0.107427	0.626
PUBLIC	1	−0.1161	0.1827	0.4034	0.5254	−0.015806	0.890
BANK	1	0.1105	0.1764	0.3927	0.5309	0.017396	1.117
TRANS	1	0.6769	0.2027	11.1448	0.0008	0.086728	1.968
TRADE	1	0.1498	0.1693	0.7831	0.3762	0.032116	1.162
BUILD	1	−0.0590	0.1724	0.1170	0.7323	−0.008460	0.943
OMAN	1	1.0554	0.1761	35.9186	0.0001	0.196426	2.873
MANU	1	1.0486	0.1890	30.7802	0.0001	0.158596	2.854
MINC	1	0.5241	0.2001	6.8602	0.0088	0.059908	1.689
AGRIC	1	0.0801	0.2579	0.0966	0.7560	0.007213	1.083
PROF	1	−0.7820	0.1753	19.8984	0.0001	−0.168240	0.458
AGRI	1	−0.8942	0.2535	12.4394	0.0004	−0.084380	0.409
CLER	1	−0.4103	0.1754	5.4754	0.0193	−0.090045	0.663
SALE	1	−0.4165	0.1874	4.9413	0.0262	−0.067167	0.659
SERV	1	−0.4808	0.1781	7.2891	0.0069	−0.088732	0.618
PROD	1	−0.8315	0.1763	22.2417	0.0001	−0.212720	0.435

Association of Predicted Probabilities and Observed Responses

Concordant	=	79.8%	Somers' D	=	0.605
Discordant	=	19.3%	Gamma	=	0.611
Tied	=	1.0%	Tau-a	=	0.092
(96783540 pairs)			c	=	0.802

YEAR OF SURVEY = 1991   COUNTRY = Italy

Number of Observations: 50716

Value	FIXED	Count
1	0	47938
2	1	2778

Criteria for Assessing Model Fit

Criterion	Intercept Only	Intercept and Covariates	Chi-Square for Covariates
AIC	21540.435	18764.485	—
SC	21549.269	19011.837	—
–2 LOG L	21538.435	18708.485	2829.950 with 27 DF (p = 0.0001)
Score	—	—	3470.544 with 27 DF (p = 0.0001)

Analysis of Maximum Likelihood Estimates

Variable	DF	Parameter Estimate	Standard Error	Wald Chi-Square	Pr > Chi-Square	Standardised Estimate	Odds Ratio
INTERCPT	1	4.2808	0.4311	98.6153	0.0001	—	72.296
FEMALE	1	−0.4859	0.0592	67.2752	0.0001	−0.128856	0.615
HEAD	1	0.2417	0.0924	6.8409	0.0089	0.066562	1.273
SPOUSE	1	−0.1874	0.1115	2.8286	0.0926	−0.041858	0.829
AGE1	1	−1.0995	0.1092	101.3656	0.0001	−0.115457	0.333
AGE2	1	−0.8462	0.0909	86.6874	0.0001	−0.147714	0.429
AGE3	1	−0.6086	0.0821	54.9296	0.0001	−0.115477	0.544
AGE4	1	−0.1924	0.0847	5.1649	0.0230	−0.036856	0.825
AGE6	1	0.3607	0.0967	13.9243	0.0002	0.069382	1.434
AGE7	1	0.4625	0.1084	18.2115	0.0001	0.078709	1.588
AGE8	1	0.2168	0.1016	4.5571	0.0328	0.035170	1.242
AGE9	1	0.1639	0.1165	1.9785	0.1596	0.020962	1.178
AGE10	1	−0.3082	0.1442	4.5672	0.0326	−0.025538	0.735
AGE11	1	0.8594	0.2110	16.5922	0.0001	0.034160	2.362
NATIOEC	0	0	—	—	—	—	—
NONEC	0	0	—	—	—	—	—
EDUC1	1	−0.6600	0.1025	41.4327	0.0001	−0.176429	0.517
EDUC2	1	−0.2265	0.1047	4.6820	0.0305	−0.057238	0.797
SINGLE	1	−0.2902	0.0920	9.9534	0.0016	−0.073023	0.748
WIDISEP	1	−0.2533	0.1241	4.1660	0.0412	−0.026233	0.776
UNEMPAGO	0	0	—	—	—	—	—
EDUCAGO	0	0	—	—	—	—	—
INACAGO	0	0	—	—	—	—	—
EMSELF	0	0	—	—	—	—	—
OSERV	1	−1.4769	0.3602	16.8166	0.0001	−0.339499	0.228
PUBLIC	1	−0.7098	0.3673	3.7354	0.0533	−0.126685	0.492
BANK	1	−0.7011	0.3742	3.5110	0.0610	−0.087706	0.496
TRANS	1	−0.6025	0.3774	2.5485	0.1104	−0.082241	0.547
TRADE	1	−1.0721	0.3612	8.8096	0.0030	−0.198493	0.342
BUILD	1	−1.6845	0.3612	21.7531	0.0001	−0.274925	0.186
OMAN	1	−0.4417	0.3643	1.4695	0.2254	−0.080207	0.643
MANU	1	−0.3016	0.3733	0.6527	0.4192	−0.045311	0.740
MINC	1	−0.2698	0.3949	0.4669	0.4944	−0.029308	0.763
AGRIC	1	−3.0126	0.3606	69.7891	0.0001	−0.361945	0.049
PROF	0	0	—	—	—	—	—
AGRI	0	0	—	—	—	—	—
CLER	0	0	—	—	—	—	—
SALE	0	0	—	—	—	—	—
SERV	0	0	—	—	—	—	—
PROD	0	0	—	—	—	—	—

Association of Predicted Probabilities and Observed Responses

Concordant = 77.6%   Somers' D = 0.564
Discordant = 21.2%   Gamma = 0.570
Tied = 1.2%   Tau-a = 0.058
(133171764 pairs)   c = 0.782

YEAR OF SURVEY = 1991   COUNTRY = Luxembourg

Number of Observations: 8830

Value	FIXED	Count
1	0	8617
2	1	213

Criteria for Assessing Model Fit

Criterion	Intercept Only	Intercept and Covariates	Chi-Square for Covariates
AIC	2009.507	1728.132	—
SC	2016.593	2011.568	—
−2 LOG L	2007.507	1648.132	359.376 with 39 DF (p = 0.0001)
Score	—	—	626.101 with 39 DF (p = 0.0001)

Analysis of Maximum Likelihood Estimates

Variable	DF	Parameter Estimate	Standard Error	Wald Chi-Square	Pr > Chi-Square	Standardised Estimate	Odds Ratio
INTERCPT	1	25.4760	1.1340	504.6829	0.0001	—	999.000
FEMALE	1	−0.5594	0.2056	7.4056	0.0065	−0.147675	0.572
HEAD	1	0.1175	0.2314	0.2578	0.6117	0.032309	1.125
SPOUSE	1	−0.8243	0.3186	6.6942	0.0097	−0.176484	0.439
AGE1	1	−0.9276	0.3676	6.3659	0.0116	−0.092204	0.396
AGE2	1	−0.3630	0.2970	1.4937	0.2216	−0.068421	0.696
AGE3	1	0.0491	0.2807	0.0307	0.8610	0.010226	1.050
AGE4	1	0.00237	0.2787	0.0001	0.9932	0.000468	1.002
AGE6	1	0.2953	0.3141	0.8842	0.3471	0.054253	1.344
AGE7	1	0.3562	0.3582	0.9891	0.3200	0.059452	1.428
AGE8	1	1.0542	0.5076	4.3124	0.0378	0.153915	2.870
AGE9	1	0.5398	0.5479	0.9707	0.3245	0.062986	1.716
AGE10	1	−0.3133	0.6310	0.2466	0.6195	−0.019162	0.731
AGE11	0	−21.4849	—	—	—	—	0.000
NATIOEC	1	−0.1319	0.1741	0.5741	0.4486	−0.033821	0.876
NONEC	1	−1.3942	0.2938	22.5164	0.0001	−0.115211	0.248
EDUC1	1	0.2832	0.2952	0.9200	0.3375	0.066972	1.327
EDUC2	1	−0.0594	0.2856	0.0433	0.8352	−0.011563	0.942
SINGLE	1	−0.4813	0.2701	3.1763	0.0747	−0.124446	0.618
WIDISEP	1	−0.9898	0.3104	10.1701	0.0014	−0.146563	0.372
UNEMPAGO	1	−2.3625	0.3047	60.1272	0.0001	−0.127184	0.094
EDUCAGO	1	−2.2559	0.2605	74.9901	0.0001	−0.162304	0.105
INACAGO	1	−1.2724	0.2961	18.4636	0.0001	−0.095279	0.280
EMSELF	1	−0.9452	1.0564	0.8006	0.3709	−0.025385	0.389
OSERV	1	−1.3503	1.0320	1.7117	0.1908	−0.291276	0.259
PUBLIC	1	−0.9961	1.0448	0.9090	0.3404	−0.170645	0.369
BANK	1	−0.6573	1.0412	0.3986	0.5278	−0.123937	0.518
TRANS	1	−0.4189	1.0719	0.1527	0.6959	−0.061245	0.658
TRADE	1	−0.7389	1.0347	0.5100	0.4752	−0.156197	0.478
BUILD	1	0.0407	1.0839	0.0014	0.9700	0.006678	1.042
OMAN	1	0.6071	1.1422	0.2825	0.5950	0.085851	1.835
MANU	1	0.3958	1.1524	0.1180	0.7312	0.041092	1.486
MINC	1	0.5492	1.1757	0.2182	0.6404	0.086075	1.732
AGRIC	1	−0.7140	1.3884	0.2644	0.6071	−0.029243	0.490
PROF	1	1.4093	0.5271	7.1474	0.0075	0.260841	4.093
AGRI	1	0.8747	0.8556	1.0451	0.3066	0.054677	2.398
CLER	1	1.7559	0.5266	11.1168	0.0009	0.439563	5.788
SALE	1	1.8627	0.6393	8.4883	0.0036	0.241559	6.441
SERV	1	1.4609	0.5580	6.8556	0.0088	0.275735	4.310
PROD	1	0.8808	0.5582	2.4903	0.1145	0.233260	2.413

Association of Predicted Probabilities and Observed Responses

Concordant	=	81.6%	Somers' D	=	0.651
Discordant	=	16.5%	Gamma	=	0.664
Tied	=	2.0%	Tau-a	=	0.031
(1835421 pairs)			c	=	0.826

YEAR OF SURVEY = 1991   COUNTRY = Netherlands

Number of Observations: 28699

Value	FIXED	Count
1	0	26226
2	1	2473

Criteria for Assessing Model Fit

Criterion	Intercept Only	Intercept and Covariates	Chi-Square for Covariates
AIC	16853.276	14057.552	—
SC	16861.541	14388.136	—
−2 LOG L	16851.276	13977.552	2873.724 with 39 DF (p = 0.0001)
Score	—	—	3289.909 with 39 DF (p = 0.0001)

Analysis of Maximum Likelihood Estimates

Variable	DF	Parameter Estimate	Standard Error	Wald Chi-Square	Pr > Chi-Square	Standardised Estimate	Odds Ratio
INTERCPT	1	2.5043	0.4205	35.4612	0.0001	—	12.235
FEMALE	1	−0.1659	0.0636	6.8070	0.0091	−0.044589	0.847
HEAD	1	−0.2923	0.0712	16.8423	0.0001	−0.079938	0.747
SPOUSE	1	−0.8998	0.1179	58.2595	0.0001	−0.199765	0.407
AGE1	1	−0.8223	0.1328	38.3520	0.0001	−0.113679	0.439
AGE2	1	−0.8665	0.1032	70.5430	0.0001	−0.168077	0.420
AGE3	1	−0.3842	0.0937	16.8171	0.0001	−0.077140	0.681
AGE4	1	−0.2373	0.0942	6.3491	0.0117	−0.045524	0.789
AGE6	1	0.0460	0.1024	0.2016	0.6534	0.008646	1.047
AGE7	1	0.5208	0.1333	15.2765	0.0001	0.084739	1.683
AGE8	1	0.5218	0.1591	10.7555	0.0010	0.071054	1.685
AGE9	1	0.5457	0.2039	7.1615	0.0074	0.060058	1.726
AGE10	1	0.4271	0.3552	1.4456	0.2292	0.022480	1.533
AGE11	1	0.8162	0.3717	4.8211	0.0281	0.022512	2.262
NATIOEC	1	−0.6645	0.2017	10.8544	0.0010	−0.036011	0.515
NONEC	1	−1.0202	0.1409	52.4141	0.0001	−0.069495	0.361
EDUC1	1	0.3343	0.0809	17.0705	0.0001	0.089513	1.397
EDUC2	1	0.4655	0.0692	45.3206	0.0001	0.126267	1.593
SINGLE	1	−0.9911	0.0883	126.1204	0.0001	−0.262487	0.371
WIDISEP	1	−0.8921	0.1322	45.5094	0.0001	−0.101456	0.410
UNEMPAGO	1	−2.2679	0.1170	375.6150	0.0001	−0.144950	0.104
EDUCAGO	1	−1.6282	0.0747	475.6606	0.0001	−0.259579	0.196
INACAGO	1	−1.4625	0.0730	400.9959	0.0001	−0.228851	0.232
EMSELF	1	−1.5081	0.4124	13.3765	0.0003	−0.033622	0.221
OSERV	1	0.5852	0.1644	12.6680	0.0004	0.143780	1.795
PUBLIC	1	0.4229	0.1831	5.3344	0.0209	0.056133	1.526
BANK	1	0.7894	0.1719	21.0923	0.0001	0.132963	2.202
TRANS	1	0.9170	0.1854	24.4545	0.0001	0.126619	2.502
TRADE	1	0.9079	0.1668	29.6449	0.0001	0.194067	2.479
BUILD	1	1.2548	0.1951	41.3796	0.0001	0.178740	3.507
OMAN	1	0.8540	0.1746	23.9137	0.0001	0.138005	2.349
MANU	1	0.7532	0.1799	17.5328	0.0001	0.110248	2.124
MINC	1	1.0073	0.2302	19.1442	0.0001	0.095005	2.738
AGRIC	1	0.4117	0.3020	1.8587	0.1728	0.031342	1.509
PROF	1	−0.4524	0.1635	7.6524	0.0057	−0.106627	0.636
AGRI	1	0.0231	0.3104	0.0055	0.9408	0.001833	1.023
CLER	1	−0.2180	0.1655	1.7350	0.1878	−0.048036	0.804
SALE	1	0.6661	0.1827	13.2992	0.0003	0.110248	1.947
SERV	1	0.1261	0.1719	0.5380	0.4633	0.023268	1.134
PROD	1	−0.4888	0.1669	8.5788	0.0034	−0.118748	0.613

Association of Predicted Probabilities and Observed Responses

Concordant	=	79.7%	Somers' D	=	0.600
Discordant	=	19.7%	Gamma	=	0.604
Tied	=	0.7%	Tau-a	=	0.094
(64856898 pairs)			c	=	0.800

YEAR OF SURVEY = 1991   COUNTRY = Portugal

Number of Observations: 27130

Value	FIXED	Count
1	0	22455
2	1	4675

Criteria for Assessing Model Fit

Criterion	Intercept Only	Intercept and Covariates	Chi-Square for Covariates
AIC	24936.828	20335.071	—
SC	24945.036	20663.407	—
−2 LOG L	24934.828	20255.071	4679.757 with 39 DF (p = 0.0001)
Score	—	—	5247.661 with 39 DF (p = 0.0001)

Analysis of Maximum Likelihood Estimates

Variable	DF	Parameter Estimate	Standard Error	Wald Chi-Square	Pr > Chi-Square	Standardised Estimate	Odds Ratio
INTERCPT	1	4.5880	0.5164	78.9268	0.0001	—	98.296
FEMALE	1	−0.3471	0.0498	48.6391	0.0001	−0.094462	0.707
HEAD	1	0.1048	0.0681	2.3688	0.1238	0.028546	1.110
SPOUSE	1	−0.0356	0.0755	0.2226	0.6371	−0.008379	0.965
AGE1	1	−1.4194	0.0893	252.7242	0.0001	−0.224335	0.242
AGE2	1	−1.2002	0.0808	220.6966	0.0001	−0.217326	0.301
AGE3	1	−0.9138	0.0742	151.6682	0.0001	−0.171739	0.401
AGE4	1	−0.3200	0.0773	17.1262	0.0001	−0.060439	0.726
AGE6	1	0.2262	0.0906	6.2413	0.0125	0.039817	1.254
AGE7	1	0.5070	0.1028	24.3161	0.0001	0.082638	1.660
AGE8	1	0.3881	0.1068	13.1988	0.0003	0.056569	1.474
AGE9	1	0.5453	0.1269	18.4550	0.0001	0.067645	1.725
AGE10	1	0.5135	0.1552	10.9485	0.0009	0.049602	1.671
AGE11	1	−0.00778	0.2208	0.0012	0.9719	−0.000419	0.992
NATIOEC	1	0.1571	0.4007	0.1538	0.6950	0.003966	1.170
NONEC	1	−0.3025	0.2233	1.8343	0.1756	−0.011516	0.739
EDUC1	1	−0.7259	0.1117	42.2393	0.0001	−0.154637	0.484
EDUC2	1	−0.6418	0.1147	31.3239	0.0001	−0.098178	0.526
SINGLE	1	−0.2604	0.0634	16.8626	0.0001	−0.064377	0.771
WIDISEP	1	−0.2586	0.1093	5.6006	0.0180	−0.028507	0.772
UNEMPAGO	1	−2.1437	0.0880	593.6416	0.0001	−0.188938	0.117
EDUCAGO	1	−1.6525	0.1054	245.6774	0.0001	−0.120844	0.192
INACAGO	1	−1.6673	0.1133	216.7087	0.0001	−0.108170	0.189
EMSELF	1	−1.2762	0.1395	83.7030	0.0001	−0.068418	0.279
OSERV	1	−0.2816	0.1911	2.1703	0.1407	−0.060836	0.755
PUBLIC	1	−0.1289	0.1957	0.4336	0.5102	−0.020808	0.879
BANK	1	−0.4160	0.2006	4.2992	0.0381	−0.051498	0.660
TRANS	1	−0.3112	0.1993	2.4374	0.1185	−0.041256	0.733
TRADE	1	−0.4561	0.1883	5.8648	0.0154	−0.089283	0.634
BUILD	1	−0.7538	0.1878	16.1022	0.0001	−0.121401	0.471
OMAN	1	0.0807	0.1873	0.1857	0.6666	0.017659	1.084
MANU	1	−0.1913	0.1974	0.9391	0.3325	−0.023499	0.826
MINC	1	−0.0348	0.2017	0.0298	0.8629	−0.004123	0.966
AGRIC	1	−0.9775	0.2409	16.4632	0.0001	−0.111158	0.376
PROF	1	−1.2123	0.4320	7.8745	0.0050	−0.217497	0.298
AGRI	1	−1.5098	0.4577	10.8822	0.0010	−0.171901	0.221
CLER	1	−0.7537	0.4312	3.0542	0.0805	−0.162966	0.471
SALE	1	−0.9580	0.4365	4.8170	0.0282	−0.126626	0.384
SERV	1	−1.2903	0.4328	8.8874	0.0029	−0.253186	0.275
PROD	1	−1.1829	0.4307	7.5418	0.0060	−0.322508	0.306

Association of Predicted Probabilities and Observed Responses

Concordant	=	79.8%	Somers' D	=	0.601
Discordant	=	19.7%	Gamma	=	0.604
Tied	=	0.5%	Tau-a	=	0.171
(104977125 pairs)			c	=	0.800

YEAR OF SURVEY = 1991   COUNTRY = Spain

Number of Observations: 46863

Value	FIXED	Count
1	0	31467
2	1	15396

Criteria for Assessing Model Fit

Criterion	Intercept Only	Intercept and Covariates	Chi-Square for Covariates
AIC	59343.138	42328.796	—
SC	59351.893	42678.996	—
–2 LOG L	59341.138	42248.796	17092.341 with 39 DF (p = 0.0001)
Score	—	—	15694.983 with 39 DF (p = 0.0001)

Analysis of Maximum Likelihood Estimates

Variable	DF	Parameter Estimate	Standard Error	Wald Chi-Square	Pr > Chi-Square	Standardised Estimate	Odds Ratio
INTERCPT	1	4.4148	0.3625	148.3323	0.0001	—	82.666
FEMALE	1	−0.3500	0.0375	87.0030	0.0001	−0.090429	0.705
HEAD	1	0.2211	0.0472	21.9349	0.0001	0.060931	1.247
SPOUSE	1	−0.1201	0.0620	3.7554	0.0526	−0.023545	0.887
AGE1	1	−1.9975	0.0758	694.5216	0.0001	−0.235303	0.136
AGE2	1	−1.6297	0.0531	941.1266	0.0001	−0.308176	0.196
AGE3	1	−1.0285	0.0471	476.5762	0.0001	−0.204209	0.358
AGE4	1	−0.3858	0.0466	68.4017	0.0001	−0.075666	0.680
AGE6	1	0.1917	0.0534	12.8795	0.0003	0.033320	1.211
AGE7	1	0.3108	0.0576	29.1113	0.0001	0.049575	1.364
AGE8	1	0.4212	0.0629	44.8678	0.0001	0.060765	1.524
AGE9	1	0.5753	0.0668	74.2396	0.0001	0.079470	1.778
AGE10	1	0.9164	0.0907	102.1877	0.0001	0.096264	2.500
AGE11	1	−0.4534	0.2728	2.7622	0.0965	−0.012946	0.635
NATIOEC	1	−0.4686	0.2844	2.7159	0.0994	−0.010929	0.626
NONEC	1	−0.5128	0.2785	3.3895	0.0656	−0.011671	0.599
EDUC1	1	−0.2413	0.0573	17.7496	0.0001	−0.063041	0.786
EDUC2	1	−0.0307	0.0561	0.2999	0.5839	−0.006671	0.970
SINGLE	1	−0.2511	0.0482	27.1712	0.0001	−0.066154	0.778
WIDISEP	1	−0.6055	0.0727	69.3563	0.0001	−0.058928	0.546
UNEMPAGO	1	−2.2867	0.0501	2083.4658	0.0001	−0.344312	0.102
EDUCAGO	1	−1.5536	0.0928	280.4315	0.0001	−0.121641	0.211
INACAGO	1	−1.5609	0.0689	512.9211	0.0001	−0.145586	0.210
EMSELF	1	−1.2105	0.1137	113.3728	0.0001	−0.062896	0.298
OSERV	1	−0.8003	0.1475	29.4383	0.0001	−0.178367	0.449
PUBLIC	1	−0.5504	0.1515	13.1975	0.0003	−0.081072	0.577
BANK	1	−1.0205	0.1528	44.5876	0.0001	−0.132665	0.360
TRANS	1	−0.7314	0.1523	23.0463	0.0001	−0.092038	0.481
TRADE	1	−1.0609	0.1454	53.2240	0.0001	−0.222893	0.346
BUILD	1	−2.2396	0.1448	239.2841	0.0001	−0.385985	0.107
OMAN	1	−0.6764	0.1455	21.5969	0.0001	−0.122087	0.508
MANU	1	−0.6818	0.1480	21.2116	0.0001	−0.102185	0.506
MINC	1	−0.7426	0.1542	23.1905	0.0001	−0.083363	0.476
AGRIC	1	−1.5049	0.1819	68.4242	0.0001	−0.190032	0.222
PROF	1	−0.7885	0.1929	16.7101	0.0001	−0.149973	0.455
AGRI	1	−1.9370	0.2231	75.3561	0.0001	−0.242238	0.144
CLER	1	−0.5683	0.1911	8.8417	0.0029	−0.117374	0.567
SALE	1	−0.8023	0.1962	16.7206	0.0001	−0.114409	0.448
SERV	1	−1.2479	0.1932	41.7103	0.0001	−0.242398	0.287
PROD	1	−1.3152	0.1912	47.3205	0.0001	−0.356409	0.268

Association of Predicted Probabilities and Observed Responses

Concordant	=	85.0%	Somers' D	=	0.702
Discordant	=	14.7%	Gamma	=	0.704
Tied	=	0.3%	Tau-a	=	0.310
(484465932 pairs)			c	=	0.851

189

YEAR OF SURVEY = 1991   COUNTRY = United Kingdom

Number of Observations: 59831   Value   FIXED   Count
                                      1   0   56666
                                      2   1   3165

Criteria for Assessing Model Fit

| | | Intercept | |
| | Intercept | and | |
Criterion	Only	Covariates	Chi-Square for Covariates
AIC	24767.759	21389.762	—
SC	24776.759	21749.734	—
–2 LOG L	24765.759	21309.762	3455.997 with 39 DF (p = 0.0001)
Score	—	—	4814.838 with 39 DF (p = 0.0001)

Analysis of Maximum Likelihood Estimates

Variable	DF	Parameter Estimate	Standard Error	Wald Chi-Square	Pr > Chi-Square	Standardised Estimate	Odds Ratio
INTERCPT	1	2.2985	0.2144	114.9724	0.0001	—	9.959
FEMALE	1	−0.0829	0.0597	1.9257	0.1652	−0.022842	0.920
HEAD	1	0.3297	0.0891	13.6833	0.0002	0.090819	1.390
SPOUSE	1	−0.1453	0.1128	1.6604	0.1975	−0.037586	0.865
AGE1	1	−0.6499	0.1040	39.0406	0.0001	−0.088352	0.522
AGE2	1	−0.00281	0.0902	0.0010	0.9752	−0.000484	0.997
AGE3	1	0.3096	0.0847	13.3775	0.0003	0.057177	1.363
AGE4	1	0.0695	0.0811	0.7351	0.3913	0.012549	1.072
AGE6	1	0.2376	0.0833	8.1415	0.0043	0.044773	1.268
AGE7	1	0.2669	0.0921	8.3928	0.0038	0.045316	1.306
AGE8	1	0.2987	0.0986	9.1808	0.0024	0.046994	1.348
AGE9	1	0.0944	0.1028	0.8440	0.3583	0.013369	1.099
AGE10	1	−0.1260	0.1124	1.2552	0.2626	−0.013567	0.882
AGE11	1	1.3690	0.1223	125.3378	0.0001	0.081619	3.931
NATIOEC	1	−0.3946	0.1380	8.1764	0.0042	−0.025791	0.674
NONEC	1	−0.6539	0.1245	27.5805	0.0001	−0.042959	0.520
EDUC1	1	0.5817	0.0548	112.4878	0.0001	0.157625	1.789
EDUC2	1	0.4224	0.0653	41.9054	0.0001	0.090694	1.526
SINGLE	1	−0.2604	0.0895	8.4691	0.0036	−0.060635	0.771
WIDISEP	1	−0.1640	0.1048	2.4474	0.1177	−0.020263	0.849
UNEMPAGO	1	−1.5798	0.0909	302.2018	0.0001	−0.115006	0.206
EDUCAGO	1	−1.4987	0.0739	411.6668	0.0001	−0.140037	0.223
INACAGO	1	−1.6309	0.0653	624.0700	0.0001	−0.155236	0.196
EMSELF	1	−1.5869	0.1322	144.0094	0.0001	−0.079407	0.205
OSERV	1	−0.1058	0.1348	0.6165	0.4323	−0.024734	0.900
PUBLIC	1	0.1824	0.1503	1.4740	0.2247	0.026331	1.200
BANK	1	0.3531	0.1441	6.0022	0.0143	0.060758	1.423
TRANS	1	0.5048	0.1642	9.4534	0.0021	0.068024	1.657
TRADE	1	−0.1103	0.1363	0.6547	0.4184	−0.024263	0.896
BUILD	1	0.1774	0.1631	1.1826	0.2768	0.021065	1.194
OMAN	1	0.5465	0.1527	12.8151	0.0003	0.087067	1.727
MANU	1	0.6684	0.1546	18.6881	0.0001	0.112399	1.951
MINC	1	0.8263	0.2112	15.3121	0.0001	0.083067	2.285
AGRIC	1	0.2009	0.2512	0.6399	0.4237	0.012113	1.223
PROF	1	−1.1574	0.1165	98.6463	0.0001	−0.246117	0.314
AGRI	1	−1.2861	0.2181	34.7736	0.0001	−0.082785	0.276
CLER	1	−0.9872	0.1171	71.0871	0.0001	−0.221291	0.373
SALE	1	−0.7036	0.1285	29.9770	0.0001	−0.114238	0.495
SERV	1	−1.1023	0.1188	86.0304	0.0001	−0.210887	0.332
PROD	1	−0.8792	0.1209	52.8572	0.0001	−0.210908	0.415

Association of Predicted Probabilities and Observed Responses

Concordant	=	77.7%	Somers' D	=	0.566
Discordant	=	21.1%	Gamma	=	0.573
Tied	=	1.3%	Tau-a	=	0.057
(179347890 pairs)			c	=	0.783

NOTES

1 INTRODUCTION

1 The pattern is less clear-cut if differential age structures are taken into account. It is well known that most European countries have a working population which is older than in the United States. Older populations are responsible for longer tenure profiles of workers. Furthermore, tenure profiles look different if attention is paid to male and female shares in the labour force as well as to the percentage of service sector jobs with shorter duration.

2 However, it has been emphasised in recent debates of developments in the United States that short-tenure profiles of employment can have a negative impact on investment in on-the-job training schemes (Stern and Ritzen 1991, Schömann 1994).

3 This perspective has been further developed in Janoski and Hicks (1994).

4 We are particularly indebted to Geoffrey Thomas, Laurent Freysson and Didier Lesnicki from Eurostat for their kind assistance in carrying out the calculations for this project and in sharing their knowledge of difficulties in data collection for the survey.

2 LEGAL AND ECONOMIC THEORIES OF LABOUR MARKET REGULATION

1 See also Däubler's 1989 proposal of a European Charter of Basic Rights (*Europäische Grundrechtsakte*) centred around concerns with social protection, in particular art. 37: fixed-term contracts are only legal if they are concluded either on request of the employee or in order to replace another employee who is temporarily absent.

2 These statements appear to have been developed mainly reflecting on the practice in smaller firms. But even in larger firms, the closing down of units or organisational reshuffling reflects only indirectly a change in relative prices.

3 In Spain, with its high percentage of fixed-term employees, the transition rates after fixed-term employment in more permanent jobs are still quite low (compare Alba-Ramírez 1991 for more details).

4 The figure is based on a mathematical model originally developed by Mincer (1974). E_s, and E_{s-d} refer to earnings streams for a person with s years of schooling and $s-d$ years of schooling. The dashed line for E_s reflects the possible interruptions of the working life due to spells of unemployment after expirations of fixed-term contracts.

5 It has to be mentioned that the time structure of discrete shifts in regulation does not create the focus of our analysis in Chapter 3 which is mainly concerned with comparative aspects of labour law reform. However, some temporal effects are investigated in Chapter 4 of the *International Handbook of Labour Market Policy and Evaluation* which discusses longitudinal designs in evaluation studies (Schmid *et al.* 1996).

6 It appears astonishing to the authors that most reports on fixed-term employment within or across countries do not treat this wage dimension in more detail despite the indications of economic theories to do so. This is a serious neglect particularly for economic studies of this subject like the analyses presented by the OECD (1993, 1996).

7 In this analysis we do not dispose of commonly collected earnings data to carry out these analyses. We can rely only on a few countries' reported results. This should be remedied eventually with the availability of the European Household Panel to researchers provided by Eurostat.

8 Whether such a way of accounting is useful in forward looking systems of human resource accounting is questionable, but we cannot deal with these aspects in more detail in the context of this study.

3 EMPLOYMENT PROTECTION SYSTEMS AND REGULATION OF FIXED-TERM CONTRACTS IN THE EUROPEAN UNION

1 Belgian labour law has so far not been consolidated into one Labour Law Code.

2 The 'Global Crisis Plan' on employment, competitiveness, and social security, which the Belgian government launched in October 1993 following the breakdown of nego-tiations on a tripartite Social Pact and which first provoked a general strike in November 1993 but then led to new negotiations between the three national actors in December, includes as a key element the reduction of notice periods. See EIRR 239, December 1993: 5, and EIRR 240, January 1994: 4–5.

3 Law of 16 March 1971. However, the dismissal of a pregnant employee for reasons other than pregnancy is not excluded.

4 The original law of 1985 specified that a full-time career break should normally last between six and twelve months, and that a part-time career break is allowed for up to five years. In sectors and companies with a collective agreement regulating the right to a career break, the employee is exempted from having to seek consent from his or her employer for the break. A Royal Decree issued in 1990 allows for a reduced-length career break of a minimum of 12 weeks after the birth of a child for both parents. See 'Belgium: Career breaks after the birth of a child', EIRR 198, July 1990: 3.

5 On the legislative history of regulations on temporary work and fixed-term contracts see Rojot 1993: 91–120, Lyon-Caen 1993, and Bonnetête and Clavel 1990.

6 The *Günstigkeitsprinzip* is currently challenged by concession bargaining at company level, e.g. the 1994 agreement concluded at VW. See Adomeit 1994.

7 The 1972 law on temporary employment was created in reaction to a decision of the Federal Constitutional Court outlawing the previous general ban on temporary work agencies (BVerfGE 21: 261–71). Prior to this verdict, temporary agencies were con-sidered an infringement on the public monopoly of labour exchange exercised exclusively by the official labour administrations.

8 The German trade unions view this law as an infringement of their constitutional right of autonomous collective bargaining. However, the Federal Constitutional Court has recently decided the constitutional right of academic freedom ranks higher than autonomous collective bargaining. Decision of the FCC of 30 July 1996.

9 Trade unions argued, without success, that the deregulation approach was unconsti-tutional. See Mückenberger 1985a: 518.

10 Kravaritou 1993: 91: 'Greek labour legislation is riddled with inconsistencies, dogged by a lack of precision, the indiscriminate spread of provisions over a wide range of het-erogeneous texts, clogged with a surfeit of details or, by contrast, parsimonious to a degree, it expresses itself in rough-hewn demotics.'

11 Redmond calculates that at least 20 per cent of Irish employees are excluded from dis-missal protection. Redmond 1982: 132.

12 The Italian law requires for a few types of employment a written contract, e.g. mariners.

13 The Italian law went beyond the minimum standards of the European Commission Directive on Collective Dismissals. See Galantino 1991: 427.

14 It has been reported that Dutch employers increasingly try to use summary dismissal in order to circumvent the administrative authorisation procedure. See Smitskam 1990.

15 The general obligation for the employer to provide work derives from decision-making of the *Hoge Raad* against 'de-activisation' (*non-actief stellen*). See Kronke 1990: 125 and 246.

16 Also known as the Dutch 'revolving door' policy. See Asscher-Vonk 1993: 222.

17 The Constitutional Court found the Bills to be formally and materially in violation of the Constitution. The Bills were seen as failing to conform with the requirement of full consultation with the unions prior to any amendment to labour legislation, and also with the fundamental rights to work and employment enshrined in the Constitution. See EIRR 174, July 1988: 8.

18 The following remarks do not always apply to Northern Ireland, which has its own employment regulations.

19 The report of the Royal Commission on Trade Unions and Employers' Associations was issued in 1968.

20 The strict contractual test in constructive dismissal was introduced in *Western Excavating Ltd.* v. *Sharp* [1978] ICR 221 (Lord Denning, Court of Appeal).

21 TUPE was the British response to the European Commission Directive on transfer of undertakings.

22 See *Polkey* v. *A.E. Dayton Services* [1987] ICR 142. This House of Lords decision reversed the liberal approach to procedures adopted by the Employment Appeal Tribunal in *British Labour Pump* v. *Byrne* [1979] IRLR 94.

23 The British median compensation amounts are published annually in the *Employment Gazette* issued by the Department of Employment (since 1995 Department of Education and Employment). See also Hepple and Fredman 1992: 171–2.

24 *Wickens* v. *Champion* [1984] ICR 365 (Employment Appeal Tribunal), and *Ironmonger* v. *Movefield Ltd.* [1988] IRLR 461 (Employment Appeal Tribunal). See also the land-mark decision on agency work before the enactment of the Employment Agencies Act 1973: *Construction Industry Training Board* v *Labour Force Ltd.* [1970] 3 *All England Reports* 220 (Divisional Court, Queen's Bench Division).

4 FIXED-TERM EMPLOYMENT PATTERNS IN THE EUROPEAN UNION

1 This explains why there have been comparatively few studies which take a comparative perspective (an exception is Walwei 1991). The predominant type of analysis is still single country studies.

2 This can be assumed to be the case until the labour force survey of 1991. In 1992 some countries introduced the duration of a fixed-term contract as an additional item for the first time and, apparently, the non-response rates on this question reached in some instances very high percentages (in Germany for example close to 50 per cent).

3 In Belgium the number of women entering the labour market grew every year since 1983. Similarly the growth in fixed-term employment is based on the steady growth of women working with fixed-term contracts. Only in 1987, when the Law on Temporary Work was introduced, was there a heavy decline in both male and female fixed-term employment of 24 per cent compared to the previous year (compare annual rates of change in Table 4.8).

4 It needs to be kept in mind that in Luxembourg fixed-term employment is of very little importance.

5 Unfortunately this has also led to much confusion in attempts to disentangle the labour market processes at work. Also the complexity of legal systems, where part-time work and fixed-term contracts are very different domains, has increased confusion rather than contributed to meaningful comparisons.

6 The staff of Eurostat, Division of the Labour Force Survey advised us not to use a more differentiated classification. These difficulties of the comparisons of educational levels are currently under revision at Eurostat.

7 Data for Italy is not available on this item.

5 MULTIVARIATE ANALYSIS OF COUNTRY PATTERNS

1 Since in the interpretation we discuss mainly the issue of who is likely to hold a fixed-term contract we report the opposite sign of coefficients as in the appendix which shows estimates of the probability to hold a permanent job.

2 It should be kept in mind that we excluded all apprentices from the analyses since they are considered to be in education rather than in employment. This is of particular importance in the analysis for West Germany since the number of fixed-term employments is reduced to about a half compared to other publications of Eurostat on the same issue.

3 In the summary Table 5.1 we report the number of negative and significant coefficients for the young age groups. A value of + 4 \ means that the four first age groups have a higher risk of fixed-term employment than the reference group (age group 5 between 35 and 39 years of age) and the sign indicates that the size of the coefficient is decreasing for older age groups.

4 Due to problems in the regrouping of educational levels there are no data for France in 1991 at Eurostat to be used in this analysis.

5 Unfortunately the ELFS does not provide the information whether respondents were on a fixed-term contract or on a permanent appointment in the previous year, although this information might be retrieved from some Member States.

6 In Italy these questions have not been included in the Labour Force Survey in 1991 and the previous years.

7 Nomenclature générale des activités économiques dans les Communautés européennes.

8 The privatisation of branches of British water and energy industries might have been accompanied by a larger use of fixed-term employment in these reference category industries which causes effects in other services and public administration to become statistically insignificant after 1988.

6 FIXED-TERM CONTRACTS AND THEIR RELATIONSHIP TO MACRO-ECONOMIC CONDITIONS

1 Source: El Pais, 17 March 1997

2 Ministerio de Trabajo y Seguridad Social, Guia Laboral 1995; see also Chapter 3, Spain, for a further description of reasons for fixed-term contracts.

3 Source: El Pais, 7 April 1997, InforMISEP Policies, Issues No. 58.

7 CONCLUSIONS

1 Discussed in Chapter 4 and in Rogowski and Schömann 1996.

2 Legally, jobs grant basic rights to employees, including protection against discrimination. A particular problem is the issue of unpaid household activity. See the discussion of Schmid (1993, 1994) within the framework of the equality and efficiency trade-off.

3 See also the recent report by the European Commission (1997) on equal opportunities for women which deals with the subject in many more aspects. Unfortunately the mechanisms for how unequal treatment occurs are treated in much less detail.

4 A more detailed assessment of privatisation programmes is a research project of its own, since not only the number of industries but also the size and the number of firms in such sectors which have been privatised have to be considered.

5 Recent developments of a Directive on part-time work and part-time work in the transition to retirement show the slow movement in this direction.

6 Since an 'implicit' agreement on the critical point in the balance of equity and efficiency on the labour market is something like a shared vision for the future development of regulation and European policy-making, not just in the domain of labour market policy but for social policy at large, we indirectly opt for a political solution first, which then could be implemented through Directives. In retrospect it appears as if the Council Directive 91/383 of 25 June 1991 on atypical employment was trying to harmonise developments without the political consensus being established before.

REFERENCES

Adamy, W. (1988) 'Deregulierung des Arbeitsmarktes – Zwischenbilanz des Beschäftigungsförderungsgesetzes', *WSI-Mitteilungen* 8, 475–82.

Adomeit, K. (1994) 'Arbeitsplätze und Solidarität', *Neue Juristische Wochenschrift* 1994, 837–8.

Akerlof, G. A. (1982) 'Labor contracts as partial gift exchange', *Quarterly Journal of Economics* 97: 543–69.

Alaluf, M. (1989) 'Atypical employment and the trade unions in Belgium', in G. Rodgers and J. Rodgers (eds) *Precarious Jobs in Labour Market Regulation. The Growth of Atypical Employment in Western Europe*, Geneva: ILO (International Institute for Labour Studies), 249–66.

Alba-Ramírez, A. (1991) 'Fixed-term employment contracts in Spain. Labor market flexibility or segmentation?' Working Paper 91–29, Departamento de Economia Universidad Carlos III de Madrid.

Asscher-Vonk, I. (1993) 'The Netherlands', in R. Blanpain (ed.) *Temporary Work and Labour Law*, Deventer: Kluwer, 211–32.

Auer, P. (1993) 'Sequences in rigidity and flexibility and their implications for the Italian labor market', in C. F. Buechtemann (ed.) *Employment Security and Labor Market Behavior – Interdisciplinary Approaches and International Evidence*, Ithaca, NY: ILR Press, 414–22.

Becker, G. S. (1964) *Human Capital*, New York: Columbia University Press.

Bentolila, S. and Saint-Paul, G. (1991) 'The macroeconomic impact of flexible labor contracts with an application to Spain', Documento de Trabajo 9106 del CEMFI, Madrid.

Bertola, G. (1990) 'Job security, employment and wages', *European Economic Review* 34(4): 851–79.

Bettio, F. and Villa, P. (1989) 'Non-wage work and disguised wage employment in Italy', in G. Rodgers and J. Rodgers (eds), *Precarious Jobs in Labour Market Regulation. The Growth of Atypical Employment in Western Europe*, Geneva: ILO (International Institute for Labour Studies), 149–78.

Bispinck, R. (1993) 'Kündigungsfristen und Kündigungsschutz in Tarifverträgen', *WSI-Mitteilungen* 5: 322–5.

Blanc-Jouvan, X. (1993) 'Du bon usage de la méthode comparative en droit du travail', in *Mélanges offerts à André Colomer*, Paris: Litec, 73–85.

Blanke, T. (1994) Autonomisation of labour law through judicial interpretation', in

R. Rogowski and T. Wilthagen (eds), *Reflexive Labour Law. Studies in Industrial Relations and Employment Regulation*, Deventer: Kluwer, 207–47.

Blankenburg, E. and Rogowski, R. (1986) 'German labour courts and the British industrial tribunal system. A socio-legal comparison of degrees of judicialisation', *Journal of Law and Society* 13: 67–92.

Blankenburg, E., Schönholz, S. and Rogowski, R. (1979) *Zur Soziologie des Arbeitsgerichtsverfahrens. Die Verrechtlichung von Arbeitskonflikten*, Darmstadt: Luchterhand.

Blanpain, R. (1985) 'Belgium', *International Encyclopedia for Labour Law and Industrial Relations*, Vol. II, Deventer: Kluwer.

Blanpain, R. (ed.) (1993) *Temporary Work and Labour Law*, Deventer: Kluwer.

Blanpain, R. and Köhler, E. (1988) *Legal and Contractual Limitations to Working-Time in the European Community Member States*, Deventer: Kluwer.

Blanpain, R. and Oversteyns, B. (1993) 'Belgium', in R. Blanpain (ed.) *Temporary Work and Labour Law*, Deventer: Kluwer, 45–75.

Bonnetête, M.-C. and Clavel, M.-F. (1990) 'Contrat à durée determinée', *Liaisons sociales*, numéro spécial 25 October 1990.

Bosch, G. (1986) 'Hat das Normalarbeitsverhältnis eine Zukunft?', *WSI-Mitteilungen* 3: 163–76.

Büchtemann, C. F. (1984) 'Zusätzliche Beschäftigung durch befristete Arbeitsverträge?', *Wirtschaftsdienst* 10: 542–8.

Büchtemann, C. F. (1993) 'Employment security and deregulation: the West German experience', in C. F. Büchtemann (ed.) *Employment Security and Labor Market Behavior – Interdisciplinary Approaches and International Evidence*, Ithaca, NY: ILR Press, 272–96.

Büchtemann, C. F. and Höland, A. (1989) 'Befristete Arbeitsverträge nach dem Beschäftigungsförderungsgesetz', Research Report 183, Bonn: Bundesminister für Arbeit und Sozialordnung.

Calmfors, L. (1994) 'Active labour market policy and unemployment – a framework for the analysis of crucial design features', in *OECD Economic Studies* 22: 7–4.

Casey, B. (1991) 'Survey evidence on trends in non-standard employment', in A. Pollert (ed.) *Farewell to Flexibility*, Oxford: Basil Blackwell, 179–99.

Coase, R. (1937) 'The nature of the firm', *Economica* 4: 386–405.

Coase, R. (1984) 'The new institutional economics', *Journal of Institutional and Theoretical Economics* 140: 229–31.

Collins, H. (1993) *Justice in Dismissal. The Law of Termination in Employment*, Oxford: Clarendon.

Commission of the European Communities (1991) 'Arbeitsmarktentwicklungen in der Gemeinschaft – Ergebnisse einer Umfrage bei Unternehmern und Arbeitnehmern', *Europäische Wirtschaft* 47: 7–164.

Commission of the European Communities (1992) 'The regulation of working conditions in the Member States of the European Community', Vols 1 and 2, *Social Europe*, Supplement 4/92 and 5/93.

Commission of the European Communities (1993) 'Spanien: Die Arbeitsmarktreform in Spanien', *inforMISEP* 44: 4–5.

Commission of the European Communities (1994) 'Employment in Europe', Luxembourg: Office for Official Publications of the European Communities.

Contratti di formazione/lavoro, Quaderni di Formazione, ISFOL, 2/84 and 5–6/85.

Däubler, W. (1986) 'Labour law research in the Federal Republic of Germany', in S. Edlund (ed.) *Labour Law Research in Twelve Countries*, Stockholm: Almqvist & Wiksell (The Swedish Work Environment Fund), 81–100.

Däubler, W. (1989) *Sozialstaat EG? Die andere Dimension des Binnenmarktes (Strategien und Optionen für die Zukunft Europas)*, Gütersloh: Bertelsmann.

Deakin, S. (1990) 'Equality under a market order: the Employment Act 1989', *Industrial Law Journal* 19: 1–19.

Deakin, S. and Mückenberger, U. (1989) 'From deregulation to a European floor of rights: labour law, flexibilisation and the European single market', *Zeitschrift für internationales Arbeits- und Sozialrecht* 3: 153–207.

de Leede, L. J. M. (1987) 'Flexibilisierung des Arbeitsrechts', *Zeitschrift für internationales Arbeits- und Sozialrecht* 1: 340–1.

Delsen, L. (1995) *Atypical Employment: An International Perspective – Causes, Consequences and Policy*, Groningen: Wolters-Noordhoff.

Department of Trade and Industry (1985) *Burdens on Business*, London: HMSO.

Dickens, L. (1994) 'Deregulation and employment rights in Great Britain', in R. Rogowski and T. Wilthagen (eds), *Reflexive Labour Law. Studies in Industrial Relations and Employment Regulation*, Deventer: Kluwer, 225–47.

Dickens, L., Hart, M., Jones, M. and Weekes, B. (1986) *Dismissed. A Study of Unfair Dismissal and the Industrial Tribunal System*, Oxford: Blackwell.

Doeringer, P. B. and Piore, M. H. (1971) *Internal Labor Markets and Manpower Analysis*, Lexington, MA: D. C. Heath.

Domergue, D. (1987) 'La convention de conversion', *Droit Social*, 250–5.

El Pais, 17 March 1997 and 7 April 1997.

Emerson, M. (1988) 'Regulation or deregulation of the labour market', *European Economic Review* 32(4): 775–817.

Enclos, P. (1990) 'Les conventions de conversion', *Droit social*, 335–8.

Esping-Andersen, G. (1990) *The Three Worlds of Welfare Capitalism*, Cambridge: Polity Press.

European Commission (1993) *Employment in Europe*, Bruxelles.

European Commission (1997) *Equal Opportunities for Women and Men in the European Union 1996. Annual Report*, Luxembourg: Office for Official Publications of the European Union.

European Foundation for the Improvement of Living and Working Conditions (1992) 'New forms of work and activity. Survey of experiences at establishment level in eight European countries', Dublin.

European Industrial Relations Review (EIRR) (1977) 'Individual dismissals in Ireland. New dimension to Irish labour law', 42: 2–3 and 32–6.

European Industrial Relations Review (1987) 'Spain: Regulations governing employment contracts', 158: 15–17.

European Industrial Relations Review (1988) 'Portugal: Labour Bills rule unconstitutional', 174: 8.

European Industrial Relations Review (1988) 'Survey of fixed-term contracts', 179: 22–3.

European Industrial Relations Review (1989) 'Belgium: Trends in the level of collective bargaining' Part I and Part II 183: 24–6 and 186: 20–2.

European Industrial Relations Review (1989) 'Luxembourg: Law on fixed-term contracts', 191: 13–14.

European Industrial Relations Review (1990) 'Belgium: New law regulates part-time work', 195: 17–19.

European Industrial Relations Review (1990) 'Belgium: Career breaks after the birth of a child', 198: 3.

European Industrial Relations Review (1990) 'Greece: Employee participation', 195: 21–2.

European Industrial Relations Review (1991) 'Greece: Strike law reformed', 204: 20–1.

European Industrial Relations Review (1991) 'Ireland: The Programme for Economic and Social Progress', 207: 16–19.

European Industrial Relations Review (1992) 'Belgium: National agreement on out-placement', 221: 18–20.

European Industrial Relations Review (1992) 'France: First assessment of the 1990 law on precarious employment', 222: 21–2.

European Industrial Relations Review (1992) 'Spain: Radical labour market reform', 220: 13.

European Industrial Relations Review (1992) 'Portugal: Termination of contract', 224: 18–21.

European Industrial Relations Review (1993) 'Belgium: Radical government plan replaces social pact', 239: 5.

European Industrial Relations Review (1993) 'Denmark: Bargaining breakthrough in industry', 230: 5–6.

European Industrial Relations Review (1993) 'Greece: Education, training and recruit-ment', 238: 30–1.

European Industrial Relations Review (1993) 'Greece: Third-party intervention', 228: 26–7.

European Industrial Relations Review (1993) 'Luxembourg: New law on part-time work-ing', 232: 31–2.

European Industrial Relations Review (1993) 'Luxembourg: New employment promotion law', 237: 29.

European Industrial Relations Review (1993) 'Spain: Dismissals and the politics of flex-ibility', 236: 24–6.

European Industrial Relations Review (1994) 'Belgium: Union protests fail to halt global plan', 240: 4–5.

European Industrial Relations Review (1994) 'France: Five-year employment law: part one', 242: 17–18.

European Industrial Relations Review (1994) 'Ireland: Programme for Competitiveness and Work', 243: 14–16.

European Industrial Relations Review (1994) 'Spain: Labour market reform', 242: 22.

European Industrial Relations Review (1994) 'Harmonisation of notice periods', 241: 22–3.

Eurostat (1988) *Labour Force Survey. Methods and Definitions*, Luxembourg: Office of Official Publications of the European Communities.

Eurostat (1991) *A Social Portrait of Europe*, Luxembourg: Office of Official Publications of the European Communities.

Eurostat (1992) *Labour Force Survey. Methods and Definition*, Luxembourg: Office of Official Publications of the European Communities.

Eurostat (1993), *Labour Force Survey 1983–1991*, Luxembourg: Office of Official Publications of the European Communities.

Eurostat (1997) 'Labour Force Survey. Principal Results', Statistics in Focus Population and Social Conditions 1997 No. 8, Luxembourg: Office of Official Publications of the European Communities.

Falke, J., Höland, A., Rohde, B. and Zimmermann, G. (1981) 'Kündigungspraxis und Kündigungsschutz in der Bundesrepublik Deutschland', Research Report 47, Bonn: Bundesminmister für Arbeit und Sozialordnung.

Fourcade, B. (1992) 'Evolution des situations d'emploi particulières de 1945 à 1990', *Travail et Emploi* 52: 4–19.

Franz, W. (1994) 'Chancen und Risiken einer Flexibilisierung des Arbeitsrechts aus ökonomischer Sicht', *Zeitschrift für Arbeitsrecht* 25: 439–62.

Galantino, L. (1991) 'Der Kündigungsschutz in Italien', *Zeitschrift für internationales Arbeits- und Sozialrecht* 5: 414–39.

Gaul, F. (1990) *Der Betriebsübergang*, Munich: Beck.

Gold, M. (1993) 'Overview of the social dimension', in M. Gold (ed.) *The Social Dimension. Employment Policy in the European Community*, London: Macmillan, 10–40.

Guergoat, J-C. and Hocquaux, C. (1991) 'L'utilisation du CDD et de l'intérim par les entreprises', *Dossiers statistiques du travail et de l'emploi*, Paris: SES-Ministère des Affaires Sociales et de l'Emploi, 75–6.

Hashimoto, M. and Raisian, J. (1992) 'Aspects of labor market flexibility in Japan and the United States', in K. Koshiro (ed.) *Employment Security and Labor Market Flexibility – An International Perspective*, Detroit: Wayne State University Press, 78–101.

Heilmann, J. (1986) 'Labour law research in the Federal Republic of Germany: current status and future trends', in S. Edlund (ed.) *Labour Law Research in Twelve Countries*, Stockholm: Almqvist & Wiksell (The Swedish Work Environment Fund), 101–21.

Henry, R. and Guergoat, J-C. (1987) 'Le salaire des travailleurs intérimaires en octobre 1984', *Dossiers statistiques du travail et de l'emploi* 33, Paris: SES-Ministère des Affaires Sociales et de L'Emploi.

Hepple, B. (1993) 'United Kingdom', in R. Blanpain (ed.) *Temporary Work and Labour Law*, Deventer: Kluwer, 259–83.

Hepple, B. and Fredman, S. (1992) *Labour Law and Industrial Relations in Great Britain* 2nd ed., Deventer: Kluwer, 40–50.

Höland, A. (1985) *Das Verhalten des Betriebsrats bei Kündigungen*, Frankfurt/New York: Campus.

Hunt, J. (1993) 'Firing costs, employment fluctuations and average employment: an examination of Germany', unpublished manuscript, Department of Economics, Yale University.

InforMISEP Employment Observatory Policies, Issue No. 42, 43, 44, 45, 46, 47, 53, 57, 58, 59, Bruxelles: Commission of the European Communities.

Infratest (1994) 'Befristete Beschäftigung und Arbeitsmarkt. Empirische Untersuchung über befristete Arbeitsverträge nach dem Beschäftigungsförderungsgesetz' (BeschFG 1985/1990), Report, Munich.

Jacobs, A. (1992) 'The Netherlands', in B. Veniziani (ed.) *Law, Collective Bargaining and Labour Flexibility in EC Countries*, Rome: ASAP, 437–65.

Jacobsen, P. (1987) 'Aspects of flexibility of labour law', *Zeitschrift für internationales Arbeits- und Sozialrecht* 1: 250–6.

Jacobsen, P. (1993) 'Denmark', in R. Blanpain (ed.) *Temporary Work and Labour Law*, Deventer: Kluwer, 77–90.

Janoski, T. (1991) 'Synthetic strategies in comparative sociological research: methods and problems of internal and external analysis', in C. Ragin (ed.) *Issues and Alternatives in Comparative Social Research*, Leiden: E. J. Brill, 59–81.

Janoski, T. and Hicks, A. M. (1994) *The Comparative Political Economy of the Welfare State*, Cambridge: Cambridge University Press.

Jessop, B., Kastendiek, H., Nielsen, K. and Pedersen, O. K. (eds) (1991) *The Politics of Flexibility: Restructuring State and Industry in Britain, Germany and Scandinavia*, Aldershot: Elgar.

Jimeno, J. F. and Toharia, L. (1991) 'Productivity and wage effects of fixed-term employment: evidence from Spain', unpublished manuscript, Department of Economics, London School of Economics.

Jimeno, J. F. and Toharia, L. (1993) 'Spanish labour markets: institutions and outcomes', in J. Hartog and J. Theeuwes (eds) *Labour Market Contracts and Institutions. A Cross-National Comparison*, Amsterdam: North-Holland, 299–322.

Jimeno, J. F. and Toharia, L. (1994) *Unemployment and labour market flexibility: Spain*, Geneva: International Labour Office.

Kahn-Freund, O. (1983) *Labour and the Law*, 3rd ed., by P. Davies and M. Freedland, London: Stevens.

Karakatsanis, A. G. (1987) 'Flexibilisierung des Arbeitsrechts in Griechenland', *Zeitschrift für internationales Arbeits- und Sozialrecht* 1: 277–82.

Keller, B. and Seifert, H. (1993) 'Regulierung atypischer Beschäftigungsverhältnisse', *WSI-Mitteilungen* 9: 538–45.

Keller, B. and Seifert, H. (1997) 'Zwischenbilanz der Deregulierung', *WSI-Mitteilungen* 8: 478–89.

Kessler, F. (1991) 'Der Kündigungsschutz in Frankreich', *Zeitschrift für internationales Arbeits- und Sozialrecht* 5: 406.

Koniaris, T. (1982) 'Greece', *International Encyclopedia for Labour Law and Industrial Relations*, Vol. V, Deventer: Kluwer.

Koniaris, T. (1993) 'Hellas', in R. Blanpain (ed.) *Temporary Work and Labour Law*, Deventer: Kluwer, 163–78.

Korver, A. (1993) 'The Netherlands: labour market, labour contracts and collective bargaining' in J. Hartog and J. Theeuwes (eds) *Labour Market Contracts and Institutions. A Cross-National Comparison*, Amsterdam: North-Holland, 385–414.

Kraft, K. (1993) 'Eurosclerosis reconsidered: employment protection and work force adjustment in West Germany', in C. F. Büchtemann (ed.), *Employment Security and Labor Market Behavior – Interdisciplinary Approaches and International Evidence*, Ithaca, NY: ILR Press, 297–304.

Kraft, K. (1994) 'A comparison of employment adjustment patterns in France, Germany, Great Britain and Italy', Discussion Paper FS I 94–207, Wissenschaftszentrum Berlin für Sozialforschung.

Kraft, K. (1997) 'Hiring and dismissal costs in theory and practice: a comparison of institutional constraints and employment adjustment patterns in six OECD countries', *Kyklos* 50(3): 341–68.

Kravaritou, Y. (1993) 'Greece', in Commission of the European Communities (ed.) 'The regulation of working conditions in the Member States of the European Community', Vol. 2, *Social Europe*, Supplement 5/93: 82–102.

Kronke, H. (1990) *Regulierungen auf dem Arbeitsmarkt. Kernbereiche des Arbeitsrechts im internationalen Vergleich*, Baden-Baden: Nomos.

Larrea Gayarre, J. (1992) 'Labour market flexibility and work organisation activities in Spain' in *New Directions in Work Organisation. The Industrial Relations Response*, Paris: OECD: 136–54.

Lefebvre, F. (1991) *Travail temporaire – Contrat à durée déterminée*, Paris: Editions Francis Lefebvre.

Leighton, P. (1986) 'Marginal workers' in R. Lewis (ed.) *Labour Law in Britain*, Oxford: Blackwell, 509–12.

Levine, D. J. (1989) 'Just-cause employment policies. When unemployment is a worker discipline device', *American Economic Review*, 79: 902–5.

Linne, G. and Voswinkel, S. (1989) *Vielleicht ist ja noch alles offen – Eine empirische Untersuchung über befristete Arbeitsverhältnisse*, Hamburg: Institut für sozialwissenschaftliche Forschung.

Lutz, B. (1993) 'Economic change, internal labor markets, and workers' protection: toward an agenda for the 1990s', in C. F. Buechtemann (ed.) *Employment Security and Labor Market Behavior*, Ithaca, NY: ILR Press, 450–5.

Lyon-Caen, A. (1987) 'La conversion: nouvelles orientations', *Droit Social*, 241–9.

Lyon-Caen, A. (1993) 'Workers' protection and the regulation of labor relations in France during the 1980s', in C. F. Buechtemann (ed.) *Employment Security and Labor Market Behavior*, Ithaca, NY: ILR Press, 347–57.

Matsuda, Y. (1992) 'Job security in Japan', in K. Koshiro (ed.) *Employment Security and Labor Market Flexibility – An International Perspective*, Detroit: Wayne State University Press.

Meulders, D., Plasman, O. and Plasman, R. (1994) *Atypical Employment in the EC*, Aldershot: Elgar.

Michon, F. and Ramaux, F. (1993) 'Temporary employment in France: a decade statement', *Labour* 7(3): 93–116.

Mincer, J. (1974) *Schooling, Experience, and Earnings*, New York: Columbia University Press.

Ministère du Travail et de la Formation Professionnelle (1992) 'Evolution récente du travail précaire', Rapport au Parlament, Paris.

Ministerio de Trabajo y Seguridad Social (1993) *Guía Laboral 1991*, Madrid.

Ministerio de Trabajo y Seguridad Social (1995) *Guía Laboral*, Madrid.

Mosley, H. and Kruppe, T. (1993) 'Employment protection and labor force adjustment. A comparative evaluation', Discussion Paper FS I 92–9, Wissenschaftszentrum Berlin für Sozialforschung.

Mosley, H. G. (1994) 'Employment protection and labor force adjustment in EC countries', in G. Schmid (ed.) *Labor Market Institutions in Europe: A Socioeconomic Evaluation of Performance*, Armonk, NY: M. E. Sharpe, 59–82.

Mückenberger, U. (1985a) 'Der verfassungsrechtliche Schutz des Dauerarbeitsverhältnisses', *Neue Zeitschrift für Arbeitsrecht*, 518–26.

Mückenberger, U. (1985b) 'Die Krise des Normalarbeitsverhältnisses', *Zeitschrift für Sozialreform* 7: 415–33, and 8: 457–74.

Mückenberger, U. (1989) 'Non-standard forms of employment in the Federal Republic of Germany: the role and effectiveness of the State', in G. Rodgers and J. Rodgers (eds) *Precarious Jobs in Labour Market Regulation. The Growth of Atypical Employment in Western Europe*, Geneva: International Institute for Labour Studies, 267–85.

Mückenberger, U. (1990) 'Normalarbeitsverhältnis: Lohnarbeit als normativer Horizont sozialer Sicherheit?', in C. Sachsse and H. T. Engelhardt (eds) *Sicherheit und Freiheit. Zur Ethik des Wohlfahrtsstaats*, Frankfurt am Main: Suhrkamp, 158–78.

Mückenberger, U. (1993) 'Ist der "Sozialraum Europa" noch auf der historischen Agenda? Neue Beschäftigungsformen und deren europäische Regulierung', *WSI-Mitteilungen* 9: 593–600.

Nielsen, K. (1991) 'Towards a flexible future – theories and politics', in B. Jessop, H. Kastendiek, K. Nielsen and O. K. Pedersen (eds) *The Politics of Flexibility*, Aldershot: Elgar: 3–32.

OECD (1986) *Flexibility in the Labour Market. The Current Debate*, Paris: OECD.

OECD (1990) *Labour Market Policies for the 1990s*, Paris: OECD.

OECD (1991) *Evaluating the Impact of Labour Market Training Programmes – The State of a Complex Art*, Paris: OECD.

OECD (1993) *Employment Outlook*, Paris: OECD.

OECD (1994) *The Jobs Study, Evidence and Explanations*, Paris: OECD.

OECD (1995) *Employment Outlook*, Paris: OECD.

OECD (1996) *Employment Outlook*, Paris: OECD.

OECD (1997) *Employment Outlook*, Paris: OECD.

Oechsler, W. A. (1988) 'Employee severance-regulations and procedures', in G. Dlugos, W. Dorow, K. Weiermair and F. C. Danesy (eds) *Management Under Differing Labour Market and Employment Systems*, Berlin: De Gruyter, 397–410.

Péllisier, J. (1986) 'Ambiguités et logique du contrôle de la Cour de Cassation', *Droit Social*, 180–2.

Pinto, M. (1987) 'Portugal: Die Flexibilisierung des Arbeitsrechts – eine europäische Herausforderung?', *Zeitschrift für internationales Arbeits- und Sozialrecht* 1: 346–53.

Pinto, M., Martins, P. F. and de Carvalho, A. E. (1993) 'Portugal', in R. Blanpain (ed.) *Temporary Work and Labour Law*, Deventer: Kluwer, 233–51.

Pollert, A. (1991) 'Introduction', in A. Pollert (ed.) *Farewell to Flexibility?*, Oxford: Blackwell, xvii–xxxv.

Prondzynski, F. von (1993) 'Ireland', in Commission of the European Communities (ed.) 'The regulation of working conditions in the Member States of the European Community', Vol. 2, *Social Europe*, Supplement 5/93: 104–11.

Ragin, C. (1987) *The Comparative Method*, Berkeley: University of California Press.

Ragin, C. (1991) *Issues and Alternatives in Comparative Social Research*, Leiden: E. J. Brill.

Redmond, M. (1982) *Dismissal Law in Ireland*, Dublin: Sweet & Maxwell.

Redmond, M. (1985) 'Ireland', *International Encyclopedia for Labour Law and Industrial Relations*, Vol. VI, Deventer: Kluwer.

Redmond, M. (1993) 'Ireland', in R. Blanpain (ed.) *Temporary Work and Labour Law*, Deventer: Kluwer, 179–200.

Rodriguez-Sanudo, F. (1993) 'Spain', in R. Blanpain (ed.) *Temporary Work and Labour Law*, Deventer: Kluwer, 253–8.

Rogowski, R. (1996a) 'The art of mirroring. Comparative law and social theory', in G. Wilson and R. Rogowski (eds) *Challenges to European Legal Scholarship*, London: Blackstone, 215–32.

Rogowski, R. (ed.) (1996b) *Civil Law*, Aldershot: Dartmouth.

Rogowski, R. (1997) 'The regulation of employment relations', *Work, Employment & Society* 11(1): 153–65.

Rogowski, R. (forthcoming) *The Resolution of Labour Conflicts. An International Comparison*, Baden-Baden: Nomos.

Rogowski, R. and Schmid, G. (1997) 'Reflexive Deregulierung – Ein Ansatz zur Dynamisierung des Arbeitsmarkts', *WSI-Mitteilungen* 8: 521–36.

Rogowski, R. and Schömann, G. (1996) 'Legal regulation and flexibility of employment contracts', in G. Schmid, J. O'Reilly and K. Schömann (eds) *International Handbook of Labour Market Policy and Evaluation*, Aldershot: Elgar: 623–51.

Rogowski, R. and Wilthagen, T. (eds) (1994) *Reflexive Labour Law. Studies in Industrial Relations and Employment Regulation*, Deventer: Kluwer.

Rojot, J. (1993) 'France', in R. Blanpain (ed.) *Temporary Work and Labour Law*, Deventer: Kluwer, 91–120.

Rosanvallon, P. (1988) *La question syndical*, Paris: Calman-Levy.

Royal Commission on Trade Unions and Employers' Associations 1965–1968, Chairman: Lord Donovan, *Report*, London: HMSO, Cmnd. 3623.

Schaub, B. (1992) *Arbeitsrechts-Handbuch*, 7th ed., Munich: Beck.

Schettkat, R. (1995) 'Asymmetric Labour Market Flows over the Business Cycle', Discussion Paper FS I 95-304, Wissenschaftszentrum Berlin für Sozialforschung.

Schintgen, R. (1993) 'Luxembourg', in Commission of the European Communities (ed.) 'The regulation of working conditions in the Member States of the European Community', Vol. 2, *Social Europe,* Supplement 5/93: 130–48.

Schliemann, K. (1991) 'Die Rechtsprechung des 7. Senats des BAG zur Befristung von Arbeitsverhältnissen', *Arbeitsrecht der Gegenwart* 1991: 113–19.

Schmid, G. (1993) 'Coordinated flexibility: the future of labor market regulation', in C. F. Büchtemann (ed.) *Employment Security and Labor Market Behavior – Interdisciplinary Approaches and International Evidence*, Ithaca, NY: ILR Press, 456–8.

Schmid, G. (1994) 'Equality and efficiency in the labor market: toward a socioeconomic theory of cooperation', in G. Schmid (ed.) *Labor Market Institutions in Europe*, Armonk, NY: M. E. Sharpe, 243–80.

Schmid, G. (1995) 'Is full employment still possible? Transitional labour markets as a new strategy of labour market policy', *Economic and Industrial Democracy* 16: 429–56.

Schmid, G., O'Reilly, J. and Schümann, K. (eds) (1996) *International Handbook of Labour Market Policy and Evaluation*, Aldershot: Elgar.

Schmidt, C. M. and Zimmermann, K. F. (1991) 'Work characteristics, firm size and wages', *The Review of Economics and Statistics* 73: 705–10.

Schömann, K. (1994) *The Dynamics of Labor Earnings over the Life Course – A Comparative and Longitudinal Analysis of Germany and Poland*, Max-Planck-Institut für Bildungsforschung, Berlin: Edition Sigma.

Schömann, K. and Kruppe, T. (1993) 'Fixed-term employment and labour market flexibility – theory and longitudinal evidence of East and Est Germany', Discussion Paper FS I 93-204, Wissenschaftszentrum Berlin für Sozialforschung.

Schömann, K. and Kruppe, T. (1994) 'Who enters fixed-term contracts: evidence from East and West Germany', *Vierteljahreshefte zur Wirtschaftsforschung* 1/2: 69–74.

Schömann, K., Rogowski, R. and Kruppe T. (1994) 'Fixed-term contracts in the European Union', European Commission, *inforMISEP, Employment Observatory of the Commission of the European Communities* 47: 30–9.

Schweizer, J. (1991) 'Befristete Arbeitsverträge an den Hochschulen', *Juristenzeitung*: 709–11.

Segura, J., Durán, F., Toharia, L. and Bentolila, S. (1991) *Análisis de la Contratación Temporal en España*, Madrid: Ministerio de Trabajo y Seguridad Social.

Selwyn, N. (1993) *Law of Employment*, 8th ed., London: Butterworths.

Shapiro, C. and Stiglitz, J. E. (1984) Equilibrium unemployment as a worker discipline device, *American Economic Review* 74: 433–44.

Sisson, K. (1987) *The Management of Collective Bargaining*, Oxford: Blackwell.

Smith, A. (1976) *An Inquiry into the Nature and Causes of the Wealth of Nations*, Oxford: Oxford University Press.

Smith, I. T., Wood, J. C. and Thomas, G. (1993) *Industrial Law*, 5th ed., London: Butterworths.

Smitskam, C. (1990) *Flexibele Arbeidsrelaties*, Deventer: Kluwer.

Standing, G. (1993) 'Labor regulation in an era of fragmented flexibility', in C. F. Büchtemann (ed.) *Employment Security and Labor Market Behavior – Interdisciplinary Approaches and International Evidence*, Ithaca, NY: ILR Press, 425–41.

Stern, D. and Ritzen, J. M. M. (1991) *Market Failure in Training? New Economic Analysis and Evidence on Training of Adult Employees*, Berlin and New York: Springer.

Stinchcombe, A. S. (1979) 'Social mobility and the industrial labor process', *Acta Sociologica* 22: 217–45.

Streeck, W. (1990) 'Status and contract: basic categories of a sociological theory of industrial relations', in D. Sugarman and G. Teubner (eds) *Regulating Corporate Groups in Europe*, Baden-Baden: Nomos, 105–45.

Streeck, W. (1996) 'Neo-voluntarism: a new European social policy regime', in G. Marks, F. W. Scharpf, P. C. Schmitter and W. Streeck, *Governance in the European Union*, London: Sage, 64–94.

Teubner, G. (1986) 'After legal instrumentalism: strategic models of post-regulatory law', in G. Teubner (ed.) *Dilemmas of Law in the Welfare State*, Berlin and New York: De Gruyter, 299–325.

Thurow, L. (1979) 'A theory of groups and economic redistribution', *Philosophy and Public Affairs* 9: 25–41.

Treu, T. (1993a) 'Employment protection and labor relations in Italy', in C. F. Buechtemann (ed.) *Employment Security and Labor Market Behavior*, Ithaca, NY: ILR Press, 385–95.

Treu, T. (1993b) 'Italy' and 'Addendum', in R. Blanpain (ed.) *Temporary Work and Labour Law*, Deventer: Kluwer, 201–10 and 285–6.

Treu, T., Geroldi, G. and Maiello, M. (1993) 'Italy: labour relations', in J. Hartog and J. Theeuwes (eds) *Labour Market Contracts and Institutions. A Cross-National Comparison*, Amsterdam: North-Holland, 323–49.

Tronti, L. (1993) 'Employment security and labor market segmentation: economic implications of the Italian Cassa Integrazione Guadagni', in C. F. Buechtemann (ed.) *Employment Security and Labor Market Behavior*, Ithaca, NY: ILR Press, 396–413.

van der Ven, H. (1984) 'De gevolgen van het weigeren van een ontslagvergunning door het GBA – Een kwantitatieve oriëntatie', SMA 1984, 815.

Vissers, A. and Dirven, H. J. (1994) 'Fixed-term contracts in the Netherlands: some evidence from panel data', Discussion Paper FS I 94–212, Wissenschaftszentrum Berlin für Sozialforschung.

Walwei, U. (1991) 'Fixed-term contracts in EC countries', *Intereconomics* 1/2: 25–31.

Lord Wedderburn (1986) *The Worker and the Law*, 3rd ed., Harmondsworth: Penguin.

Weekes, B. C. M., Mellish, M., Dickens, L. and Lloyd, J. (1975) *Industrial Relations and the Limits of Law*, Oxford: Blackwell.

Zielinski, T. (1982) 'Les problèmes méthodologiques dans la science du droit du travail', *Bulletin de droit comparé du travail et de la sécurité sociale*, 363–86.

Zöllner, W. and Lorenz, K.-G. (1992) *Arbeitsrecht*, 4th ed., Munich: Beck.

Zweigert, K. and Kötz H. (1987) *An Introduction to Comparative Law*, 2nd ed., Oxford: Clarendon.

INDEX OF AUTHORS CITED

Adamy, W. 156
Akerlof, G.A. 18
Alaluf, M. 27
Alba-Ramírez, A. 72, 111, 142–3, 150,
  165
Asscher-Vonk, I. 55

Becker, G.S. 15
Bentolila, S. and Saint-Paul, G. 150; *see
  also* Segura, J. *et al.*
Bertola, G. 14, 150
Bettio, F. and Villa, P. 48
Bispinck, R. 39
Blanc-Jouvan, X. 4–5
Blankenburg, E. 40; and Rogowski, R.
  68
Blanpain, R. 3, 25; and Köhler, E. 3; and
  Oversteyns, B. 27–8
Bosch, G. 11
Büchtemann, C.F. 6, 149, 158; and
  Höland, A. 72

Calmfors, L. 4
Casey, B. 70
Coase, R. 14, 22, 165
Collins, H. 68

Däubler, W. 38
de Carvalho, A.E. *see* Pinto, M. *et al.*
de Leede, L.J.M. 56
Deakin, S. 66; and Mückenberger, U.
  10
Delsen, L. 72
Dickens, L. 164; *et al.* 68; *see also*
  Weekes, B. *et al.*
Dirven, H.J. 142–3, 165
Doeringer, P.B. and Piore, M.H. 16
Domergue, D. 34
Durán, F. *see* Segura, J. *et al.*

Emerson, M. 6, 76
Enclos, P. 34
Esping-Andersen, G. 4

Franz, W. 165
Fredman, S. 65

Geroldi, G. *see* Treu, T. *et al.*
Gold, M. 70
Guergoat, J.-C. 156; and Hocquaux, C.
  156

Hart, M. *see* Dickens, L. *et al.*
Hashimoto, M. and Raisian, J. 4
Heilmann, J. 38
Henry, R. and Guergoat, J.-C. 156
Hepple, B. 68–9; and Fredman, S.
  65
Hocquaux, C. 156
Höland, A. 38, 72
Hunt, J. 156

Jacobs, A. 55–6
Jacobsen, P. 31–2
Janoski, T. 5
Jessop, B. *et al.* 158
Jimeno, J.F. and Toharia, L. 63, 150–2
Jones, M. *see* Dickens, L. *et al.*

Kahn-Freund, O. 65
Karakatsanis, A.G. 43
Kastendiek, H. *see* Jessop, B. *et al.*
Keller, B. and Seifert, H. 11, 42
Kessler, F. 34–5
Köhler, E. 3
Koniaris, T. 43
Korver, A. 54
Kötz, H. 5
Kraft, K. 155–6

Kronke, H. 25, 28–30, 35, 42, 45, 51–2, 55, 57–9, 61, 64
Kruppe, T. 6, 52, 142–3, 165

Larrea Gayarre, J. 63
Lefebvre, F. 36
Leighton, P. 68
Levine, D.J. 18
Linne, G. and Voswinkel, S. 156
Lloyd, J. *see* Weekes, B. *et al.*
Lorenz, K.-G. 41
Lutz, B. 158
Lyon-Caen, A. 32, 34

Maiello, M. *see* Treu, T. *et al.*
Martins, P.F. *see* Pinto, M. *et al.*
Matsuda, Y. 4
Mellish, M. *see* Weekes, B. *et al.*
Meulders, D. *et al.* 72
Michon, F. and Ramaux, F. 72, 76, 156, 164
Mincer, J. 15
Mosley, H. 158; and Kruppe, T. 6, 52, 165
Mückenberger, U. 10–11

Nielsen, K. 1; *see also* Jessop, B. *et al.*

Oechsler, W.A. 38
O Reilly, J. *see* Schmid, G. *et al.*
Oversteyns, B. 27–8

Pedersen, O.K. *see* Jessop, B. *et al.*
Péllisier, J. 33
Pinto, M. 57–8; *et al.* 58–9
Piore, M.H. 16
Plasman, O. and R. *see* Meulders, D. *et al.*
Pollert, A. 158
Prondzynski, F. von 45

Ragin, C. 5
Raisian, J. 4
Ramaux, F. 72, 76, 156, 164
Redmond, M. 45, 47
Rodriguez-Sanudo, F. 62
Rogowksi, R. 4–5, 38, 68, 158; and Schmid, G. 9, 11; and Schömann, G. 12; and Wilthagen, T. 11, 24

Rosanvallon, P. 27

Saint-Paul, G. 150
Schaub, G. 39–42
Schettkat, R. 76
Schliemann, K. 41
Schmid, G. 3, 9, 11, 158–9, 166; *et al.* 6
Schmidt, C.M. and Zimmermann, K.F. 17
Schömann, G. 12
Schömann, K. 6, 16, 22; and Kruppe, T. 142–3, 165; *see also* Schmid, G. *et al.*
Segura, J. *et al.* 72, 150, 152
Seifert, H. 11, 42
Selwyn, N. 70
Shapiro, C. and Stiglitz, J.E. 17–19
Sisson, K. 65
Smith, Adam 13, 22
Smith, I.T. *et al.* 66
Standing, G. 9, 164
Stiglitz, J.E. 17–19
Stinchcombe, A.S. 16
Streeck, W. 9–10

Teubner, G. 11
Thomas, G. *see* Smith, I.T. *et al.*
Thurow, L. 159
Toharia, L. 63, 150–2; *see also* Segura, J. *et al.*
Treu, T. 50–1; *et al.* 49
Tronti, L. 52

van der Ven, H. 54
Villa, P. 48
Vissers, A. and Dirven, H.J. 142–3, 165
Voswinkel, S. 156

Walwei, U. 6, 72
Wedderburn, Lord 68
Weekes, B. *et al.* 66; *see also* Dickens, L. *et al.*
Wilthagen, T. 11, 24
Wood, J.C. *see* Smith, I.T. *et al.*

Zielinski, T. 4
Zimmermann, K.F. 17
Zöllner, W. and Lorenz, K.-G. 41
Zweigert, K. and Kötz, H. 5

SUBJECT INDEX

absenteeism 61
academic personnel 41, 64, 148
active labour market policy 45
activity rates 92; *see also* women:
  participation
age of employees 101–11, 134–5, 151
agency work 3, 26–7, 30–1, 40, 43, 46–7,
  50, 55, 58, 68–9, 72, 152, 156, 166
agriculture 128, 144–5
apprenticeships 64, 73–4, 133, 141, 152
atypical forms of employment 2, 8–12,
  20, 166; EU draft directives on 70–1

Belgium 25–9, 76, 80, 84, 87, 92–3, 96,
  101, 111, 117, 122, 128, 134, 145,
  148, 168–9
beneficiality 38
business, burden on 9

career breaks 26
case law 45
casual employment contracts 64
causality principle 151
centralised wage bargaining 44
child care 26
co-ordination between European countries
  9
collective agreements 25, 29, 56, 65,
  128, 130, 144–7, 152–7 *passim*
collective dismissals 49; *see also*
  redundancy payments, redundancy
  procedures
common law 45
community work 65
comparative method of research 4–6
compensation: for loss of job 40, 43, 46,
  61, 68, 166, 167; *see also* wages and
  wage differentials
compensation criterion 1

conciliation 62
Conseil National du Travail (CNT), Belgian
  25, 27
constitutional courts 57
construction industry 64, 128, 144–5
constructive dismissal 60, 67
contracting out 72
contracts of employment (as distinct from
  employment relationships) 10
cultural changes 11
cyclical variations 149

Denmark 29–32, 76, 80, 84, 87, 92, 96,
  101, 111, 117, 122, 128, 134, 139,
  145, 148, 170–1
deregulation *see* regulation
disabled employees 39
discrimination in employment 66, 68,
  70, 139–40, 151, 165
dismissal: costs of 22; null and void 61;
  procedures 33, 52, 54, 57–8, 61–2,
  164; reasons for 26, 30–1, 33–4, 39,
  45–7, 49, 57–61, 67, 155; *see also*
  constructive dismissal
distributional effects of policy changes 6
Donovan Commission 65–6
dummy variables 139, 142, 144, 155
duration of job tenure 2, 153

earnings, life-time patterns of 15–16; *see
  also* wages and wage differentials
economic activity, levels of 149
education contracts 51
educational level of workers 116–17,
  140–1; *see also* training
efficiency, concepts of 1, 158–9, 166
efficiency wage theory 13, 17–23 *passim*,
  143–6, 150
elasticity of demand for labour 150

employment agencies *see* agency work
employment businesses 68–9
employment creation 2, 92, 102, 132, 152
employment protection 2–4, 8–12, 20–4,
 29, 32, 38, 144, 151, 156, 164–6; in
 Belgium 25–7; in Denmark 29–31; in
 France 32–5; in Germany 38–40; in
 Greece 42–3; in Ireland 44–7; in Italy
 48–50; in Luxembourg 52–3; in the
 Netherlands 54–5; in Portugal 56–8;
 in Spain 60–2; in United Kingdom
 65–9
employment solidarity contracts 37
employment status a year earlier 130,
 141–4, 151
energy and water sector 144
entrants to the labour force 102, 139,
 151, 165
equal pay and treatment for men and
 women 66, 70, 140
equity 159–60, 166
European Household Panel 140
European Parliament· 71
European Union Directives 62, 70–1,
 116, 130, 159; *see also* Labour Force
 Survey
Eurostat 7

female participation in labour force *see*
 women
filters applied to employment status 133
fixed-term contracts: different forms
 63–4; in Belgium 27–9; in Denmark
 31–2; in France 35–7; in Germany
 40–2; in Greece 43–4; in Ireland
 47–8; in Italy 450–2; in Luxembourg
 53–4; in the Netherlands 55–6; in
 Portugal 58–60; in Spain 62–5; in
 United Kingdom 69–70; legal theories
 of 8–13, 19–23
flexibilisation 2, 8–9, 22, 27, 32, 56, 72,
 155, 158, 164
'flexible' labour 150
force majeure 37, 62
France 32–7, 72, 76, 80, 84, 92, 96,
 101–2, 111, 117, 122, 128, 130, 134,
 142–5, 156, 165, 167, 172–3
free movement of workers 70
freedom of contract 40

gender differences *see* women
Germany 38–42, 72, 80, 83–4, 92–3, 96,
 111, 117, 122, 128, 130–4, 141–7,
 155–6, 165, 174–5
Gesamtmetall 146
globalisation 9
Greece 42–4, 76, 83–4, 91–3, 96, 111,
 116–17, 122, 128, 132, 134, 139, 141,
 144, 176–7
gross misconduct 35, 37–9, 47, 49, 57,
 60, 66

hazardous working environments 130
heads of household 134
'hire and fire' practices 16
holidays 71
homeworking 64, 68
Hoogovens Agreement 56
hours of work *see* working time
household structure 134
human capital theory 13–16, 20–3, 146
hypotheses 21–2

IG Metall 146, 155–6
individual choice to make a fixed-term
 contract 3
industrial action *see* strikes
industrial sectors, comparisons between
 128, 144–7, 165
industrial tribunals 65, 67–8
inequality in employment relationships
 10
insolvency 40
institutional factors affecting employment
 144–5
integration: between countries 9; of
 entrants into the labour market 102
interdisciplinary approach to research 8,
 158
intermittent work 65
Ireland 44–8, 76, 80, 84, 92–3, 96, 101,
 111, 117, 122, 128, 132, 134, 139,
 141, 145, 148, 178–9
Italy 48–52, 76, 80, 91–3, 96, 111, 117,
 134, 141, 144–5, 180–1

job creation *see* employment creation
'just cause' dismissal 49, 57
just-in-time production 3

labour costs 22
Labour Force Survey 73–4, 116, 130,
 140–2, 151, 164
last in, first out 165
law 8–9, 11–12; comparative studies of
 4–5; as dynamic process 73

'lean' management 3, 146
learning-by-doing 14
legal competence of European bodies
9
liberalisation of labour law 9
lifestyle 11
logistic regression 133
lois Auroux 32, 36
longitudinal studies 142, 165
long-term contracts, advantages to
employers 14
long-term unemployed 59, 142, 155
Luxembourg 52–4, 76, 80, 84, 92–3,
96, 111, 132–3, 139, 145, 147,
182–3

Maastricht Treaty and criteria 71, 166
macro-economic conditions 149–50
manufacturing 145–6, 156
marital status 134
maternity leave 47–8, 51, 54; *see also*
pregnancy
military service 28, 37, 51, 54
minimum wage policies 63
mobility of labour 102, 143–4
multi-disciplinary research *see*
interdisciplinary approach
multivariate analysis 133, 155–6

nationality 139
Netherlands 54–6, 76, 80, 84, 92, 96,
101, 111, 117, 122, 128, 134, 140–2,
145–8, 165, 184–5
new contracts 154
new launch contracts 64
norms 12
notice periods 25, 29–35, 39, 43, 45, 48,
55–8, 61, 66, 69, 166

occupational structure 117–22, 147–8,
165
older workers 55, 101–2, 155
on-call labour contracts 28
Organisation for Economic Cooperation
and Development (OECD) 84, 143
outplacement 27

partial retirement 63
part-time work 11, 46, 56, 63, 80,
111–16, 152, 166
participation in the labour force *see*
activity rates
path dependency 142, 158

personnel policies and management 2–3,
9
Portugal 56–60, 76, 80, 83, 91–3, 96,
101, 111, 116–17, 122, 128, 134, 141,
144, 148, 167, 186–7
practical work contracts 64
precarious employment 37, 102, 128,
147, 155
pregnancy 26, 28, 30, 67, 69; *see also*
maternity leave
primary jobs 16, 20; *see also* segmentation
of the labour market
primary level of education 116
privatisation 165–6
probability of having a fixed-term contract
133, 168–91
probation periods 37, 41, 54–5, 58, 102,
143, 165–6
production-oriented industries 122, 128
public services 145–6

qualifications, educational 116–17
qualifying periods 45, 66, 69–70, 164

racial discrimination *see* discrimination in
employment
real wages 17
reasonable behaviour by employers
67–70
reasons for making fixed-term contracts
21, 29, 40, 42, 44, 53, 73, 83, 151,
155
redundancy payments 26, 66
redundancy procedures 30, 34–5, 39, 46,
53, 61–2, 65–8, 152
reflexive labour law 8–12, 19–24, 143
regulation, deregulation and re-regulation
of the labour market 1, 6–12 *passim*,
41, 66, 72–3, 102, 116, 128, 130, 143,
149, 156–66; hierarchical structure or
regulation 38; 'model' forms of
regulation 4
reinstatement 35, 46, 61
relief contracts 63
renewal of fixed-term contracts 27–8, 31
replacement of permanent employees 3,
51
returning to the labour market 130
rights of workers 10
'rigid' labour 150
rigidity of the labour market 1

sales personnel 147

screening periods for new employees 142–3

seasonal work 2–3, 32, 37, 41, 44, 47, 50, 53, 59, 63, 65, 69, 73–4, 80, 91, 146

secondary jobs 16–17, 20; *see also* segmentation of the labour market

secondary level of education 116

security and insecurity of employment 13–15, 19, 116, 149, 158, 167

segmentation of the labour market 13, 16–17, 20–3, 142, 146, 154, 164–5

self-employment 142

seniority 139, 156

service industries 145–6

sex discrimination *see* discrimination in employment

Shell agreement 56

shipbuilding industry 51

shirking 17–19, 150

shop floor bargaining 65

short-duration contracts 130, 144

Single European Act 70

single people 134

skilled workers 146

small firms 49, 57, 147, 151–2, 156

social plans 53

Social Policy, European 9, 70

social protection 11

socio-economic labour market theories 22–3

Spain 60–5, 72, 76, 83–4, 91–3, 96, 102, 111, 116–17, 122, 128, 130, 134, 141–4, 148–52, 155–6, 164–6, 188–9

stability in the labour market 1, 16

standard employment relationships and contracts 8–12, 19, 21, 133

strikes 43, 45, 51

summary dismissal 45, 54; *see also* gross misconduct

suspension of employees 57

technical change 61

temporary work 26–7, 30–1, 36–7, 40, 43, 50, 53–6, 59, 62–3, 68, 74, 76, 152; EU directive on 116

trade union activities 26, 30, 35, 66–7, 144, 146, 152, 155

training 15–16, 20, 23, 34, 71, 73–4, 133, 141

training contracts 152, 154

transfer of undertakings 62, 67

transitions within the labour market 166

trends and patterns in use of fixed-term contracts 74–83

turnover of labour 165

unemployment: recruitment from 132, 142–3; as a worker discipline device 18–19, 21, 23; *see also* long-term unemployed

unfair dismissal 24, 32–3, 42, 45–6, 50, 53, 61, 66–7

United Kingdom 9, 47, 65–71, 76, 80, 84, 87, 92, 96, 101, 111, 117, 128, 134, 139–45, 148, 164, 166, 190–1

United States 1–2

university graduates 117, 140–1

vintage effects 21

wages and wage differentials 13–17, 22–3, 143–4, 151–2, 165, 167; *see also* real wages

waiting lists of employees for hire 42

women: employment patterns 83–101, 134, 139, 164; participation in labour force 11, 92–3, 96, 101–2, 111; *see also* equal pay

work books 48

work experience 64, 142–3

working time 3, 116

works councils 38, 40, 57, 143

young workers 29, 59, 101–2, 139, 151, 154–5, 165